W9-BTF-835

Sources of Modern Architecture

Dennis Sharp

Sources of
Modern Architecture

A Critical Bibliography

Eastview Editions Inc.

Copyright © 1981 Dennis Sharp

Library of Congress Cataloguing in Publication Data

Sharp, Dennis
  Sources of modern architecture.
  1. Architecture, Modern – 20th century – Bibliography
  I. Title
  016.7249   Z5941.5

ISBN 0-89860-050-2

First published in Great Britain and the USA 1967
Second edition (revised and enlarged) published in Great Britain 1981 by Granada Publishing
Limited – Technical Books Division
Published in the USA 1981 by Eastview Editions Inc., PO Box 783, Westfield, NJ 07091

Printed in Great Britain
by W. & J. Mackay Limited, Chatham

Contents

Of course, literature and architecture are very, very far from each other, sometimes out of sight

Alvar Aalto

Architecture takes possession of space, marks its bounds, encloses it, imprisons it. It has the privilege of creating magic spaces, entirely works of the spirit

Auguste Perret

One cannot understand architecture as an art if one does not have some ideas about art

Gio Ponti

A style known to one in its growth and in its different stages of evolution, becomes not so much just an idea, but the illusion of a living inevitability

André Malraux

Introduction to the new edition

In bringing out a new edition of *Sources of Modern Architecture* I am principally aware of the vast increase there has been over the past two decades in the literature on modern architecture, architectural theory, aesthetics, design history, construction and planning. At times it has been difficult to keep up with the sheer volume of new material emanating not only from established authors, including many of the architects referred to in this list, but also from the scores of monographs, special publications, magazine articles and student theses, all of which have aided the elucidation of the early pioneer years of the Modern Movement in architecture. In addition to this, vast new areas of research have opened up and many definitive publications have been produced that clearly provide sources for new interpretations of 'modern architecture'. Whereas I have attempted to take into consideration many of these new publications, and thus expand the framework of the original listings, it would perhaps be wrong to take a new direction in relation to a bibliography which had a particular purpose and flavour which reflected the energetic enquiry that was going on when it was originally produced in the 1960s. Thus this new edition takes on some of the new material where it helps to expand areas of knowledge and some of the ballast from the previous edition is jettisoned. However, much of the original material is simply reinforced with references to new editions and new viewpoints. In total *Sources* has been completely updated and references increased by approximately 40 per cent; biographical details have wherever possible been brought up to date.

In retaining most of the titles that appeared in the original version it must be admitted that some of the books listed in the subject and national biographies have now gone out of print; others, it might well be argued, have lost their relevance. However, I feel that the list still indicates a certain attitude to architecture and architectural theory which was important at the time of the post-war revival of interest in the Modern Movement and although one would admit that the appearance of new works (many of which are additionally listed) has expanded the knowledge and information available in this subject area, many of the titles in the original edition have significant value as historical tracts, as well as intellectual curiosities. Now that the rivers of bibliographical reference material on the Modern Movement in architecture are in full flood, it is often worth searching out these earlier small streams of influence and interest. When the list was originally compiled, and then essentially for research purposes and not to flatter any individual, group or faction, it was my intention to provide a working document for those engaged on modern architectural research. Indirectly it was also a personal list compiled to indicate the appalling lack of material on modern architecture in British libraries, and in a provocative sense to influence libraries to dust down the covers of the pre-war books that had been consigned to inaccessible book stacks. In concise form, therefore, the bibliography set out to provide a basic list of works by and on the key architects who formulated the Modern Movement itself. This involved too a considerable amount of research into foreign-language titles, many of them seemingly unpronounceable to English readers, and a considerable number unknown in English collections. One book reviewer who felt strangely lost in the world of foreign-language book titles suggested, when he was reviewing the first edition, that all these titles should be shown in English. While I gave this considerable thought, it would of course defeat the whole aim of accurate bibliographical reference. However, whenever possible, new information was sought on those titles which indicated that limited English translations were available or where English summaries were provided within the books when they were of a general nature.

The emphasis of this list therefore is on *sources*. While it has been supplemented and extended by many new titles and bibliographical lists (particularly those of Vance Bibliographies, Montecello, Illinois, usa) nothing to my knowledge has replaced it as a reference work. When it was compiled, biographical material on the lesser known pioneers was at a premium, but now a few general publications have appeared which set out additional information on individual architects. Of these the English-language publications *Contemporary Architects* (London 1980) and *Who's Who in Architecture* (edited by J.M.Richards, London 1978) are probably the most informative, while the Gale research volumes on British and American architects, noted in detail elsewhere, edited by Laurence Wodehouse, have useful brief and often cryptic biographies as well as comments on individual publications. Where a special bibliography on an individual architect is known, this has been included in the entries for the biographical sections of this book.

Recent scholarship is reflected in the addition of considerably more material on individual architects and a corresponding increase in bibliographies completed either by individual researchers or institutions. These I believe should have priority over the addition of numerous new articles from journals which would add considerably to the length of the present listings. The journals themselves often contain adequate indexes which may be readily consulted for specific studies. The position over magazines such as *Lotus* and *Oppositions* and annuals such as *Architecture in Greece* (which has produced a number of useful articles on Greek modernists) and *Zodiac*, etc. is more difficult. Frequently they have carried important research articles which do not lend themselves to easy classification.

One of the more perplexing developments for any Western compiler of source material is the influx of important studies from Japanese publishers: the late flowering of Modern Movement scholarship, albeit aided and abetted by Western historians and critics, has produced a bumper harvest of new material. *A + U, Global Architect* and *Japan Architect* have all featured studies at great length on the origins and evolution of Modern Movement ideas and personalities, often illustrating their articles with hitherto unknown, or more often, extremely rare, material. Because of the important nature of this information some references are included to it but users of this bibliography are recommended to consult the *Avery Index* for more general and comprehensive coverage of these valuable sources. Nothing galls the bibliographer more than the knowledge that his list may well leave out some of the more recent, as well as the hard to find, foreign-language material. Possibly nothing irritates the researcher more than the suspicion that he may have missed a reference in a language he does not know which might illumine his work. I have therefore whenever possible given clues as to where English-language references can be found even if only partially related.

The bibliography as a whole follows the same pattern as the earlier edition but is expanded in content and subject areas. The addition of a list of general sources of information should prove useful and has been placed at the commencement of the 'Subject Bibliography'. The periodicals section, on which so little information was available when the list was originally compiled, has been expanded to take into account more accurate information on publishing histories as well as the proliferation of new impressions and reprints of magazines pertinent to modern architecture.

In the earlier edition of this bibliography architectural books were treated very much as sources in their own right, as repositories of information on and by architects and about buildings. One of the interesting developments amongst collectors, if not so apparent to scholars, has been the concern with the progeny of the books themselves: who designed them, illustrated them, what type-styles were adopted and who printed them. It is a fascinating subject and one not entirely beyond the scope of this new edition; although its expansion as a subject area can only be briefly summarised and, of course, illustrated.

One of the unexpected spin-offs from a bibliography such as this has been its use by antiquarian booksellers throughout the world as a reference publication and also, most unfortunately, as a guide to the rarity value (and therefore the high cost) of individual items. I can only stress that at the outset it was not meant for this purpose but was aimed at providing as complete a list as possible of the basic literary sources of the new movement in architecture, collecting together from a multitude of languages the key works which would themselves provide clues to the approaches of individual architects to their work. It was originally seen too as part of a trilogy, and in consequence must still be viewed as a complement to two other books. It provided a reservoir of references for my own *Visual History of 20th Century Architecture* (London 1972) and for the anthology produced jointly with Tim and Charlotte Benton in 1977, *Form and Function*, which was prepared essentially for the use of the students of the Open University pursuing the A305 course on Architecture and Design. Over the years it has also found its place as a complement to other publications such as Ulrich Conrads' *Programmes and Manifestoes on 20th-century Architecture* and some of the course books provided for the Open University under the general editorship of Mr Benton.

I am pleased to record that this revised edition has been brought about by a consistent demand for the original edition, first published as an Architectural Association Paper by Lund Humphries, London, and by the notion that that now somewhat dated version is still used and presumably provides a useful source of information for architects, researchers and students.

This new edition would not have been possible without the unstinting help of Wendy Aldhous who has aided me and the publishers in every way possible through her meticulous checking of items in the text, through the rectifying of a few previous errors (largely typographical) and in helping to assess the importance of things to be kept in or left out. We are both aware that this still leaves room for controversy; the list still remains a personal anthology. How could it be otherwise? Its emphasis is essentially Western as the sources of the real Modern Movement were most precisely Continental, but wherever possible the connections between the originators of the new architecture and their successors reflect the whole diaspora of ideas, whether these were in Europe, the USA or Australasia.

One reviewer gave the impression when the first edition was issued that the bibliography was like a Hall of Heroes and that I had not really presented enough material on British architects. While allowing for the reviewer's chauvinism, I can only mitigate the omissions by expanding the periods of British – more specifically English – architectural sources within the Arts and Crafts Movement and the work that was carried out by key architects around the turn of the century. The re-establishment of the figures from that period, Baillie Scott (under 'B' here, to save confusion), Voysey, even Morris and Ruskin, reflected upon by only a few historians of the 1920s and 1930s, are now much more closely connected through recent studies to Continental trends and developments. I trust that with the current interest in the late nineteenth-century period, a book on sources of modern architecture at least does justice to this previously neglected area of study, although I must confess that I am still not tempted to place the much praised – but utterly 'un-modern' – Edwin Lutyens amongst my pioneers!

Dennis Sharp
Epping Green
1979

Introduction to the first edition

A considerable amount of interest was shown when this bibliography first appeared as two separate supplements to the *Architectural Association Journal*. It is now presented in a completely different form. Due to the speed with which rough drafts were turned into final typescript the original version contained numerous errors, transferred from a badly typed manuscript. A large number of typographical errors also added to the confusion. It seems that detailed bibliographical work cannot be adequately sorted out under the pressures that attend the production of a monthly magazine.

In this new version the mistakes have been rectified and the bibliography itself has been expanded to include biographies of individual architects. Also a good deal of the recent literature on the Modern Movement has been included.

The work involved in producing a list such as this has been considerable and the effects of sifting and noting has created certain prejudices on the part of the compiler. For instance, the German contribution has been considered to be of prime importance.

The problem created by the lack of readily available material on the Modern Movement in the national and university libraries in Britain means that the student has a limited number of titles at his disposal. Wherever possible, therefore, the bias is towards those books that can be readily obtained. It is to be hoped that the libraries will use this list to help them fill the more obvious gaps in their collections. Whilst this list is in no way fully comprehensive it has been compiled selectively to provide the student with the main sources and the most authoritative supporting material. It has been arranged so that each section allows for cross-reference. Each section is, however, self-contained and an effort has been made to avoid repetition. Over 1000 books and magazine articles are listed and a selection of magazines concerned with Modern Movement developments is included. These should provide the key to many unopened doors.

The choice of articles on the work of individual architects needs a few words of defence. Out of the wide range of contributions, both descriptive and topical, I have chosen to list those that seem to me to have a distinct historical or analytical importance.

The arrangement of the bibliography is as follows: the first section is devoted to books and articles on individual architects and to one or two influential critics and painters. This section is arranged alphabetically. After a brief biography each part is arranged in date order with the books and articles written *by* the person appearing first; then follow the books or monographs *on* the individual by other writers, and finally articles *on* the individual. These divisions are indicated by rules. The second section, the subject bibliography, is concerned with general works on modern architecture and theory; aesthetics; the Bauhaus and Art Nouveau. The last section is devoted to books concerned with national trends in modern architecture. Entries for both these sections are arranged alphabetically by author. A selective list of magazines terminates the bibliography.

Wherever possible the first date and original place of publication are given. Where any doubt occurs this is noted by brackets around the date. The same method is used to indicate later editions. When it is known that a paper-bound edition is available, or that the book has appeared only as a paperback, this is noted: (p.b.). The compilation of this list terminated in the early part of 1966 and any future editions will be brought up-to-date to include important publications that appear after this date.

Dennis Sharp
January 1967

Acknowledgements to First Edition

So many people have helped with the compilation and production of this list that it would be impossible to mention them all by name; to all of them I am most grateful. I would, however, like to thank the following individually: James Palmes and David Dean and the staff of the RIBA Library; Slavoj Halmann, also of the RIBA Library, for his help with periodicals and for his encouragement; Professor Nikolaus Pevsner, Arthur Korn and Dr Reyner Banham for comments on earlier drafts; Dr J.Quentin Hughes of the Liverpool School of Architecture for help with the early drafts; Professor Serge Chermayeff; Professor Hermann Finsterlin; Mrs Oud-Dinaux; George E.Pettengill, Librarian, American Institute of Architects; Van den Broek and Bakema; W.M.Dudok; The Secretary, Zentralvereinigung der Architekten Österreichs; Basil Ward for advice on Lethaby and Connell, Ward and Lucas; Miss Enid Caldicott, Miss Elizabeth Dixon and the staff of the Architectural Association Library, who have all spent a lot of time over the years looking out early material for me and checking proofs; Edward Carter and George Wiltshire of the Architectural Association for their encouragement and for help in finding suitable portrait photographs when the compiler's sources were exhausted.

I also extend my grateful thanks to a number of national and local libraries whose assistance has been invaluable: The Victoria and Albert Museum Library; Picton Arts Library, Liverpool; The School of Architecture and Cohen Library, Liverpool University; Central Library, Manchester; the School of Architecture and Arts Faculty Library, Manchester University; Bedfordshire County Library and Luton Public Library.

DS

Note

Further help has been received from numerous sources but my acknowledgements must still be to the people listed above who made the original publication possible. Although some of them are now deceased their help and advice went far beyond this list. In addition I would however like to couple the names above with those who gave me additional advice over the years: John Vloemans, Otto Koenigsberger, Julius Posener as well as generations of students at the AA School who have found practical use in this bibliography. To John Taylor and Charlotte Burri of Lund Humphries Publishers I owe a great deal for their patient supervision of the texts and careful proof-reading.

DS

Biographical bibliography

Bibliographies, biographies and general publication lists on individual architects are to be found in the following publications: Lawrence Wodehouse, *American Architects from the Civil War to the First World War* and *American Architects from the First World War to the Present*, 2 vols, Gale Research Company, Detroit, Michigan 1976–7; Lawrence Wodehouse, *British Architects, 1840–1976*, Gale, Detroit 1978; David M.Sokel, *American Architecture and Art*, Gale, Detroit 1976; Anatole Senkevitch, Jr, *Soviet Architecture 1917–62*, University Press of Virginia, Charlottesville 1974; J.M. Richards (ed.), *Who's Who in Architecture from 1400 to the Present Day*, London, New York, 1977.
Note also:
H-R. Hitchcock, *American Architectural Books*, 1946 (1962), Da Capo, New York 1976. An expanded version of the 1962 edition which lists books, portfolios and pamphlets on architecture and related subjects published in the usa before 1895.
The various volumes of 'The American Association of Architectural Bibliographers', Charlottesville, usa, some of which are mentioned in the individual biographical sections of this bibliography.

Alvar AALTO (1898–1976)

Henrik Hugo Alvar Aalto, born at Kuortane, near Jyväskylä, 1898. Died Helsinki, 1976.

Studied at Helsinki Polytechnic under Frosterus until 1921.

Elected Member, Academy of Finland, 1955; Honorary Member, Akademie der Künste, Berlin; RIBA Royal Gold Medallist 1957; Professor of Experimental Architecture, MIT, 1946–7.

Aalto wrote very little (all collected in *Sketches*, see below); his work demands to be seen in its setting and enjoyed for its richness of form and sympathetic use of natural materials. Among his best-known works are the Paimio Sanatorium (1929–33), Municipal Library, Viipuri (1935), Villa Mairea (1938–9), Town Hall, Säynätsalo (1951), Pedagogical Institute, Jyväskylä (1957), National Pensions Building, Helsinki (1956), Church, Imatra (1958).

The comprehensive volumes edited by Karl Fleig, *Alvar Aalto*, show the variety and development of the architect's work. The book by the Neuenschwanders is a study in depth of Aalto's work in 1950–1 and shows the method of working in his office. Since Aalto's death, many new books, catalogues and articles have appeared. A comprehensive bibliography has yet to be published although the recent books noted contain selected lists. See Vance Bibliography A-172.

AALTO, ALVAR. 'Zwischen Humanismus und Materialismus', *Der Bau*, Nos.7–8, Vienna 1955; reprinted in *Baukunst und Werkform*, Vol.9, No.6, 1956, pp.298–300.

AALTO, ALVAR. 'Problemi di architettura', *Quaderni ACJ*, Turin 1956.

AALTO, ALVAR. 'RIBA Annual Discourse 1957', *RIBA Journal*, May 1957, pp. 258–63.

MCANDREW, J., & BREINES, S. *Alvar Aalto: Architecture and Furniture*, New York 1938.

LABÒ, G. *Alvar Aalto*, Milan 1948.

GIEDION, S. *Space, Time and Architecture*, Cambridge, Mass., London, 1949 (2nd edn). Included in all later editions, section: 'Alvar Aalto: Elemental and Contemporary.' (In 4th edn pp.565–605).

NEUENSCHWANDER, E. & C. *Alvar Aalto and Finnish Architecture*, Zürich, London, 1954. A monograph covering the 1950–1 period in detail.

GUTHEIM, F. *Alvar Aalto*, New York, London, 1960. A short survey of Aalto's work.

SCHILDT, G. & MOSSO, L. *Alvar Aalto*, Jyväskylä 1962.

FLEIG, K. (ed.) *Alvar Aalto 1922–62*, Zürich, London, New York, 1963 and *Alvar Aalto 1963–*, *loc.cit.*, 1970. Also pb. précis of 2 vols, London 1975.

BAIRD, G. *Alvar Aalto*, London, New York, 1970. Photographs by Futugawa.

RUUSUVUORI, A. (ed.) *Alvar Aalto 1898–1976*, Helsinki 1978. The English-language catalogue for the 1978 exhibition.

SCHILDT, G. (ed.) *Alvar Aalto: Sketches*, Cambridge (Mass.), London 1978. Aalto's writings and drawings.

SHAND, P.M. 'Tuberculosis Sanatorium, Paimio, Finland', *Architectural Review*, September 1933, pp.85–90.
SHAND, P.M. 'The Library at Viipuri, Eastern Finland', *Architectural Review*, March 1936, pp.107–14.
WOOD, J. (ed.) 'Alvar Aalto 1957', *Architects' Year Book*, No.8, London 1957, pp.137–88.

BANHAM, R. 'The One and the Few: The Rise of Modern Architecture in Finland', *Architectural Review*, April 1957, pp.243–59. A first-class survey of Finnish architecture with particular reference to Aalto's achievements.
SHARP, D. 'Aalto and his Influence', *Architecture and Building*, December 1957, pp.476–9.
SANTINI, P.C., & SCHILDT, G. 'Alvar Aalto from Sunila to Imatra: ideas, projects and buildings', *Zodiac 3*, Milan 1958, pp.27–82.
MOSSO, L. 'La luce nell' architettura di Aalto', *Zodiac 7*, Milan, pp.66–115.
ANON. 'Alvar Aalto', *L'Architecture d'Aujourd'hui*, April–May 1964, pp.112–17. A pictorial summary of Aalto's work.

Erik Gunnar ASPLUND (1885–1940)

Born Stockholm, 1885. Died Stockholm, 1940.
Initially Asplund's ambition was to be a painter; he sketched and painted with some talent. He studied at Royal Institute of Technology, Stockholm, Division of Architecture 1905–1909, and also privately under Begsten, Tengbom, Westman and Östberg, and visited old Swedish buildings in vacations. He travelled widely in Europe. After 1909 he entered many competitions, winning – in 1912 and 1913 – two for schools. One of these was later commissioned. In 1913 won first prize for extension to Law Courts, Gothenburg, – completed in 1937 – after much controversy over style of façade. In 1914, with Sigurd Lewerentz, he won the international competition for the layout of Stockholm's South Cemetery – surely one of the truly great twentieth-century developments? From 1912–13 he was assistant lecturer in Stockholm; 1917–18, special instructor in Ornamental Art. In 1917–20 he was made Editor of *Teknisk Tidskrift Arkitektur*. Practice continued with private houses, cemeteries and chapels, early showed strong personal and romantic idiosyncracies contrasting with his later demands for harmony of material and design, form and technique.
In 1920 visited USA on research for public library for Stockholm City Council. His Skandia Cinema, Stockholm, dates from 1922. Asplund designed the layout for the Stockholm exhibition 1930; his Paradiset Restaurant was considered by many as *the* best building. The exhibition itself contained an extensive modern housing section and aimed 'to point the way to a new architecture and a new life . . . to explore the new ways in which architecture might socially serve man'.
From 1931–1940 he was Professor of Architecture, Royal Institute of Technology, Stockholm. Asplund's last important works included two Stockholm Laboratories, a department store and the Woodland Cemetery at Skogskyrogarden.

ASPLUND, GUNNAR, MARKELIUS, S. *et al. Acceptera – Manifesto*, Stockholm 1931. Swedish text.

ZEVI, B. *Erik Gunnar Asplund* in the *Architetti del Movimento Moderno* Series 6, Milan 1948.
HOLMDAHL, GUSTAV *et al. Gunnar Asplund Architect 1885–1940*, Stockholm 1950. French/English. A beautifully produced publication which does Asplund great service.
HILL, O. *Fair Horizons: buildings of today*, London 1950, see pp.49–51.
DE MARÉ, E. *Gunnar Asplund. A great modern architect*, London 1955.
WREDE, S. *The Architecture of Erik Gunnar Asplund*, Cambridge (Mass.), London, 1980.

SHAND, P. MORTON. Illustrated memoir of Asplund. *Architectural Review*, May 1941.
SHAND, P.MORTON. 'E. Gunnar Asplund', *AA Journal*, Jan. 1959.

Mackay Hugh BAILLIE SCOTT   (1865–1945)

Born near Ramsgate, Kent, 1865. Died Brighton, 1945.
Baillie Scott's father was a 'gentleman' of considerable means; the eldest of four children he was educated privately in Worthing and Royal Agricultural College, Cirencester, from where he graduated in 1885 with Silver Medal. On visit to London decided to become architect. In 1886 began as articled pupil to Bath City Architect, Major Charles E.Davis, from whom he learned 'only to draw out the orders'. He always 'remained essentially a countryman' and of his fellow architects he seems to have known only Voysey personally, digesting the works of others through magazines.
In his early twenties settled in Isle of Man, building a number of small houses, village halls, etc.; his sketches of 'An Ideal Country Cottage' in *The Studio* magazine inspired a reader to commission its erection in Cheshire. Other commissions followed in England and abroad: Rumania, Italy, Poland, Switzerland, America and particularly Germany, including decorations for the Grand Ducal Palace at Darmstadt.
In 1903 he moved his practice to Bedford. He built a pair of cottages at the 1905 Letchworth exhibition – acknowledged outstanding success and resulted in many commissions for small houses and cottages all over Britain.
Contributed articles to books on town planning and garden suburbs. In 1914 planned a garden city for Kharkov.
Resumed practice in 1919 with A.Edgar Beresford in London, continuing small country-house building.
He wrote two books on houses and gardens (his own) and many magazine articles mainly for *The Studio* and chiefly on furniture and decoration. His aim was to create: 'sane practical planning for actual requirements of normal people . . . disdaining artificial conventions, social or architectural . . . to re-establish rural traditions . . . and attack the prevalent vogue of vulgar mechanically produced ornament . . .' He chose to use only 'shapes and materials which blend with background'. The AR obituary refers to him as 'one of the great British pioneers of Art Nouveau'.

BAILLIE SCOTT, M.H. *Haus eines Kunstfreundes*, Vol.I, Darmstadt, London 1902. Introduction by H.Muthesius.

BAILLIE SCOTT, M.H. *Houses and Gardens*, London 1906.

BAILLIE SCOTT, M.H., RAYMOND UNWIN *et al. Town Planning and Modern Architecture in the Hampstead Garden Suburb*, London 1909. Includes 'The Englishman's Home', pp.11–17.

BAILLIE SCOTT, M.H. *et al. Garden Suburbs, Town Planning and Modern Architecture*, London 1911.

BAILLIE SCOTT M.H. and A.EDGAR BERESFORD. *Houses and Gardens*, London 1933. A substantial revision of the 1906 book.

DAVISON, T.RAFFLES. (ed.) *The Arts connected with Building*, London 1909. Lectures delivered to Worshipful Company of Carpenters including 'Ideals in Building, False and True', pp.139–152 by Baillie Scott.

KORNWOLF, JAMES D. *M.H.Baillie Scott and the Arts and Crafts Movement*, Baltimore and London 1972. The definitive biography with comprehensive bibliography.

MEDICI MALL, K. *Das Landhaus Waldbühl von M. H. Baillie Scott. Ein Gesamtkunstwerk zwischen Neugotik und Jugendstil*, Bern 1979.

TAYLOR, NICHOLAS. 'Baillie Scott's Waldbühl', *Architectural Review*, Dec. 1965, pp.456–8.

Otto BARTNING (1883–1959)

Born Karlsruhe, 1883. Died Darmstadt, 1959.
Studied at Charlottenburg and Karlsruhe Technical High Schools and Berlin University. Commenced practice in Berlin in 1905.
Director, Staatliche Bauhochschule in Weimar. Responsible for a large number of buildings including churches, offices, factories, private and public housing, estate developments in Berlin, the Rhineland, Austria and Czechoslovakia. Particularly well known for his Protestant churches: 'Sternkirche', 1922; Steel Church, Cologne, 1928; the circular planned Church of the Resurrection, Essen, 1930. No writings in English.

BARTNING, OTTO. *Vom neuen Kirchbau*, Berlin 1919.

BARTNING, OTTO. *Was ist Bauen?*, Stuttgart 1952. Presidential address to the BDA. (6pp.)

BARTNING, OTTO. *Otto Bartning in kurzen Worten*, Hamburg 1954.

BARTNING, OTTO. *Erde Geliebte*, Hamburg 1955.

BARTNING, OTTO, & WEYRES, W. *Kirchen: Handbuch für den Kirchenbau*, Munich 1959. Bartning was editor for the second part of this comprehensive volume on German church building: Buch II, *Evangelischer Kirchenbau*.

MAYER, H.K.F. *Der Baumeister Otto Bartning und die Wiederentdeckung des Raumes*, Heidelberg 1951.

Peter BEHRENS (1868–1940)

Born Hamburg, 1868. Died Berlin, 1940.
Began his career as a painter, attended Karlsruhe and Düsseldorf Art Schools,
1886–9. Founder member of the Munich Sezession, 1893. Specialized in
graphic and applied art work. 1896 Travelled in Italy. 1898 Studied problems
of industrial mass production.
Invited to help form the Art Colony at Darmstadt by the Grand Duke Ernst
Ludwig of Hessen in 1899. Designed his first building – his own house – at
Darmstadt, 1901.
Became Head of Düsseldorf Art School in 1903. Appointed designer to the
electrical combine AEG in Berlin, 1907, for whom he designed products and a
number of industrial buildings, as well as workers' housing. Private practice in
Berlin brought a number of important commissions and also brought to his
office three pupils, Walter Gropius, Mies van der Rohe and – for a short period
in 1910 – Charles-Édouard Jeanneret (Le Corbusier). Designed
Bassett-Lowke House, England in 1924.
Behrens became Director of Architecture, Vienna Academy in 1922 and later
Director of the Department of Architecture at the Prussian Academy in Berlin
from 1936.
The books by Hoeber and Cremers are excellent records of the built work of
Peter Behrens. The book edited by Grimme on the Master School at the
Vienna Academy indicates the excellence of his students. The recent Berlin
catalogue is excellent, with bibliography.

BEHRENS, PETER. *Feste des Lebens und der Kunst*, Jena 1900.
BEHRENS, PETER. *Beziehungen der künstlerischen und technischen Probleme*, Berlin
1917. Also published in *Wendingen*, Nos.3–4, 1920, pp.4–20.
BEHRENS, PETER. *Das Ethos und die Umlagerung der künstlerischen Probleme*,
Darmstadt 1920.
BEHRENS, PETER. 'Die Baugesinnung des Faschismus', *Die Neue Linie*,
November 1933, pp.11–13.

HOEBER, F. *Peter Behrens*, Munich 1913.
CREMERS, P.J. *Peter Behrens, sein Werk von 1909 bis zur Gegenwart*, Essen 1928.
GRIMME, K.M. (ed.) *Peter Behrens und seine Wiener Akademische Meisterschule*, Vienna
1930. With a contribution by Peter Behrens.
WEBER, W. (ed.) *Peter Behrens (1868–1940)*, Kaiserslautern, 1966/7. Exhibition
catalogue. Foreword by Walter Gropius.
BUDDENSEIG, TILMAN *et al. Industriekultur: Peter Behrens und die AEG 1907–1914*,
Berlin 1979. The Berlin exhibition catalogue.

NIEMEYER, W. 'Peter Behrens und die Raumästhetik seiner Kunst', *Dekorative
Kunst*, 1906–7, pp.137–65.
POSENER, J. 'L'Œuvre de Peter Behrens', *L'Architecture d'Aujourd'hui*, March
1934, pp.8–29.
SHAND, P.M. 'Peter Behrens', *Architectural Review*, September 1934, pp.39–42.
Reprinted in SHARP, D. (ed.) *The Rationalists*, London 1978, pp.6–15.
ROGERS, E., *et al*. 'Numero dedicato a Peter Behrens', *Casabella Continuità*,
Special No.240, 1960. An important collection of articles on Behrens's work,
with numerous illustrations.

Max BERG   (1870–1947)

Born Stettin, 1870. Died 1947.
Studied at the Technical High School, Charlottenburg, under Schaeffer. City
Architect, Breslau (now Wroclaw).
Berg's claim to fame rests on one major building of international importance,
the Jahrhunderthalle of 1913 in Breslau. This enormous, heavy concrete dome
(now used as the People's Palace) was not only a monument to human
engineering skill but also an early example of architect/engineer collaboration;
the engineer was Trauer. Berg later gave up architecture.

BERG, MAX. 'Hochhäuser im Stadtbild', *Wasmuths Monatshefte für Baukunst*, Year
6, 1921–2, p.101.

H. P. BERLAGE   (1856–1934)

Hendrik Petrus Berlage was born in Amsterdam in 1856. Died The Hague,
1934.
Studied at Zürich under Semper, 1875–78. In 1878 he returned to Holland for
a short period before travelling extensively in Europe. He settled in Holland in
1881 setting up practice in 1889. He became the greatest name in Dutch
architecture, designing and carrying out many important buildings and
convincingly putting down his ideas and philosophy in writing. This
philosophy was of considerable importance to his followers in the so-called
'Amsterdam School', de Klerk, Kramer, Van de Meij and Wijdeveld. He was
also instrumental in introducing Frank Lloyd Wright's work to Dutch and
Swiss architects in 1912 after visit to USA in 1911. His best known buildings
include the Exchange, Amsterdam, 1897–1903; Diamond-Workers' House,
Amsterdam, 1899–1900; Holland House, City of London, 1914, etc. Settled in
The Hague, 1911.
Berlage's work was principally founded on geometry and in his most famous
book, *Grundlagen und Entwicklung der Architektur* (the four Zürich lectures) he
quotes Sheraton: 'Time alters fashions . . . but that which is founded on
geometry and real science will remain unalterable'.
The major monograph on Berlage is by Pieter Singelenberg and contains a
comprehensive bibliography.

BERLAGE, HENDRIK PETRUS. *Over Stijl in Bouw- en Meubelkunst*, Rotterdam 1904
(2nd edn 1908; 3rd edn 1917).
BERLAGE, HENDRIK PETRUS. *Gedanken über Stil in der Baukunst*, Leipzig 1905.
BERLAGE, HENDRIK PETRUS. *Grundlagen und Entwicklung der Architektur*, Berlin,
Rotterdam, 1908.
BERLAGE, HENDRIK PETRUS. *Studies over Bouwkunst, Stil en Samenleving*, Rotterdam
1910.
BERLAGE, HENDRIK PETRUS. *Een drietal Lezingen in Amerika gehouden*, Rotterdam
1912.
BERLAGE, HENDRIK PETRUS. *Schoonheid en Samenleving*, Rotterdam 1919 (2nd edn
1924).

BERLAGE, HENDRIK PETRUS. *L'Art et La Societé*, Brussels 1921.
BERLAGE, HENDRIK PETRUS. *De Ontwikkeling der moderne bouwkunst in Holland*, Amsterdam 1925, Sorbonne lecture.
BERLAGE, HENDRIK PETRUS. *Het wezen der Bouwkunst en haar geschiedenis: aesthetische beschouwingen*, Haarlem 1934.
BERLAGE, H.P. 'Over Architectuur', *Tweemaandelijks Tijdschrift*, Vol.11, Pt1, Amsterdam 1896.
BERLAGE, H.P. 'Scritti di H.P.Berlage', *Casabella*, No.249. Extracts from Berlage's writings.

BAZEL, K.P.C. DE, *et al. Dr H.P.Berlage en zijn werk*, Rotterdam 1916. Festschrift on 60th birthday includes essays on town planning, furniture, etc.
GRATAMA, J. *Dr H.P.Berlage Bouwmeester*, Rotterdam 1925. 70th birthday Festschrift.
HAVELAAR, J. *Dr H.P.Berlage*, Amsterdam, n.d. (*c.*1927). In the series *Nederlandsche Bouwmeesters* No.3, p.b.
SINGELENBERG, P. *H.P.Berlage: Idea and Style. The Quest for Modern Architecture*, Utrecht 1972. An excellent study of Berlage's work and ideas in relation to contemporary developments.

MISC. 'H.P.Berlage', Special No., *Bouwkundig Weekblad Architectura*, No.51, 1934. The 'commemorative' issue.
GRASSI, G. 'Immagine di Berlage', *Casabella*, No.249.

Max BILL   (1908–   )

Born Winterthur, Switzerland, 1908.
A man of many parts: sculptor, painter, designer and architect, Bill studied at the Kunstgewerbeschule, Zürich and from 1927 to 1929 at the Dessau Bauhaus. Set up practice as architect in 1930. Member of the 'abstraction création' group, 1932–7. Responsible for the exhibition 'Die gute Form'. In 1936 he was awarded the Prix d'Honneur at the Milan Triennale.
He was co-founder of the Hochschule für Gestaltung, Ulm and served as Rector from 1951 to 1956. He also designed the buildings of the School.
Formerly Head of Department of Architecture and Design, Ulm.

BILL, MAX (ed.) *Le Corbusier et P. Jeanneret, œuvre complète*, 1934–8, Zürich 1939 (2nd edn 1945).
BILL, MAX (ed.) *Moderne Schweizer Architektur*, Basel 1942 (1950).
BILL, MAX (ed.) *Die gute Form*, Bern and Zürich 1949.
BILL, MAX (ed.) *Robert Maillart*, Zürich 1949. (London 1969)
BILL, MAX. *Form: Balance sheet of mid-twentieth century trends in design*, Basel 1952.
BILL, MAX (ed.) 'The Bauhaus Idea', *Architects' Year Book*, No.5, London 1953, pp.29–32.

MALDONADO, T. *Max Bill*, Buenos Aires 1955. (Stuttgart 1956). Full bibliography.
GOMRINGER, E. (ed.) *Max Bill*, Teufen 1958.
STABER, M. *Max Bill*, London 1964.

ROGERS, E. N. 'Max Bill', *Magazine of Art*, No.46, May 1953, pp.226–230.
STABER, M. 'Max Bill und die Umweltgestaltung', *Zodiac 9*, Milan 1962, pp.60–94.

Dominikus BÖHM   (1880–1955)

Born Jettingen, near Ulm, 1880. Died Cologne, 1955.
Studied at the Technical High School, Stuttgart, under Theodor Fischer.
Leader of the Roman Catholic new church architecture movement in
Germany. Designed the wooden Offenbach church, 1919, probably his
best-known church, St Engelbert, Cologne-Riehl, in 1930; the concrete church
at Neu-Ulm, 1923; church at Bischofsheim, 1925. Was also a teacher at
Bingen, Offenbach and Cologne schools of architecture. His work is
characterized by its simplicity and ingenious use of structural shapes for
symbolic purposes. Won the international competition for a Cathedral at San
Salvador in 1953. Father of Gottfried Böhm whose concrete buildings have
had great influence in 1960s and 1970s.

HOFF, A., & MUCK, H. *Böhm: Leben und Werk*, Munich, Zürich, 1962.

SCHWARZ, R. 'Dominikus Böhm', *Baukunst und Werkform*, No.2, 1955,
pp.72–131.

Max Bill
Victor Bourgeois

pour Augsbourg.

Paul BONATZ (1877–1951)

Born Solgne, Lorraine, 1877. Died Berlin, 1951.
Studied at the Technical High Schools at Munich and Charlottenburg. At first
assistant to, later successor of, Theodor Fischer as Professor of Architecture at
Stuttgart Technical High School, 1902–7, 1908. Responsible for a number of
university, commercial and industrial buildings. The well-known railway
station at Stuttgart was designed by Bonatz in association with F. Scholar and
erected 1914–28. Bonatz's work – much of it of a conservative nature – is well
represented in the illustrated books and magazines of the period.

BONATZ, PAUL. *Leben und Bauen*, Stuttgart 1950 (4th edn 1958).
BONATZ, P., & LEONHARDT, F. *Brücken*, Königstein-im-Taunus 1951. One of *Die
Blauen Bücher* series.

GRAUBNER, G. (ed.) *Paul Bonatz und seine Schüler*, Stuttgart 1930.
TAMMS, F. (ed.) *Paul Bonatz, Arbeiten aus den Jahren 1907–37*, Stuttgart 1937.

Victor BOURGEOIS (1897–1962)

Born Charleroi, Belgium, 1897. Died Brussels, 1962.
Studied at the Académie Royale des Beaux-Arts, Brussels, 1914–19. He

became in the inter-war period the leading Belgian architect-urbanist. An original signatory of the CIAM La Sarraz Manifesto, he was a vice-president of CIAM from 1928 to 1947.

He was honoured for his work by many Belgian and foreign organizations. Included among his awards was an honorary citizenship of New York. He was Professor at the École Nationale Supérieure d'Architecture at Brussels. Bourgeois was also the director or co-director of a number of influential reviews, including *Au Volant* (1919); *Les Geste* (1920); *Sept Arts* (1922–8); *Bruxelles* (1932–3); *Sept Arts* (1948–). He was also responsible with Van Eesteren, Steiger and Giedion for the published report *Rationelle Bebauungsweisen* on the 2nd CIAM Congress (Frankfurt-am-Main 1931).

BOURGEOIS, VICTOR. *De l'architecture au temps d'Érasme à l'Humanisme social de notre architecture*, Brussels 1946. In collaboration with R. de Cooman.
BOURGEOIS, VICTOR. *Victor Bourgeois: Architectures 1922–52*, Brussels 1952.
BOURGEOIS, VICTOR. *L'architecte et son espace*, Brussels 1955. In the collection *Sept Arts* (see above).
BOUGEOIS, V. 'Reflexions sur l'architecture moderne en Belgique', *Le Document*, Brussels, April 1924.

FLOUQUET, P.L. *Victor Bourgeois – Architecture 1922–1952*, Brussels 1952.
LINZE, G. *Victor Bourgeois*, Brussels 1960. Brief, but it contains a bibliographical section and list of works. In the series *Monographies de l'art Belge*.

Marcel BREUER (1902–)

Born Pecs, Hungary, 1902. Lives in New York.

He went to Vienna in 1920 with the intention of becoming a painter and sculptor. But he was embarrassed by the eclectic air at the Academy and hearing about Gropius's new venture at Weimar moved on. He has become the most celebrated of the first-generation Bauhaus students. In 1924 he took over the direction of the furniture workshops at the Bauhaus. He left Dessau in 1928 and set up practice in Berlin during the 'lean' period. Travelled extensively. In 1932 he built his first house at Wiesbaden; in 1933 he designed the famous Dolderthal apartments for Giedion in conjunction with the Roths. Moving to England he was in partnership with F.R.S. Yorke in 1936–7. Then Breuer moved to the USA to join Walter Gropius, the newly appointed Chairman of the Architecture Department at Harvard. They were partners in practice, 1937–41. Moved to New York in 1946. In 1952 he was selected as one of the three architects for UNESCO HQ in Paris.

His views are presented in the book *Sun and Shadow* (1956) and his work collected in the volume edited by Cranston Jones. See Vance bibliographies, *Marcel Breuer: Architect and Designer*, A-53 and *The Architecture of Marcel Lajos Breuer*, A–202.

BREUER, MARCEL. *Sun and Shadow. The Philosophy of an Architect*, London, New York, 1956. (Peter Blake, ed.).
BREUER, MARCEL. *Marcel Breuer: 1921–1961: Buildings and Projects*, New York, London, 1962. Intro. and notes by C. Jones. German version:
BREUER, MARCEL. *Marcel Breuer 1921–62*, Stuttgart 1962.

BLAKE, P. *Marcel Breuer: Architect and Designer*, New York 1949.
ARGAN, G.C. *Marcel Breuer*, Milan 1957.
MISC. *Marcel Breuer*, New York 1972. Exhibition cat. with essay by W. von Eckardt. Issued in French version, 1974.

HITCHCOCK, H-R. 'Marcel Breuer and the American Tradition in Architecture', 1938. Typewritten, RIBA exhibition catalogue. (18 pp.)

J.H. Van den BROEK (1898–1978) and J.B. BAKEMA (1914–)

J.H. van den Broek was born in Rotterdam in 1898. Died The Hague, 1978. Studied at Delft Technical College, graduating in 1924. Began his own practice in Rotterdam in 1927. In 1937 he joined J.A. Brinkman (b.1902) in partnership, replacing L.C. van der Vlugt (b.1894) who had died in 1936. He has held a professorship at Delft for many years. In 1947 he took into partnership J.B. Bakema. Brinkman died in 1949. This succession of architects working together has produced some of the most significant modern architecture in the Netherlands. Mart Stam (q.v.) was assistant.
Jacob B. Bakema was born at Groningen in 1914.
Studied engineering and architecture at Groningen, at Amsterdam and at Delft. His early experience was gained in Van Eesteren's town planning office in Amsterdam and in the office of Van Tijen and Maaskant. Since 1963 Professor of Architectural Design, Delft.
The work of Van den Broek and Bakema has been published in the 'Documents of Modern Architecture' series (Stuttgart) edited by Jürgen Joedicke.

BROEK, J.H.VAN DEN (ed.) *Habitations*, Vols. 1–3, Rotterdam 1945–65.
BROEK, J.H.VAN DEN. *Creatieve Krachten in de Architectonische Conceptie*, Delft 1948.
BAKEMA, J. *L. C. van der Vlucht*, Rotterdam 1968.
BAKEMA, J.B. 'Dutch Architecture Today', *Architects' Year Book*, No.5, 1953, pp.67–82.
BAKEMA, J.B. 'Architecture by Planning/Planning by Architecture', *Architects' Year Book*, No.8, pp.23–42.

NEWMAN, O. (ed.) CIAM *'59 in Otterlo*, London 1961. Important contributions by Bakema, etc.
JOEDICKE, J. (ed.) *Architektur und Städtebau. Das Werk der Architekten van den Broek und Bakema*, Stuttgart 1963.
JOEDICKE, J. (ed.) *Architektur-Urbanismus* Stuttgart 1976.

VAN TIJEN, W. 'Het Bureau van den Broek en Bakema', *Forum*, No.6, Amsterdam 1957, pp.166–202.

MISC. 'Jacob Berend Bakema', *Der Aufbau*, November 1958, pp.439–44.

PERUGINI, G. 'Costruzioni degli architetti Jacob Bakema e Johannes van den Broek', *L'Architettura*, No.47, September 1959, pp.324–39.

MISC. 'Van den Broek und Bakema', Special No., *Bauen und Wohnen*, October 1959.

HOUSDEN, B. (ed.) 'M.Brinkman, J.A. Brinkman, L.C. van der Vlugt, J.H. van den Broek, J.B. Bakema', *Architectural Association Journal*, December 1960. A special issue with information on all the partners of the firm.

NEWMAN, O. 'Jacob Bakema: Holland', *Canadian Architect*, May 1962, pp.43–50.

Daniel Hudson BURNHAM (1846–1912)
and John Wellborn ROOT (1850–91)

Daniel Burnham was born in Henderson, New York, in 1846. Died Heidelberg, 1912. After vain attempts to gain an education at Harvard and Yale, Burnham entered an architectural office in Chicago in 1872 where he met John Wellborn Root (b. Lumpkin 1850). They formed a partnership in 1873 and began experiments in steel-framed construction for which they became justly famous. Designed the Rookery in 1886, the Reliance Building, Chicago (with C.Atwood) in 1890–4, and the battered load-bearing yet elegant Monadnock Building, Chicago in 1889–91. The firm was commissioned to prepare the World's Columbian Exposition for 1893 at the turn of the decade and Burnham saw it through; Root, the designer-philosopher, died in 1891. Firm renamed D.H.Burnham and Co. From the planning of the exposition Burnham gained insight into the problems of planning and drew out proposals for Washington D.C. in 1902. His famous Chicago Plan dates from 1907; the famous Flatiron Building, New York from 1902.

ROOT, J.W. *The meaning of architecture: Buildings and writings by John Wellborn Root*, New York 1967. (Collected and introduced by Donald Hoffmann).

ROOT, J.W. 'Art of pure color', *Inland Architect and Builder*, Vol.I, No.5, June 1883, pp.66–67; Vol.I, No.6, July 1883, pp.80, 82; Vol.II, No.1, Aug. 1883, p.89; Vol.II, No.2, Sep. 1883, p.106.

ROOT, J.W. 'A great architectural problem', *Inland Architect and News Record*, Vol.XV, No.5, June 1890, pp.67–71. A paper first read at the Art Institute of Chicago, June 1890.

ROOT, J.W. 'Architects of Chicago', *America* (Chicago), Vol.5, 11 Dec. 1890. A special issue of the magazine with the article published anonymously and later reprinted in the *Inland Architect and News Record*, Vol.XVI, No.8, Jan. 1891, pp.91–92.

MONROE, H. *John Wellborn Root: A study of his life and work*, Boston, New York, 1896. (Park Forest, Ill., Prairie School reprint, 1966).

HOFFMANN, D. *The architecture of John Wellborn Root*, Baltimore 1973.

MOORE, C.H. *Daniel H. Burnham: Architect and Planner of Cities*, 2 vols, Boston 1921.

HINES, T. *Burnham of Chicago: Architect and Planner*, Chicago 1974.

Felix Candela

Felix CANDELA (1910–)

Born in Madrid, 1910. Lived and worked in Mexico 1939–71. Now in USA.
Studied at the High School for Architecture, Madrid. Graduated 1935.
Candela is best known for adventurous use of reinforced concrete and for his
interest in shell vaulting. He, with his fellow countryman Eduardo Torroja,
has translated the science of engineering into the art of architecture. Beauty of
form has been produced from the economy of structure and an intuitive
understanding of materials and their performance under stress. In 1947
adopted Mexican nationality and with brothers set up a constructional and
architectural practice. Built hotels and apartments before specialising in
catenary structures. Candela has been honoured by many countries and is also
a recipient of the UIA Auguste Perret Prize for Architecture.

FABER, C. *Candela: Adventurer in New Structural Forms*, New York 1961.
FABER, C. *Candela: The Shell Builder*, London 1963.
SMITH, C.B. *Builders in the Sun: Five Mexican Architects*, New York 1967;
pp.93–129 on Candela.

Serge Chermayeff

Serge CHERMAYEFF (1900–)

Born in Russia, 1900. Lives in New Haven, Conn.
Educated at the Royal Drawing Society School and Harrow School. Studied
art and architecture in Germany, Austria, France and Holland. He began his
career as a member of the editorial staff, Amalgamated Press, London,
1918–23. Later he became well known as a furniture and industrial designer.
In 1930 he set up in architectural practice on his own. He carried out a number
of commissions for buildings and exhibitions in England in the thirties,
including the Bexhill Pavilion, won while in partnership with Eric
Mendelsohn. Wrote in *AJ* and *AR*. After the period with Mendelsohn
(1933–6) he continued his practice independently in England and California.
He was appointed Chairman, Department of Design, and Professor of
Architecture, Brooklyn College and held these positions 1942–6. In practice in
New York City, 1946–51 and President, Institute of Design, Chicago.
Professor of Architecture, Harvard Graduate School of Design, 1953–62;
Professor at Yale, 1962–1969. Chermayeff became an American citizen in
1946.
He has contributed to many journals on a variety of subjects, including
housing, planning, design, education and architecture.

CHERMAYEFF, S. & ALEXANDER, C. *Community and Privacy. Towards a New Architecture of Humanism*, New York 1963; Harmondsworth 1966 (p.b.).
CHERMAYEFF, S. & TZONIS, A. *Shape of Community*, Harmondsworth 1971 (p.b.)
CHERMAYEFF, S. & RICHARDS, J.M. 'A Hundred Years Ahead', *AJ*, LXXXI, 1935.
CHERMAYEFF, S. 'Multiple Dwellings and their possibilities' in Zucker, P. *New Architecture and City Planning*. New York 1944, pp.278–89.

ANON. 'Serge Chermayeff', *Der Aufbau*, September 1957, pp.369–70. Biographical notes and illustrations.

Wells COATES (1895–1958)

Wells Wintemute Coates was born in Tokyo in 1895 of Canadian parents. Died Vancouver, 1958.

His mother was an architectural pupil of Louis Sullivan and was a contemporary of Frank Lloyd Wright. He was educated privately in Japan and later studied for a number of years at McGill in Canada. In 1924 after coming to England he received his Ph.D. from London University for a study of diesel engines. He began his professional career as a journalist for the *Daily Express* and worked for some time in Paris, coming into close contact with the work of contemporary architects and painters at the Paris Exhibition in 1925. He began work as an engineer-architect in about 1927, employed by 'Crysede' to design shop fittings, etc. In the early thirties he became actively involved in architectural design and began to encourage his colleagues to form groups for the furtherance of modern ideas in architecture and design. He was a faithful disciple of CIAM and the founder of the English MARS Group (1933).

In the post-war years he was responsible for a series of designs for cheap mass housing and for the Telekinema at the 1951 Festival of Britain. In 1952 he was appointed architect-planner to the new town of Iroquois, Ontario, Canada. He also taught at Harvard in 1955–6.

His most important lecture, to the 20th Century Group, entitled 'A Sketch Plan for a New Aesthetic' (February 1931) has never been published. His writings cover a wide field of interests and a few of the key articles on architecture and design are listed below. Cantacuzino's book now provides a definitive source.

COATES, WELLS. Work of the architect in *Unit One*, London 1934, pp.105–115.
COATES, WELLS. 'Inspiration from Japan', *Architects' Journal*, 4 November 1931, pp.586–7.
COATES, WELLS. 'Materials for Architecture', *Architects' Journal*, 4 November 1931, pp.388–9.
COATES, WELLS. 'Response to Tradition', *Architectural Review*, November 1932, pp.165–8.
COATES, WELLS. 'The Conditions for an Architecture for Today', *Architectural Association Journal*, April 1938, pp.447–57.
RICHARDS, J.M. 'Wells Coates 1893–1958', *Architectural Review*, December 1958, pp.357–60.
CANTACUZINO, S. *Wells Coates: A monograph*, London 1978.

Amyas Connell

Basil Ward

Amyas CONNELL (1900–80), Basil WARD (1902–78) & Colin LUCAS (1906–)

Amyas Douglas Connell was born in New Zealand in 1900. Died London, 1980. Educated at New Plymouth High School and as articled pupil. Met Ward, both desired to travel. On coming to London they continued their studies at the Bartlett School, University College, London. Connell won the Rome Prize in Architecture for 1926. In 1928, after travelling Europe extensively with Ward, he commenced practice in London. On return from Rome built the controversial house 'High and Over' at Amersham for the Director of the British School, Sir Bernard Ashmole. Ward joined the practice in 1932; Lucas in 1933. This practice – it continued until 1939 – was without doubt one of the most important factors in the development of modern architecture in England. All three partners were original members of the MARS Group. After war service Connell went to East Africa and built among other buildings Parliament House and the Aga Khan Hospital in Nairobi.

Basil Robert Ward was born in New Zealand in 1902. Died Ambleside, 1978. Educated at Napier College. Ward was placed second in the Rome Scholarship in 1926. After going to Rome, Ward went to Rangoon for three years. During the war he was in the Research and Experiment Department, Ministry of Home Security. Then became Lt-Commander, RNVR. At the end of the war the firm Murray, Ward and Partners was formed. He also became Professor (later Lethaby Professor) in Architecture at the Royal College of Art. Taught at Manchester, Lancaster, etc, after retirement.

Colin Anderson Lucas was born in London in 1906.

Educated at Cheltenham, studied architecture at Cambridge. He began his architectural career by forming his own building company. He built a number of reinforced concrete houses. Lucas headed development section of the LCC

Colin Lucas

and was leader of the group responsible for Roehampton Lane Housing Scheme. Formerly with GLC.

The work of the practice is recorded in the magazines of the period, and in books devoted to the modern house, e.g. those by F.R.S. Yorke. A number of key magazine issues are listed in the monograph published by the Architectural Association in 1956.

BLOMFIELD, R. & CONNELL, A. 'For and Against Modern Architecture', *The Listener*, XII, 1934, pp.885–8.

LUCAS, COLIN. On his own work in *Unit One*, London 1934, pp.118–124.

MISC. 'Reinforced Concrete Houses', *RIBA Journal*, July 1937, pp.901–9. Featuring Moor Park and Wentworth houses.

MISC. 'Connell, Ward and Lucas 1927–1939', Special No., *Architectural Association Journal*, November 1956.

Biographical notes by Brian Housden; captions by Arthur Korn; articles by H-R.Hitchcock and T.Stevens.

WARD, B. 'Connell, Ward and Lucas', in D. Sharp (ed.) *Planning and Architecture*, London 1967. Ward's own account of working in the partnership.

WARD, B. 'Houses in the Thirties', *Concrete Quarterly*, 85, April–May 1970, pp.11–15.

Lúcio COSTA (1902–)

Born Toulon, France 1902.

Studied at the National School of Fine Arts in Rio de Janeiro. On leaving he entered into practice with a Russian architect who had settled in Brazil,

Lúcio Costa

Gregori Warchavchik. In 1931 he was appointed Director of the Rio School of
Fine Arts. He worked on the Ministry of Health building as chief architect
with Le Corbusier. Since the war Costa has been largely involved in town
planning, his best-known work being the plan for the new capital of Brazil,
Brasilia. Most of Costa's writings are in Portuguese or Spanish, but
descriptions of his work in contemporary European and American magazines
are available.

COSTA, LÚCIO. *Arquitecture Brasiliera*, Rio de Janeiro 1952, in the series '*Os
Cadernos da Cultura*'. See also *Considerações sobre arte contemporâncea*, in the same
series.
COSTA, LÚCIO. *About my work in Brazil*, Rio de Janeiro 1958. Text in English,
French and Portuguese.

GAZENCO, J.O., & SCARONE, M.M. *Lúcio Costa*, Buenos Aires 1959, in the series
Arquitectos americanos contemporaneos, No.4. Spanish text.
MAGALHÃES, A., & FELDMAN, E. *Doorway to Brasilia*, Philadelphia 1959. Includes
contributions by Costa.

FERRAZ, G. 'Individualidades na história da atual arquitectura no Brasil',
Habitat No.35, São Paulo, October 1956, pp.28–43.

Theo van DOESBURG (1883–1931)

Theo van Doesburg was but one of the many pseudonyms used by
C.E.M.Küpper who was born in Utrecht in 1883. Died Davos, 1931.
Began his career as a painter and held his first exhibition at The Hague in
1908. Also poet.
After military service in the first world war he worked in collaboration with
J.J.P.Oud and Jan Wils in Leiden. They founded the group 'de Sphinx' in
1916. In 1917 the 'Stijl' group was formed. He took the ideas of de Stijl (in a
lecture tour) to Germany in 1921. He expounded the doctrinaire foundations
of the group to students of the Bauhaus at Weimar in 1922. The first exhibition
of architectural designs by the group was shown, including the work of Van
Eesteren and Rietveld, at Paris in 1923. The Elementarist manifesto was
issued in 1926, the year that Van Doesburg was commissioned to reconstruct
the cabaret l'Aubette in Strasbourg. Moved to Paris; built studio 1930–1.
He edited the review *de Stijl* for part of its life and the last edition, which
appeared in 1932, was posthumously devoted to him. H.L.C.Jaffé's
monograph on the group, *de Stijl 1917–1931*, contains almost everything there
is to know about the work of Van Doesburg.

VAN DOESBURG, THEO. *De nieuwe beweging in de schilderkunst*, Delft 1917.
VAN DOESBURG, THEO. *Drie voordrachten over de nieuwe beeldende Kunst*, Amsterdam
1919.
VAN DOESBURG, THEO. *Gronbegrippen der nieuwe beeldende Kunst*, Amsterdam 1919.
German trans. *Grundbegriffe der neuen gestaltenden Kunst*, Bauhaus Book, No.6,
Munich 1925.
English version. *Principles of Neo-plastic Art*, London 1969.
VAN DOESBURG, THEO. *Klassiek, barok, modern*, Antwerp 1920. French trans.
Classique, baroque, moderne, Paris 1921.
VAN DOESBURG, THEO. *Wat is Dada?* The Hague 1924.

SWEENY, J.J. (ed.) *Theo van Doesburg*, New York 1947. Retrospective exhibition
catalogue.
JAFFÉ, H.L.C. *de Stijl – 1917–1931, The Dutch Contribution to Modern Art*,
Amsterdam 1956. For full bibliography on Van Doesburg see pp.271–7.
BALJEU, J. *Theo van Doesburg*, London 1980.

Constantinos A. DOXIADIS (1914–1975)

Born Stenimachos, 1914. Died Athens, 1975.
He was trained as an architect and engineer, studying at the Technical
University, Athens and Berlin. In 1937 he became Head of the Department of
Regional and Town Planning, Ministry of Public Works, Greece. After the
war he was made Permanent Secretary for Housing Reconstruction in Greece
and between 1948 and 1951 the co-ordinator of the Recovery Programme. The
father of the 'Ekistics' (the science of human settlements) movement, he
founded the Graduate School of Ekistics at Athens Technological Institute.

He was also president of the Ekistics Centre in Athens, which publishes the magazine *Ekistics*.

His practice, Doxiadis Associates, founded in 1951, has carried out work throughout the world, acting as planning consultants on reconstruction and development and architects for individual buildings.

In an attempt to rationalize some of the problems affecting architects and planners today Doxiadis wrote *Architecture in Transition*, an enlargement of the RIBA Discourse. He has contributed numerous articles to journals on 'Ekistics', planning and architecture. Vance have produced a bibliography 'Constantinos A.Doxiades': A-237.

DOXIADIS, CONSTANTINOS APOSTULU. *Architecture in Transition*, London 1963.
DOXIADIS, CONSTANTINOS APOSTULU. *New World of Urban Man*, New York 1965, with T.B. Douglass.
DOXIADIS, CONSTANTINOS APOSTULU. *Urban Renewal and the Future of the American City*, Chicago 1965.
DOXIADIS, CONTANTINOS APOSTULU. *Ekistics: An Introduction to the Science of Human Settlements*, London, New York, 1968.
DOXIADIS, CONSTANTINOS APOSTULU. 'Architecture in Evolution', *RIBA Journal*, September 1960, pp.429–38; October 1960, pp.469–79. The RIBA Annual Discourse, 1960.

Constantinos A. Doxiadis

ANON. 'Konstantinos Apostulu Doxiadis', *Der Aufbau*, No.12, 1958, pp.471–4.
WEGENSTEIN, M. 'Dr C.A.Doxiadis und die "Oekistik"', *Schweizerische Bauzeitung*, 20 August 1959, pp.548–50.
WATSON, L.K. 'Doxiadis Associates', *RIBA Journal*, October 1960, pp.467–8.
EHRENKRANTZ, E., & TANNER, O. 'The Remarkable Dr Doxiadis', *Architectural Forum*, May 1961, pp.112–16, 154 f.
LLEWELYN-DAVIES, R. 'Ekistics, The Pattern of Human Settlements', *Architectural Review*, December 1965, pp.399–401.

Willem Marinus DUDOK   (1884–1974)

Born Amsterdam, 1884. Died Hilversum, 1974.
Studied at the Military Academy in Breda. In 1913 in charge of high buildings in Leiden. Appointed municipal engineer at Leiden in 1913, municipal architect at Hilversum, 1915. Collaborated with Oud on low-cost housing project, 1914. He also had a practice of his own.
The doyen of the 'middle of the road' Dutch architects who had a considerable influence on brick building in England and Germany, Dudok is best known for his work in Hilversum: Vondel School, 1928–9; Town Hall, 1928–31, etc. His work outside Hilversum includes the Netherlands House, University of Paris,

Willem Marinus Dudok

1927–8, and the Bijenkorf Store, Rotterdam, 1929–30 (destroyed). He was awarded the Royal Gold Medal in 1935.

A complete record of his work is included in the publication produced in Amsterdam in 1954 on the occasion of his 70th birthday. His work is also featured in numerous Dutch and foreign contemporary magazines and in all the standard works on modern Dutch architecture.

FRIEDHOFF, G. *W.M.Dudok*, Amsterdam, n.d. (*c.*1930), in the series '*Nederlandsche Bouwmeesters*'.
MISC. *Willem M.Dudok*, Amsterdam 1954.

JORDAN, R.F. 'Dudok and the Repercussions of his European Influence', *Architectural Review*, April 1954, pp.236–41.

Johannes DUIKER (1890–1935)
and Bernard BIJVOET (1889–)

Johannes Duiker was born in The Hague, 1890. Died Amsterdam, 1935.
Bernard Bijvoet was born in Amsterdam, 1889.

Both architects studied at Delft Technical College from which they graduated in 1913 under Evers for whom they both later worked. Later they became the two leading architectural practitioners in the modern Functional style, building many structures including the epoch-making Zonnestraal Sanatorium, Hilversum, and the Open Air School, Amsterdam. Duiker was a member of the 'De Stijl' and the 'De 8 en Opbouw' groups, joining the latter in 1928 and editing the joint journal until 1932. Articles in *De 8 en Opbouw* 3, 1932; 4, 1933; 5, 1934, etc.

Bijvoet met Pierre Chareau in Paris in 1919 and he left the practice in Amsterdam in 1925 to work for Chareau and others for approximately ten years. In 1935 Bijvoet returned to Amsterdam to carry out Duiker's work after his death. Worked in Paris 1937–40 with Beaudoin and Lods; remaining work, to 1970, in Holland.

MISC. 'Zonnestraal', *Forum*, Vol.16, No.1, Jan. 1962.
MISC. 'Duiker I', *Forum*, Vol.22, No.5 and 6, Nov. 1971–72.
DEAN, C. (ed.) *Johannes Duiker*, London (in preparation). Essays by Dean, Vickery, Sharp, *et al*.
BOGA, T. (ed.) *B. Bijvoet & J. Duiker 1890–1935*, Zurich, n.d.
VICKERY, R. 'Bijvoet & Duiker', *AA Quarterly*, Vol.2, No.1, 1970, pp.4–10 (See also author's expanded article, *Perspecta*, No.13/14, pp.130–61.)

Cornelius van EESTEREN (1897–)

Born Kinderdijk, 1897.

Educated at Dordrecht, then became apprentice carpenter, trainee clerk of works. Joined office of W. Kromhout (1864–1940) *c.*1915 as architectural student. In 1917 graduated from the Academy of Fine Arts and Technical

Science, Rotterdam. Also studied at the Sorbonne and the Ecole des Beaux-Arts in Paris. From 1919–1921 he worked for architects in The Hague and in Amsterdam. 1921 received the Prix de Rome and used the prize to study brick buildings in north Germany. Visited Bauhaus and met Van Doesburg. 1923 worked with Van Doesburg in Paris, became a friend of Mondrian and participated in De Stijl exhibition. Wrote for *De Stijl* (e.g. extra no. Jan. 1932). Merged his office with that of Jan Wils 1924. Joined the Rotterdam 'Opbau' group 1925. His role became increasingly that of the functionalist town planner in the late 1920s. Wrote for *i 10* with Stam and Oud. From 1929–59 successively chief architect, town planner, head town planning section, Amsterdam. 1930–47 President of CIAM. 1947–67 Professor of Town Planning, Technical University of Delft. For list of articles published see Blijstra.

DOESBURG, THEO VAN, & EESTEREN, C. 'Manifest 5', *De Stijl*, 6, 1923–4.

BLIJSTRA, R. *C. van Eesteren*, Amsterdam 1971 in the 'Art and Architecture in The Netherlands' series.

August ENDELL   (1871–1924)

Born Berlin, 1871. Died Berlin, 1924.

He studied philosophy, psychology and aesthetics, first at Tübingen and later at Munich under Theodor Lipps. He became acquainted with Lipps's ideas on 'empathy' and cultivated a friendship with the leading artists of the Jugendstil, Obrist, Riemerschmid, Pankok, etc. In 1898 he completed the decoration of the Elvira Studio in Munich with an abstract motif running over the whole width of the façade.

Endell commands a unique position in the Modern Movement as he combined the role of architect and theorist. His writings on aesthetics began in 1898 with an essay called *Um die Schönheit*. He returned to Berlin in 1901 and in the following years built up a highly successful practice. After the war, in 1918, he was appointed Director of the Breslau Academy. He stayed until the year of his death.

None of his writings, as far as I know, has been published in English. Many of them remain in the pages of contemporary magazines, valuable testimonies to an architect/teacher who successfully combined an interest in practice and theory. See also biography on Scharoun.

ENDELL, AUGUST. *Um die Schönheit. Eine Paraphrase über die Münchner Kunstausstellung 1896*, Munich 1896.

ENDELL, AUGUST. *Die Schönheit der grossen Stadt*, Stuttgart 1908. Endell's major work.

ENDELL, AUGUST. 'Möglichkeiten und Ziele einer neuen Architektur', *Deutsche Kunst und Dekoration*, Vol. 1, Darmstadt 1897–8, pp.141–53.

ENDELL, AUGUST. 'Formenschönheit und dekorative Kunst', *Dekorative Kunst*, Vol. 1, Munich 1898, pp.75–77, 119.

ENDELL, AUGUST. 'Architektonische Erstlinge', *Dekorative Kunst*, Vol.4, 1900, pp.297–317.
SEMBACH, K-J. *August Endell: Der Architekt des Photoateliers Elvira 1871–1925*, Munich 1977. Exhibition catalogue. See also Peter Green, 'August Endell', *AA Quarterly*, Vol.9, No.4, 1977, pp.36–44.

SCHEFFLER, KARL. 'August Endell', *Kunst und Künstler*, 5, 1907, pp.314–24.
SCHEFFLER, KARL. 'Neue Arbeiten von August Endell', *Kunst und Künstler*, 11, 1913, pp.350–9.

Luigi FIGINI (1903–) and Gino POLLINI (1903–)

Luigi Figini was born in Milan in 1903 and Gino Pollini in the same year at Rovereto, Trentino. Both architects graduated from Milan Polytechnic: Figini in 1926 and Pollini in 1927. They were founder members of the mainly Milanese *gruppo 7* founded in 1926 with Terragni and others. Exhibited at the Monza Biennale in 1927 but gained public attention through their artists' villa (in a park) at the Milan Triennale in 1933. Accused of being 'fashionable europeans' by Persico at about the same time along with the rest of *gruppo 7*. But they became one of the most respected firms of Italian rationalist designers producing many fine buildings for the Olivetti Company, in Ivrea, exhibition pavilions, residential buildings, etc. Their postwar church of the Madonna dei Poveri, Milan, 1952–6, constructed in concrete with narrow slit windows and a *beton brut* finish is outstanding.

FIGINI, L. 'Origines de l'architecture moderne en Italie', *L'Architecture d'Aujourd'hui*, June 1952, pp.5–9,
FIGINI, L. 'Architettura Italiana 1963'. Special issue of *Edilizia Moderna*, No.82–3, 1964.

TEDESCHI, E.G. *Figini e Pollini*, Milan 1959 (p.b).

ANON. 'Chiesa della Madonna dei Poveri a Milano', *L'Architettura*, November 1957, pp.452–7.
RYKWERT, J. 'Figini & Polini', *Architectural Design*, Aug. 1967, pp.369–78.
ANON. 'Housing at Ivrea', *Architectural Review*, May 1946, pp.147–50.
See also 'Nursery School at Ivrea', *Architectural Review*, April 1946, pp.117–20.
ANON. 'Olivetti: design in industry', *Museum of Modern Art Bulletin* (New York), Vol.20, no.1, 1952.

Hermann FINSTERLIN (1887–1973)

Born Munich, 1887. Died Stuttgart, 1973.
Studied philosophy, biology, chemistry, physics and numerous other subjects, before taking up the study of painting under Franz von Stuck in Munich. An Anthroposophist, his interest in architecture was always that of a designer rather than a practitioner – in fact he never built a building. Gropius invited him to exhibit at the 'Exhibition of Unknown Architects' organized by the

Hermann Finsterlin

Arbeitsrat für Kunst in Berlin, 1919. He joined in Bruno Taut's 'Utopian Correspondence' (pseud: 'Prometh') and thus became a member of what is termed the Glass Chain. Meyer employed him, briefly, at the Bauhaus. His paintings and drawings have been exhibited in many European centres. His essays and articles are difficult to translate and they remain by and large in their original complicated German.

FINSTERLIN, HERMANN. 'Der achte Tag', *Frühlicht*, 1920.
FINSTERLIN, HERMANN. 'Innenarchitektur', *Frühlicht*, winter, 1921–2.
FINSTERLIN, HERMANN. 'Die Genesis der Weltarchitektur oder die Deszendenz der Dome als Stilspiel', *Frühlicht*, spring, 1923. (All these articles from *Frühlicht* are reproduced in Taut, B. *Frühlicht, 1920–1922*, Berlin 1963.)
FINSTERLIN, HERMANN. 'Finsterlin: Vormenspel in de Architectuur', *Wendingen*, No.3, 1924 (special issue).
FINSTERLIN, HERMANN, *Ein Griff in ein halbes Jahrhundert*, Stuttgart 1964. Poems and drawings.

BORSI, F. (Ed.) *Hermann Finsterlin: Idea dell'architettura*, Florence 1969. Italian and German text.
SHARP, D. 'Hermann Finsterlin and Formspiel' in *Modern Architecture and Expressionism*, London 1966, pp.97–108.
SCHNEEDE, U.M. (ed.) *Hermann Finsterlin*, Stuttgart 1973. Exhibition catalogue.
MISC. *Hermann Finsterlin (1887–1973)*, Krefeld 1976. Exibition catalogue.

E. Maxwell Fry

PEVSNER, N. 'Finsterlin and Some Others', *Architectural Review*, November 1962, pp.353–7.

SHARP, D. 'Hermann Finsterlin: Prometheus unbound', *Building Design*, 15 Sept. 1972.

SHARP, D. 'The last of the German Fantasts', *Building Design*, 12 Oct. 1973.

E.Maxwell FRY (1899–)

Born Wallasey, Cheshire in 1899.

Trained at the Liverpool School of Architecture under Professor Charles Reilly. Reilly later referred to Fry's work as being 'among the best in the country'.

Fry moved to London to work for Adams and Thompson, with whom he later became a partner. This firm was responsible through Fry for Sassoon House, Peckham, 1934–5. The other low-cost, reinforced concrete housing scheme designed by Fry at that time was Kensal House, Kensington (1937). Walter Gropius joined Fry in partnership in 1934 until 1936. From 1943 to 1945 Fry acted as town planning adviser in West Africa. After the war he established a new practice with his wife, Jane Drew, 1945–50. The title of the practice changed in 1951 to Fry, Drew, Drake and Lasdun and again in 1958 to Fry, Drew and Partners. In 1973 it became Fry, Drew, Knight and Creamer. From 1950 to 1955 Fry and Drew worked in collaboration with Le Corbusier on Chandigarh. He was awarded the Royal Gold Medal for Architecture in 1964. His publications, many of which have been produced in collaboration with Jane Drew, cover many aspects of architecture, including a book that is a plea for quality in building, two studies on tropical architecture and a fascinating book for children on architecture.

FRY, E.MAXWELL. *Fine Building*, London 1944.

FRY, E.M., & DREW, J. *Architecture for Children*, London 1944.

FRY, E.M., DREW, J., & FORD, H.L. *Village Housing in the Tropics*, London 1947 (2nd edn 1953).

FRY, E.M., & DREW, J. *Tropical Architecture in the Dry and Humid Zones*, London 1964.

FRY, E.M. 'The Architect and his Time', *Architects' Year Book*, No.3, 1949, pp.9–12.

FRY, E.M. 'A Discursive Commentary', *Architects' Year Book*, No.6, 1955, pp.7–10.

FRY, E.M. 'English Architecture from the Thirties', *Architects' Year Book*, No.8, 1957, pp.53–6.

HITCHENS, S. (ed.) *Fry, Drew, Knight and Creamer: Architecture*, London 1978.

Bohuslav Fuchs

Bohuslav FUCHS (1894–1972)

Born Vsechovice, 1894. Died Brno, 1972.
Fuchs studied at the Academy of Fine Arts in Prague under Professor Jan
Kotera 1916–1919. From 1919–1921 he worked in the office of Kotera; from
1921–23 as an architect in Prague he worked in collaboration with the
architect Josef Stepanek. In the latter years he moved to Brno where he was
employed until 1929 in the architectural department of the municipality.
During this period he also had a private architectural office in Brno. Fuchs was
made Professor of Town Planning and Architecture at the Technical
University, Brno, in 1945. Was dismissed in 1958 and became architect for the
Institute for the Conservation of Historic Monuments in Brno. In 1968 he was
awarded the title of 'National Artist of Czechoslovakia' and in 1969 awarded
the Herder Prize in Vienna.

FUCHS, BOHUSLAV. *Nove Zonovani*, Prague 1967. An important study and
statement about 'The new zoning'.
FUCHS, BOHUSLAV. *In margine umeleckeho odk zu Jana Kotery*, Brno 1972.

ROSSMAN, Z. *Architekt, Bohuslav Fuchs*, Basel 1930.
KUDELKA, Z. *Bohuslav Fuchs*, Prague 1966.
MISC. *Bohuslav Fuchs*, Brno 1970. A Festschrift published by the Czech Society
of Architects.

R. Buckminster FULLER   (1895–   )

Born Milton, Mass., 1895. Lives in Carbondale, Illinois.
Studied at Harvard (1913) and the US Naval Academy at Annapolis,
Maryland, at the end of the first world war. His years in the Navy were
formative ones and he started his 'theoretical conceptioning' and work on the
'flying jet-stilts porpoise', an idea for four-dimensional transport that got into
print in 1932. In 1927 the Dymaxion (dynamic plus maximum efficiency)
Technology was formulated. The Dymaxion house design appeared that year.
Fuller now operates from the Design Department, Southern Illinois
University, but he has lectured in major universities and architectural schools
throughout the world. The genius of twentieth-century technology, Fuller has
adequately summed up in his position in the book *No More Secondhand God:*
'And I've thought through tomorrow which is also today . . . And you say
aren't you being fantastic? And knowing you I say no.' The geodesic structures
developed by Fuller were first introduced for the Ford Rotunda in 1953; they
are now to be found in most countries.
Fuller is a prolific writer and talker, and fortunately he has been well served by
his disciples and biographers. John McHale's edition of *Architectural Design* and
his book on Fuller are indispensable sources.

FULLER, R.BUCKMINSTER. *Nine Chains to the Moon*, New York 1938 (p.b.
Carbondale 1963).
FULLER, R.BUCKMINSTER. *Education Automation: freeing the scholar to return to his
studies*, Carbondale 1962.
FULLER, R.BUCKMINSTER. *No More Secondhand God and Other Writings*, Carbondale 1963.
FULLER, R.B. 'Dymaxion House', *Architectural Forum*, March 1932, pp.285–6.
FULLER, R.B. 'Experimental Probing of Architectural Initiative', *RIBA Journal*,
October 1958, pp.415–24. RIBA Annual Discourse.
FULLER, R.B. 'Universal Requirements of a Dwelling Advantage', *Architectural
Design*, March 1960, pp.101–10.
FULLER, R.B. 'Conceptuality of Fundamental Structures', *Structures in Art and
Science*, New York, London, 1965, pp.66–88.

MARKS, R.W. *The Dymaxion World of Buckminster Fuller*, New York 1960.
MCHALE, J. *R.Buckminster Fuller*, New York, London, 1962. Contains
biographical and bibliographical material.
MARKS, R.W. (ed.) *Buckminster Fuller: Ideas and Integrities: A spontaneous
autobiographical disclosure*, Englewood Cliffs, N.J., 1963.

MCHALE, J. 'Buckminster Fuller', *Architectural Review*, July 1956, pp.12–20.
MCHALE, J. (ed.) 'Richard Buckminster Fuller', *Architectural Design*, Special
Issue, July 1961.

Naum GABO   (1890–1977)

Born Briansk, Russia, 1890. Died Middlebury, Connecticut, 1977.
Gabo's work as a sculptor has always been close to architecture. He is very

much an architect's sculptor. His work is supported by fluent statements on the artist's conception of space and structure. He began studying medicine and later the arts at Munich University, but left in 1914 to go to Scandinavia. He decided to become a sculptor. In 1917 he returned to Russia. The *Realistic Manifesto*, by Gabo and his brother Antoine Pevsner, appeared in 1920. In 1922 he went to live in Berlin and remained there until 1932. In the mid-thirties he came to England and stayed until 1946 when he left for the USA. During his stay in England he produced a number of important statements on constructivist art and edited the International Survey of Constructive Art, *Circle*, with J.L. Martin and Ben Nicholson. In 1952 he became a US citizen. From 1953 to 1954 he was appointed Professor at Harvard Graduate School of Architecture. The principal monograph on his work – besides the many exhibition catalogues – is the one listed below, *Gabo: Constructions, Sculpture, Paintings, Drawings, Engravings* (1957).

GABO, NAUM. *Antoine Pevsner*, New York 1948.
GABO, NAUM. *Gabo: Constructions, Sculpture, Paintings, Drawings, Engravings*, London, Cambridge (Mass.), 1957. Introductory essay by J.L. Martin and Herbert Read. A full bibliography and a number of Gabo's writings are included.
GABO, NAUM. 'The Constructivist Idea in Art', *Circle*, London 1937, pp.1–10.
GABO, NAUM. 'Sculpture: Carving and Construction in Space', *ibid.*, pp.103–11.
GABO, NAUM. 'On Constructive Realism', *Architects' Year Book*, No.4, 1952, pp.8–14. The Trowbridge Lecture, Yale University.
GABO, NAUM. 'Naum Gabo Talks about his Work', *Studio International*, April 1966, pp.127–31. See also 'The Realistic Manifesto' in the same issue, p.126.

Tony GARNIER (1869–1948)

Born Lyon, 1869. Died La Bédoule, 1948.
His early ideas for an industrial town date back to the turn of the century. When he was a Rome Scholar he began his project for a *cité industrielle*, 1901–4. Planned for 35,000 people, it was a revolutionary concept. It did not get into print until 1917. He became the City Architect of Lyon in 1905, remaining there, and carrying out a number of projects based on ideas to be found in his city project, until 1919. He designed the town hall in the Paris suburb of Boulogne-Billancourt (1931–4) in collaboration with Debat-Ponsan. The record of achievement at Lyon is contained in the book *Les Grands Travaux de la ville de Lyon* and his work is generally recorded in one of Morancé's *L'Architecture Vivante* series.

GARNIER, TONY. *Une cité industrielle. Étude pour la construction des villes*, Paris 1917.
GARNIER, TONY. *Les Grands Travaux de la ville de Lyon*, Paris 1920.

BADOVICI, J., & MORANCÉ, A. *L'Œuvre de Tony Garnier*, Paris 1938.
VERONESI, G. *Tony Garnier*, Milan 1948.

DESHAIRS, L. *Catalogue d'exposition de Tony Garnier au Musée des Arts Décoratifs à Paris*, Paris 1925.

HERRIOT, E. & PIESSAT, L. *Tony Garnier: 1869–1948*, Lyon 1951.

BOURDEIX, P. *Tony Garnier et son œuvre*, Paris 1967.

PAWLOWSKI, C. *Tony Garnier et les débuts de l'urbanisme fonctionnel en France*, Paris 1967.

WIEBENSON, D. *Tony Garnier: La cité industrielle*, London, New York, 1968. 'Planning and Cities' series.

BOURDEIX, P. 'Tony Garnier: Précurseur de l'architecture d'aujourd'hui', *L'Architecture d'Aujourd'hui*, March 1931.

Antonio GAUDÍ (1852–1926)

Born Reus, Catalonia, 1852. Killed in a tram accident, Barcelona, 1926. Studied architecture at the Escola Superior d'Arquitectura, Barcelona. Established himself in practice even before his studies were completed. Gaudi suffered from bad health all his life. His political views and architecture were considered eccentric in Barcelona. His inventiveness, however, was never disputed and his buildings remain as testimonies to this. The Sagrada Familia Church, which occupied him from 1883 until his death in 1926, the Casa Milà

Antonio Gaudí

47

(1905–10), the layout of the Parc Güell (1900–14), are his best known works. No writings by Gaudi himself exist, as far as I know. George Collins's book, published in 1960, is the best account of Gaudi's life and work in the English language – even though the author's habit of writing a second book in the notes is trying. Ràfols's and Bergós's biographies are the most valuable source books.

RÁFOLS, J.F., & FOLGUERA, F. *Gaudí: el gran arquitecto español*, Barcelona 1928, in Catalan; 2nd edn, 1929 in Spanish.

CIRLOT, J.E. *El Arte de Gaudí*, Barcelona 1950; 2nd edn, 1954.

RÀFOLS, J.F. *Gaudí: 1852–1926*, Barcelona 1952. A full bibliography, pp.235–304.

BERGÓS, J. *Gaudí: l'home i l'obra*, Barcelona 1954.

MARTINELL, C. *Antonio Gaudí*, Milan 1955. The author's collected writings on Gaudí.

HITCHCOCK, H-R. *Gaudí*, New York 1957 (Museum of Modern Art Catalogue).

LE CORBUSIER, GOMIS, J., & PRATS-VALLES, J. *Gaudí*, Barcelona 1958, New York n.d. Photographic volume.

COLLINS, G.R. *Antonio Gaudí*, London 1960, containing an extensive bibliography, pp.131–4.

SERT, J.L., & SWEENY, J. *Antoni Gaudí*, London, New York, 1960.

PANE, R. *Antoni Gaudí*, Milan 1964.

CASANELLES, E. *Nueva vision de Gaudí*, Barcelona 1965.

GIEDION-WELCKER, C. *Park Güell*, Barcelona, New York, 1966.

CIRLOT, J.E. *Gaudí*, Barcelona 1966.

PERUCHO, J. *Gaudí una Arquitectura de Anticipation*, Barcelona 1967. English, French, Spanish and German text.

LE CORBUSIER. *Gaudí*, Barcelona 1967. English, French, Spanish, German text.

CASANELLES, E. *Antonio Gaudí, A Reappraisal*, London 1967.

BOHIGAS, O. *Architettura Modernista. Gaudí e il movimento catalano*, Barcelona 1968. Italian text.

DESCHARNES, R. *Gaudí the Visionary*, London 1971. With preface by Salvador Dali.

BORRAS, MARIA LLUISA. *Casa Batllo, Casa Mila*, Tokyo 1972 (edited with photos by Yukio Futagawa). English/Japanese text.

COLLINS, G.R. *A bibliography of Antonio Gaudí and the Catalan Movement 1870–1930*, Charlottesville 1973.

TARRAGO, S. *Gaudí*, Barcelona 1974.

WIEDEMAN, J. A. *Gaudí. Inspiration in Architektur und Handwerk*, Munich 1974.

MARTINELL Y BRUNET. *Gaudí: His Life, His Theories, His Work*, Barcelona 1975 (Translated by Judith Rohrer).

COLLINS, G. R. *The Drawings of Antonio Gaudí*, New York 1977. Exhibition catalogue with 34pp. and 13 plates.

MOWER, D. *Gaudí*, London 1977.

WAUGH, E. 'Gaudí', *Architectural Review*, June 1930, pp.309–11. The 'discovery' of Gaudí by an Englishman.

ZEVI, B. 'Un genio catalano: Antonio Gaudí', *Metron*, No.38, 1950, pp.26–53.
The post-war 'rediscovery' of Gaudí.
HITCHCOCK, H-R. 'The work of Antonio Gaudí i Cornet', *Architectural Association Journal*, November 1958, pp.86–98.
JOEDICKE, J. 'Wilkür und Bindung im Werk von Antonio Gaudí',
Bauen + Wohnen, 5, 1960, pp.181–7.
GIRARDI, V. Various articles on Gaudí's buildings in *L'Architettura*,
Nos.159–67, 1969.

Irving John GILL   (1870–1936)

Born the son of a building contractor in Syracuse, New York, 1870. Died Los Angeles, 1936.
Gill spent a short time in the office of a Syracuse architect but moved to the office of Adler and Sullivan, Chicago in 1890 where he met Frank Lloyd Wright. For health reasons he moved, in 1893, to San Diego and set up practice there in 1896. From 1898–1906 was in partnership with W.S.Hebbard building mostly locally although he did undertake a number of summer houses in Rhode Island. The radical simplification in his style and his interest in low-cost housing began in the years before 1916 when he moved to Los Angeles. In 1916 he built the famous Walter Dodge house (destroyed) in Los Angeles.

MCCOY, E. *Irving Gill 1870–1936*, Los Angeles 1958.
MCCOY, E. *Five Californian Architects*, Los Angeles 1960 (p.b.).

ANON. 'Irving Gill's Dodge House, 1916–65', *Arts and Architecture*, Sept 1965, pp.10,11.

Moisei GINSBURG   (1892–1946)

Born Minsk, 1892. Died Moscow, 1946.
Graduated from the Academy of Arts, Milan, 1914. Returned to Russia and studied at Rizhsky Polytechnic, Moscow, graduating in 1917 with engineering degree. In 1921 he moved to Moscow and took up teaching. In 1923 he became Professor at the Vkhutemas (Higher Artistic and Technical Workshops). Also taught at the Moscow Institute of Higher Technology and became an active member of the Russian Academy of Arts and Science. He published a Constructivist credo, during early 1920s was editor of *CA* in which he wrote a series of theoretical articles developing the functional design and social aspects of a programme for a new architecture. In the 1930s he edited a general history of architecture for the Academy and during the war headed a committee on prefabrication. During his last years he wrote a large treatise on architecture but only one section – on tectonics – was completed by the time of his death.
Nothing is published on Ginsburg in English. Reference should be made to Anatole Senkevitch, Jnr. *Soviet Architecture 1917–62* (Charlottesville 1974) for material in the Russian language.

Josef GOCAR (1880–1945)

Born Semin, near Pardubice, 1880. Died Prague, 1945.
The best known of all modern Czech architects, Josef Gocar studied at the
Baugewerbeschule (School of Industrial Design), Prague, 1903–05, under Jan
Kotera. He worked in Kotera's office until 1908. In 1911 joined Bohemian
Artists Group. From 1911–14 produced an artistic monthly journal. A
renowned furniture designer he was also a well liked teacher and served from
1929 as Professor at Academy of Fine Arts, Prague. Buildings include:
Department store Wenke, Jaromet, 1910; House of Black Mother of God in
Prague, 1911; St Venceslaw Church, Prague, 1928–32.

GOCAR, J., JANAK, P., KYSELA, F. *Tschechische Bestrebungen um ein Modernes Interieur*,
Prague 1915. A record of the Czech interiors for the Werkbund Exhibition,
Cologne 1914.
GOCAR, J. *Hradec Kralove*. Prague 1930. (Foreword by Z. Wirth).

WIRTH, Z. *Josef Gocar*, Geneva 1930. Text in Czech, French, German.
BENESOVA, M. *Josef Gocar*, Prague 1958.

Bruce GOFF (1904–)

Born Alton, Kansas in 1940. Lives in Bartlesville, Oklahoma.
Goff is the epitome of the American self-made man. Apprentice to Rush,
Endicott and Rush, Tulsa, Oklahoma. His first major work was the 'Art Deco'
Boston Avenue Methodist Episcopal Church, Tulsa, 1926. He had no formal
architectural education as such but has taught architecture and has produced
many buildings in the 'Prairie School' vein. His admiration for Frank Lloyd
Wright is seen in his architectural philosophy as well as his buildings. He is
best known, particularly on the British side of the Atlantic, for his
unconventional house designs, the Ford house at Aurora, Illinois (1948) and
the Bavinger house (1950–55).

GOFF, BRUCE. 'All about Goff', *Architectural Record*, November 1953, p.338 ff.
GOFF, BRUCE. 'Notes on Architecture' in Conrads, U., and Sperlich, H.G.
Fantastic Architecture, New York 1962; London 1963, p.155. An extract from the
original article in *Bauwelt*, No.4, January 1958, p.88.
GOFF, BRUCE. 'Goff on Goff', *Progressive Architecture*, December 1962, pp.102–23.
GOFF, BRUCE. 'A Young Architect's Protest for Architecture', *Perspecta*, 13/14,
1971, pp.330–57.
GOFF, BRUCE. *Bruce Goff, Architect*, Billings, Montana 1978. Limited edn
exhibition catalogue of 30 plates of Goff's work.

MOHRI, T. *Bruce Goff in Architecture*, Tokyo 1970.
MURPHY, W. & MULLER, L. *Bruce Goff, A Portfolio*, New York 1970.
DE LONG, D. *The Architecture of Bruce Goff: Buildings and Projects 1916–1974*, 2 vols.,
New York 1977. The definitive publication on Goff.
COOK, J. *The Architecture of Bruce Goff*, London, New York, 1978.

Bruce Goff

SERGEANT, J. & MOORING, S. (eds). A special issue (and also AD Profile No.16) of *Architectural Design*, Vol.48, No.10, 1978. An important survey including articles by March, Jencks, Price, Greene, Cook, etc.

MEEHAN, P.J. *Bruce Goff, Architect: Writings 1918–1978*, Monticello, Illinois, 1979. Comprehensive bibliography in the Vance 'Architecture Series', A-73.

WAECHTER, H.H. 'Architecture of Bruce Goff', *AIA Journal*, December 1959, pp.32–6.

PILLET, M. 'L'insolite Monsieur Bruce Goff', *L'Architecture d'Aujourd'hui*, June 1962, pp.50–7.

PLESSIX, F.DU, & GRAY, C. 'Bruce Goff, Visionary Architect', *Art in America*, February 1965, pp.82–7.

Charles Sumner GREENE (1868–1957)
and Henry Mather GREENE (1870–1954)

C.S. Greene was born in St Louis, 1868. Died Carmel, California, 1957.
H.M. Greene was also born in St Louis. Died Altadena, 1954.
Known colloquially as the Greene & Greene Bros.
Both brothers were largely brought up on a Virginian farm until their father, a

physician, moved to St Louis. Educated at the Manual Training High School, St Louis and later at MIT where they graduated in 1891 and 1892 respectively. Lived in Boston for some years but in 1893 visit to parents who were living on West Coast led to their settling and working there for the rest of their lives. Opened office in Pasadena but moved to Los Angeles in 1901. In 1914 Charles was invited to design house in Carmel where he eventually settled, withdrawing from the firm and ceasing practice. Henry continued until his retirement in 1930s. Their very original 'oriental' early buildings were in much demand before the first world war but the fashion dropped off due to the rise of the Spanish Colonial style interest developed after Bertram Goodhue built his structures for the San Diego Exposition in 1915.

STRAND, J. *A Greene and Greene guide*, Pasadena 1974.

CURRENT, W.R. & K. *Greene & Greene: Architects in the Residential Style*, Fort Worth 1974.

MCCOY, E. *Five California Architects*, New York 1960 and 1974 (G & G chapter by R.L.Makinson).

BANGS, J.M. 'Greene & Greene: . . .', *Architectural Forum* 89, Oct. 1948, pp.80–89.

YOST, L.M. 'Greene & Greene of Pasadena', *J. of Soc. of Architectural Historians*, 9 March 1950, pp.11–19.

MCCOY, E. 'Notes on Greene & Greene', *Arts and Architecture*, July 1953, pp.27–38.

LANCASTER, C. 'My interviews with Greene & Greene', *AIA Journal* 28, July 1957, pp.202–206.

LANCASTER, C. 'Some sources of Greene & Greene', *AIA Journal* 34, Aug. 1960, pp.39–46.

MAKINSON, R.L. 'Greene & Greene – 2 papers on Gamble House', *Prairie School Review*, 4th Q., 1968, pp.4–31.

Walter Burley GRIFFIN (1876–1937)

Born Maywood, Illinois, 1876. Died, Lucknow, 1937 after falling from scaffolding.

One of the few pioneers of modern architecture to emerge in Australasia. Griffin was a native American who worked for a time with Frank Lloyd Wright (*c*.1902–6) before going to Melboune with his talented wife Mary Mohony after Griffin had won competition for the layout of Australia's new Government city at Canberra, in 1912. Griffin was a talented original and by no means 'simply' a former Wright pupil; his interests ranged from city planning to Rudolf Steiner's work and ideas. His best known buildings in Australia are to be found in the Melbourne area where he settled 1914 after turning down an invitation to head the Architectural Department at University of Illinois. Visited Europe in 1913–14 where he met Lethaby, Wagner, etc. Settled in India in 1936 after commission in Lucknow.

Vance bibliographies have produced *Canberra and Walter Burley Griffin*, A-97.

GRIFFIN, W.B. *The Federal Capital*, Melbourne 1913 (1915).
GRIFFIN, W.B. *The U.P. Industrial and Agricultural Exhibition, Lucknow*, Lucknow 1936.

BIRRELL, J. *Walter Burley Griffin*, Brisbane 1964. The first full biography of Griffin brought out at the time of the 50th anniversary of the building of Canberra.
VAN ZANTEN, D. (ed.) *Walter Burley Griffin: Selected Designs*, Palos Park, Illinois 1970. A beautifully produced book of the exquisite drawings produced by Marion Mohony and Griffin's own lectures prepared by the Prairie School Press. Good bibliography.

JOHNSON, D. *The Architecture of Walter Burley Griffin*, Melbourne 1977.

JOHNSON, D. 'The Griffin Reico Incinerators', *AA Quarterly*, Vol.3, no.4, 1971, pp.46–55.

Walter GROPIUS (1883–1969)

Born Berlin, 1883. Died in USA, 1969.
Educated in Berlin. Studied architecture at the Technical High Schools in Charlottenburg and Munich, 1903–7. Worked in the office of Peter Behrens in Berlin, 1907–10. Started practice in Berlin, 1910. Undertook a number of industrial design commissions and produced his first important building, the factory for the Fagus Company, at Alfeld-an-der-Leine, in collaboration with Adolf Meyer, 1911. Gropius and Meyer designed the Model Factory for the 1914 Werkbund Exhibition, Cologne.
1914–18 officer in German army. In 1915 invited by Grand Duke of Saxe-Weimar to become Director of the two existing arts schools in Weimar. Restyled and united these schools under the single title Das Staatliche Bauhaus, Weimar, in 1919. Issued Bauhaus 'Proclamation' in the same year. Bauhaus to Dessau in 1925, where Gropius remained Director until 1928. Resumed private practice in Berlin after that date.
Vice-President, CIAM, 1929–57. Fled Germany in 1934 and joined Maxwell Fry in practice in London. He moved to the United States in 1937. Professor of Architecture, Harvard, 1937. Appointed Chairman of Department of Architecture, Graduate School of Design, 1938. After practice with Marcel Breuer, 1938–43, eventually in 1945 formed The Architects' Collaborative (TAC). Gropius's writings cover almost every aspect of architectural practice, theory, education, teamwork and criticism. Fortunately, comprehensive bibliographies exist, and these are listed below.

GROPIUS, WALTER. *Staatliches Bauhaus, Weimar, 1919–23*, Munich 1923. Includes the essay 'Idee und Aufbau des Staatlichen Bauhauses' by Gropius, pp.7–18.
GROPIUS, WALTER. *Internationale Architektur*, Munich 1925 (2nd edn 1927). Bauhaus Book No.1.
GROPIUS, WALTER. (ed.) *Neue Arbeiten der Bauhauswerkstätten*, Munich 1925. Bauhaus Book No.7.

GROPIUS, WALTER. *Bauhausbauten Dessau*, Munich 1930. Bauhaus Book No.12.
BAYER, H., GROPIUS, W. & I. *Bauhaus 1919–1928*, New York 1938. Second printing, Boston 1952; Stuttgart 1955.
GROPIUS, WALTER. *The New Architecture and the Bauhaus*, London 1935 (1956). Translated by P.Morton Shand, with an introduction by Frank Pick.
GROPIUS, WALTER. *Architecture and Design in the Age of Science*, New York 1952 (10pp., p.b.).
GROPIUS, WALTER. *The Scope of Total Architecture*, London 1956.
GROPIUS, W., TANGE, K., & ISHIMOTO, Y. *Katsura: Tradition and Creation in Japanese Architecture*, New Haven 1960.
GROPIUS, W. *et al. The Architects' Collaborative 1945–65*, Teufen (Switzerland), 1966.

GIEDION, S. *Walter Gropius*, Paris 1931 (15pp., p.b.). The first monograph on Gropius, in the series *Les artistes nouveaux*.
COOK, R.V. (compiler). *A Bibliography of Walter Gropius 1919–50'*, Chicago 1951. A typewritten (26pp.) list published by the American Institute of Architects. Superseded by O'Neal, W. B. *Walter Gropius, A bibliography of writings by and about Walter Gropius*, Charlottesville 1966 and supplement of 1972.
ARGAN, G.C. *Walter Gropius e la Bauhaus*, Turin 1951.
GIEDION, S. *Walter Gropius: Work and Teamwork*, London 1954.
HERBERT, G. *The Synthetic Vision of Walter Gropius*, Witwatersrand University, Johannesburg 1959.
FITCH, J.M. *Walter Gropius*, London, New York, 1960.
WEBER, H. *Walter Gropius und das Faguswerk*, Munich 1961.
WINGLER, H.M. *Das Bauhaus: 1919–1933 Weimar, Dessau, Berlin*, Bramsche 1962. See also the section devoted to the Bauhaus Books and books on the Bauhaus in Part 2 of this bibliography, pp.159–62.

SCHEFFAUER, H.G. 'The Work of Walter Gropius', *Architectural Review*, August 1924, pp.50–4.
NELSON, G. 'Architects of Europe Today, II: Walter Gropius', *Pencil Points*, August 1936, pp.422–32.
RUDOLPH, P. (ed.) 'Walter Gropius et son école', Special No., *L'Architecture d'Aujourd'hui*, February 1950.
PEVSNER, N. 'Gropius and Van de Velde', *Architectural Review*, March 1963, pp.165–8.
SHILLABER, C. (compiler). 'Walter Gropius: A Bibliography, Part I, in *Papers of the American Association of Architectural Bibliographers*, Vol. 1, 1965, pp.23–43. Published by the University of Virginia, Charlottesville.

Hector GUIMARD   (1867–1942)

Born Lyon, 1867. Died New York, 1942.
Trained at the Ecole des Arts Décoratifs and the Ecole des Beaux-Arts, Paris, where he later taught. Worked on the 1889 Paris Exhibition. Visited England in 1894. Various influences on his work include those of his teacher de Baudet,

Walter Gropius

Hector Guimard

Viollet-le-Duc's writings and the early works of Victor Horta which he saw
when he visited Brussels in 1895.

The architect of the Paris Art Nouveau, Guimard incorporated the florid
curvilinear twists of the style in his designs. He caught the attention of the
public with his designs for the Paris Métro in 1900. Like the other Art Nouveau
architects he was also a furniture designer and an interior decorator of the
most original kind. His buildings include the fashionable apartment block, the
Castel Béranger (1897–8) in the rue de la Fontaine, Paris 16e, and the
Humbert de Romans Building (1902), Paris, with its exciting cast-iron
interior.

An interesting side-light is thrown on the Art Nouveau in the article Guimard
wrote for the *Architectural Record* in 1902. His work is well represented in the
standard book on the Art Nouveau and in a number of recent magazine
articles. His monuments to the *fin de siècle* remain for everyone to see at the
entrances to several Métro stations in Paris.

GUIMARD, HECTOR. *Le Castel Béranger*, Paris 1899.
GUIMARD, H. 'An architect's opinion of l'Art Nouveau', *Architectural Record*, June
1902, pp.130–33.

MAZADE, F. 'An "Art Nouveau" Edifice in Paris' (The Humbert de Romans
Building by Guimard), *Architectural Record*, May 1902, pp.53–66.

Hugo Häring

DESBRUÈRES, M. 'Le Castel Béranger', *Bizarre*, No.27, 1963, pp.6–19. Special Issue on *Maisons 1900 de Paris*.
MISC. *Guimard, Horta, Van de Velde*, Paris 1971, pp.122–221. Exhibition catalogue.
CANTACUZINO, S. 'Hector Guimard' in Richards, J.M. and Pevsner, N. (eds) *The Anti-Rationalists*, London 1973, pp.9–31.
DUNSTER, D. *Hector Guimard*, London 1978.

Hugo HÄRING (1882–1958)

Born Biberach, Württemberg, 1882. Died Göppingen, 1958.
Studied at the Technical High School, Stuttgart under Theodor Fischer and at the Technical High School, Dresden under Gurlitt, Schumacher and Wallot. Worked as an architect in Ulm, 1903–4; Hamburg, 1904–14. After the war he became a member of the 'Novembergruppe' and established his practice in Berlin. In 1926 he was made Secretary of the enlarged Berlin 'Ring'. In the thirties he was head of a private school of art, 'Kunst und Werk' in Berlin. In 1943 he returned to Biberach.
His best-known work is the farm complex at Gut Garkau, near Lübeck. His theoretical writings, views on the relation of form and function and organic architecture, are important and many of these are collected in the book edited

57

by Heinrich Lauterbach and Jürgen Joedicke. A complete bibliography is also included.

HÄRING, HUGO. *Vom neuen Bauen. Über das Geheimnis der Gestalt*, Berlin 1957 (p.b.).
HÄRING, HUGO. 'Probleme des Bauens', Parts 1–3, *Der Neubau*, No.17, 10 September 1924, pp.201–3.
HÄRING, HUGO. 'Probleme des Bauens', Part 4, *Der Neubau*, No.13, 10 February 1925, p.43.
HÄRING, HUGO. 'Wege zur Form', *Die Form*, No.1, October 1925, pp.3–5.

LAUTERBACH, H. & JOEDICKE, J. *Hugo Häring, Schriften, Entwürfe, Bauten*, Stuttgart 1965, in the series '*Dokumente der Modernen Architektur*', No.4. This includes the text of many of Häring's writings in chronological order and a comprehensive bibliography.

JOEDICKE, J. 'Häring at Garkau', *Architectural Review*, May 1960, pp.313–18.
JOEDICKE, J. 'Hugo Häring: Zur Theorie des organhaften Bauens', *Bauen und Wohnen*, No.11, 1960, p.419–22.

Josef Havlicek

Josef HAVLICEK (1899–1961)

Born Prague, 1899. Died Prague, 1961.
Studied at Czech Technical University in Prague and at the Academy of Fine
Arts in Prague under Josef Gocar. Architect in Prague, member of Manes, of
Sdruzeni architeku, of SIA, member of CIAM. From 1928–36 in partnership
with Karel Houzik. Buildings: Insurance building, Prague 1929–33 together
with Karel Houzik, Sanatorium Podebrady, 1937.

HAVLICEK, J. and HOUZIK, K. *Stavby a plany* (Buildings and Projects). Edition
MSA, No.3. Text by Karel Teige. Prague 1931.
HAVLICEK, J. *Navrhy a stavby* (Projects and Buildings), Prague 1964.

Ludwig HILBERSEIMER (1885–1967)

Born Karlsruhe, 1885. Died in USA, 1967.
After studying in Karlsruhe he moved to Berlin where he practised until 1928.
He then joined the Bauhaus staff at Dessau.
Among his early projects was a design for an Opera House in Berlin, 1911.
Later projects included low-cost row-houses and multi-storey blocks.
Hilberseimer was an original member of the influential Berlin 'Ring' of
architects. Early in the twenties he concentrated on town planning and its
theoretical application in relation to the design of individual large-scale
structures.
After 1938 Hilberseimer taught at the Illinois Institute of Technology where
he became Director and Professor of City and Regional Planning. His books
include studies of city planning and architecture, a definitive study of the work
of his colleague Mies van der Rohe and a survey of the development of modern
architecture.

HILBERSEIMER, LUDWIG. *Grosstadtbauten*, Hanover 1925.
HILBERSEIMER, LUDWIG. *Internationale neue Baukunst*, Stuttgart 1928.
HILBERSEIMER, LUDWIG. *Grosstadtarchitektur*, Stuttgart 1927.
HILBERSEIMER, LUDWIG. *Beton als Gestalter*, Stuttgart 1928. In collaboration
with Julius Vischer.
HILBERSEIMER, LUDWIG. *Hallenbauten*, Stuttgart 1928 (Leipzig 1931).
HILBERSEIMER, LUDWIG. *The Nature of Cities: Origin, Growth and Decline*, Chicago
1955.
HILBERSEIMER, LUDWIG. *Mies van der Rohe*, Chicago 1956.
HILBERSEIMER, LUDWIG. *Contemporary Architecture. Its Roots and Trends*, Chicago
1964.

Josef HOFFMANN (1870–1956)

Born Pirnitz, Moravia, 1870. Died Vienna, 1956.
A book illustrator, furniture designer and an architect, he studied at the
Vienna Academy under Hasenhauer and Wagner, the father of modern

architecture in Austria. Also worked for a year as an assistant designer in Wagner's Vienna studio and was nominated by Wagner to replace himself as Professor of Architecture at the Academy.

Founder member with Olbrich and a number of radical painters and sculptors of the Vienna Sezession, 1897. In 1899 he became Professor at the School of Applied Arts in Vienna. With Koloman Moser he founded the Wiener Werkstätte in 1903. These workshops lasted until 1933. In 1907 he founded the *Kunstschau* with the graphic artist and painter Gustav Klimt. In between he found time to design a number of significant buildings, among the best known being the Sanatorium at Purkesdorf, 1904, and the Palais Stoclet at Brussels, 1905. His position in the Arts and Crafts atmosphere of the workshops and the Sezession seemed to Adolf Loos at the time to be diametrically opposed to modern, unornamented architecture.

KLEINER, L. *Josef Hoffmann*, Berlin, Leipzig, Vienna, 1927.
WEISER, A. *Josef Hoffmann*, Geneva 1930.
ROCHOWANSKI, L.W. *Josef Hoffmann*, Vienna 1950. A study to commemorate Hoffmann's 50th birthday.
VERONESI, G. *Josef Hoffmann*, Milan 1956 (p.b.).
SECKLER, E. *et al*. *Josef Hoffmann 1870–1956*, London 1977. Exhibition catalogue (p.b.).
SEKLER, E.F. 'The Stoclet House by Josef Hoffmann' in *Essays in the History of Architecture presented to R.Wittkower*, London 1967, pp.228–44.

EISLER, M. 'Josef Hoffmann 1870–1920', *Wendingen*, Special Nos.8–9, 1920, pp.4–20. This double issue also contains other articles on Hoffmann including an article by Hoffmann himself on Vienna.
BEHRENS, P. 'The Work of Josef Hoffmann', *Architecture* (The Journal of the Society of Architects, London), Vol.2, 1923, pp.589–99.

Victor HORTA (1861–1947)

Born Ghent, 1861. Died Brussels, 1947.

Studied at Ghent Academy and the Academy, Brussels. He left the Academy at Brussels in 1881 and took up an appointment with the neo-Classicist, Alphonse Balat. In 1885 he left to carry out a commission in Ghent but returned to Balat's office soon after for another short period. He later assumed responsibility for the office after Balat's death.

At the beginning of the 1890s Horta designed the first of his buildings that were later to be labelled Art Nouveau. Hôtel Tassel was built 1892–3; Hotel Solvay, 1895–1900; the Maison du Peuple, 1896–9, with the first glass and iron façade in Belgium.

Horta was appointed Professor of the Brussels Academy in 1912. Later he became Head, 1927–31. During 1916–19 he lived in the United States.

A number of studies of his work are available, among the best of these is *Victor Horta* by Delevoy. Madsen's book *Sources of Art Nouveau* establishes the context of his work, while the same author's article in the *Architectural Review* provides a good summary.

HORTA, VICTOR. *Considérations sur l'art moderne*, Brussels 1925.
HORTA, VICTOR. *L'Enseignement architectural et l'architecture moderne*, Brussels 1926.

DELEVOY, R.L. *Victor Horta*, Brussels 1958.
PUTTEMANS, R., & OTHERS. *Victor Horta*, Brussels 1964.
MISC. *Guimard, Horta, Van de Velde*, Paris 1971, Exhibition catalogue, see pp.17–65.

THIEBAULT-SISSON. 'The Innovator: Victor Horta', *Art et Décorations*, Vol.1, Jan.–June 1897, pp.11–18, republished in Benton, T. & C. and D. Sharp, *Form and Function*, London 1975, pp.15–17.
MADSEN, S.T. 'Horta: Works and Style of Victor Horta before 1900', *Architectural Review*, December 1955, pp.388–92. See also chapter in the same author's *Sources of Art Nouveau*, Oslo 1956, pp.311–18.
MISC. 'Lettura di Victor Horta', *L'Architettura*, Special No. on the work of Horta. Nos.23–9, 1958.
MISC. 'Victor Horta', *Rythme*, Brussels, Special No.39, April 1964.

George HOWE (1886–1955)
and William LESCAZE (1896–1969)

George Howe was born in Worcester (Mass.), 1886. Died Cambridge (Mass.), 1955.
Educated at Harvard 1904–1907 and at the Ecole des Beaux-Arts, Paris, 1908–12. Was at Harvard at the same time as Stanford White and developed an admiration for the work of McKim, Mead and White. In 1916 Howe joined Mellor and Miegs as a partner in their Philadelphia firm. Between 1929–1934 he was in partnership with William Lescaze who that year had completed his initial work at Dartington Hall, Totnes, Devon.

William Lescaze was born in Geneva, Switzerland, 1896. Died New York, 1969. Pupil of Karl Moser at the Technical High School, Zurich. From 1919–20 he worked in areas of France devastated by the first world war and in the office of Henri Sauvage in Paris. He emigrated to the USA in 1923 and worked for some time in Cleveland before setting up his own practice in New York. Although the joint practice between Howe and Lescaze was short-lived, they completed their most famous building, the Philadelphia Savings Fund Society's skyscraper, in 1932. After the dissolution of their practice Lescaze went back to working in New York while Howe was briefly associated with Louis Kahn and Norman Bel Geddes. Later he became Chairman of the Department of Architecture at Yale, 1950–54. Howe was a prolific writer and his articles appear in many architectural and other journals. Full bibliography in Stern's book.

LESCAZE, W.H. *On being an Architect*, New York 1942.

STERN, R.A. *George Howe: Towards a Modern American Architecture*, New York, London, 1975. Contains references to Lescaze.

ROBIN, A. and BARMACHO. 'Howe and Lescaze', Special Issue, *L'Architecture d'Aujourd'hui*, No.4, Nov./Dec. 1933.

GIOLLI, R. 'William Lescaze', *Casabella*, 10, 1937, pp.10–21.

JORDY, W.H. and STERN, R.A.M. (eds) Special Issue. Philadelphia Savings Fund Society Building, *Journal of the Society of Architectural Historians* (USA), No.21, May 1962.

BARBEY, G. 'William Lescaze: Sa Carrière et Son Œuvre 1915–39', *Werk*, No.58, Aug. 1971, pp.559–65.

WODEHOUSE, L. 'William Lescaze and Dartington Hall', *AA Quarterly*, Vol.8, No.2, 1976, pp.3–14.

Arne JACOBSEN (1902–1971)

Born Copenhagen, 1902. Died in Copenhagen, 1971.
Studied at the Academy of Arts, Copenhagen, completing his architectural training in 1928.
Early in his career it became obvious that he was destined to change the basis of architecture and design in his own country. It has been said that he freed Danish architecture from the stranglehold of classicism. In so doing he became Denmark's most famous architect and designer. His town hall projects include Aarhus (1939–42); Søllerød (1942) and Rødovre (1955). In Copenhagen he designed the Jespersen Office Building (1955), SAS Building (1959) and the well known Munkegaards School, Gentofte Municipality (1952–6). All these buildings have been illustrated in detail in *Arkitekten*. After the mid-fifties Jacobsen's practice became more international. He took part in a number of international competitions. In 1959 he was commissioned to design St Catherine's College, Oxford. In 1956 he became Professor of Architecture at the Academy, Copenhagen.

PEDERSEN, J. *Arkitekten Arne Jacobsen*, Copenhagen 1954.

FABER, T. *Arne Jacobsen*, London 1964.

SKRIVER, R.E. (introd.) *Arne Jacobsen, Architecture, Applied Art*, Exhibition Catalogue, RIBA, London 1959. A list of articles that have appeared on Jacobsen's work in *Arkitekten* is included.

SKRIVER, R.E. (ed.) 'L'Œuvre d'Arne Jacobsen', *L'Architecture d'Aujourd'hui*, December 1960–January 1961, pp.42–53.

MISC. 'Recent Buildings by Arne Jacobsen', *Zodiac*, 5, pp.44–53.

Philip JOHNSON (1906–   )

Born Cleveland, Ohio, 1906. Lives in New York.
Began his studies at Harvard in classics and philosophy. Became the first director of the Museum of Modern Art, New York in the 1930s. There he was responsible for the presentation of a number of influential exhibitions and for writing the accompanying catalogues. After this period at the Museum he returned to Harvard for a time to study architecture under Marcel Breuer. In

1947 he produced the first monograph on Mies van der Rohe. He also became something of a disciple. Since the time he worked in collaboration with the Master he has gained an enormous reputation as a fashionable (and unpredictable) architect, particularly with his houses. Through Johnson the rebirth of eclecticism has become a reality.

Many studies of his work exist and all his schemes have been illustrated in American and European periodicals. John Jacobus's monograph is a useful introduction. Johnson's own book (written with Henry-Russell Hitchcock in 1932) on the International Style created the collective phrase for the new functional architecture. The recent book of *Writings* is invaluable and contains a full bibliography.

JOHNSON, P. (with HITCHCOCK, H-R.) *The International Style: Architecture since 1922*, New York 1932. (Reprinted, New York 1966.)

JOHNSON, P. *Machine Art*, New York 1934. A survey of modern industrial design.

JOHNSON, P. *Mies van der Rohe*, New York 1947 (revised and enlarged edition, 1953); Stuttgart 1956.

JOHNSON, P. *Philip Johnson: Architecture 1949–65*, New York, London, 1966. Introd. by H-R. Hitchcock.

JOHNSON, P. *Philip Johnson Writings*, New York 1979. Foreword by V. Scully. Intro. by P. Eisenman. Commentary by R. Stern.

JACOBUS, J. *Philip Johnson*, New York, London, 1962.

HITCHCOCK, H-R. 'Philip Johnson', *Architectural Review*, April 1955, pp.236–47. An appreciation of the architect and his work.

HITCHCOCK, H-R. 'Current Work of Philip Johnson', *Zodiac, 8*, 1961, pp.64–81.

O'NEAL, W.B. (compiler). 'Writings by and about Philip C. Johnson', Part 1, *Papers of The American Association of Architectural Bibliographers*, Vol. 1, 1965, pp.47–80. This supersedes the same compiler's previous list, Virginia, 1954, and the bibliography compiled by Elizabeth Harrah in 1955. It brings Johnson's list of writings up to the end of June 1964. It includes all contributions to journals both by and about Johnson.

Louis I. KAHN (1901–1974)

Born Island of Osel, Russia, 1901. Went to the USA in 1905 where he died 1974. He was a student at the School of Fine Arts, University of Pennsylvania. Took up a teaching assistantship at Pennsylvania, 1923–4, after which he became Senior Assistant in the City Architect's office, Philadelphia. After a number of other jobs he began his own practice in 1934. In 1941 he began to work in association with George Howe. He was Design Critic at Yale from 1947 to 1952; Professor of Architecture at Yale, 1947–57; Professor of Architecture, University of Pennsylvania, 1957. He became the mentor of the architectural world and established the type of reputation that is in keeping with his own architectural philosophy – the creative gentleman designer.

His list of writings is incredibly long; these are carefully listed in Vincent Scully's biography (pp.122–6) and *A + U* for 1973. I will not attempt a comprehensive list here but only mention a few significant books and articles. Note, also, Vance bibliography (1980): A-190 *Louis Kahn Bibliography*.

KAHN, LOUIS. *The Notebooks and Drawings of Louis J. Kahn*, Philadelphia 1962.
KAHN, L. *et al. Louis I. Kahn*, A+U Publication, Tokyo 1975.
KAHN, L. 'Monumentality', in Zucker, P. (ed.). *New Architecture and City Planning*, New York 1944, pp.577–88.
KAHN, L. 'Form and Design', *Architectural Design*, No.4, 1961, pp.145–54.

SCULLY, JR., V. *Louis I. Kahn*, New York, London, 1962.
See biographical and bibliographical sections.

MCQUADE, N. 'Louis Kahn and his Strong-Bone Structures', *Architectural Forum*, October 1957, pp.134–43. See also *Architectural Forum*, March 1958, pp.114–19.
SMITHSON, A. & P. 'Louis Kahn', *Architects' Year Book*, 9, pp.102–18.
SMITHSON, A. & P. 'Louis Kahn, Architect and Townplanner', *Integral* (Caracas), No.13, 1958, pp.18–23.
BANHAM, R. 'On Trial 2. Louis Kahn, the Buttery-Hatch Aesthetic', *Architectural Review*, March 1962, pp.203–6.
KATAN, E. & R. 'Louis Kahn', *L'Architecture d'Aujourd'hui*, No.105, 1962–3, pp.1–39.
CHANG, CHING-YU (ed.), 'Louis I. Kahn – Silence and Light', *Architecture and Urbanism*, 73/101, Special issue. Also book.

Frederick KIESLER (1896–1965)

Born Vienna, 1896. Died New York, 1965.
Studied at the Technical High School and the Academy, Vienna. With his unusual spatial designs Kiesler quickly established a name for himself in the *avant-garde* groups of the early twenties. His first contact with the Dutch 'de Stijl' group was in 1923. He was also closely associated with the 'G' Group founded by Werner Graeff, Hans Richter and Mies. He designed the Austrian Theatre and the Architecture section at the 1925 Paris Exposition.
In 1926 he went to the USA, where he taught and worked until his death. For thirteen years he was scenic director at the Juillard School of Music. He was also director of the Laboratory, School of Architecture, Columbia University. His architectural notoriety seems to rest on the designs he made for 'endless' spaces. His space house was designed in 1937. The article listed below, 'Kiesler's Pursuit of an Idea', is an excellent introduction to his work with very good illustrations and biographical material. His widow has prepared an extensive typewritten bibliography.

KIESLER, FREDERICK. *Inside the Endless House*. Art, People and Architecture: A Journal, New York 1966.
KIESLER, FREDERICK. 'Kiesler's Pursuit of an Idea', *Progressive Architecture*, July 1961, pp.104–16.

ANON. 'Design's Bad Boy', *Architectural Forum*, February 1947, pp.81–91.

Michel de KLERK (1889–1923)

Born Amsterdam, 1884. Died Amsterdam, 1923.
The leading exponent of the Amsterdam school; influenced by H.P.Berlage and the older generation of Revivalists. With Van der Meij and Kramer, de Klerk was responsible for the weirdest of all the Amsterdam 'Arts and Crafts Expressionist' buildings, the Shipping Offices, built during 1913–17, in the centre of the city. This is the key building of the Amsterdam school. This loosely organized group produced the magazine *Wendingen* through the society of architects and designers called 'Architectura et Amicita' which was formed in the middle of the nineteenth century. De Klerk was not only an architect and furniture designer of considerable imaginative skill but also a draughtsman and graphic artist of distinction. His drawings and photographs of his housing schemes were reproduced in *Wendingen* as well as in all the now standard works on modern Dutch architecture. See Fanelli's book listed under National Bibliography: Holland and Belgium, and J.J. Vriend's *Amsterdam School*, Amsterdam 1970.

BAZEL, K.P.C.DE. 'Onze Tijd en het werk van M. de Klerk', *Wendingen*, No.2, 1919, pp.2–12.
MIERAS, J.P. 'Over het Teekenwerk van M. de Klerk', *Wendingen*, No.2, 1924. A special issue devoted to the graphic work of de Klerk.
STAAL, J.F. 'Onuitgevoerde ontwerpen', *Wendingen*, Nos.4–5, 1924. A selection of projects by de Klerk.
KRAMER, P. 'De Bouwwerken van Michel de Klerk', *Wendingen*, Nos. 9–10, 1924. The housing schemes including the Eigen Haard development.
SHARP, D. 'Michel de Klerk and the Eigen Haard Development', *GA Houses*, No.3, pp.8–23.

Louis H. De KONINCK (1896–   )

Born Brussels, 1896. Lives in Brussels.
Studied at Brussels Academy (1912–1916) under Horta and also studied civil engineering and reinforced concrete at the Industrial School. During 1912–13 he attended lecture series by Berlage and Van de Velde, which further influenced his development, but during this period his main influence was that of Austrian Art Nouveau, until the early work of Le Corbusier became the main formative influence upon him. Between 1915–17 he was working on agricultural buildings – both traditional and modern. By 1917 he was experimenting in prefabricated building elements (tested in 1921 in some experimental low-cost houses), and by 1919 he was working on demountable, light-weight, prefabricated structures. In 1920 he designed a low-cost, prefabricated housing system, followed by experiments in prefabricated agricultural buildings. These experiments continued in wood, metal and concrete, gaining international recognition with a prototype emergency shelter for disaster victims in 1945. At the same time, he continued to investigate more permanent concrete structures (largely housing), making

advances in both construction and shuttering methods. The development of his various influences and experiments are perhaps best seen in the development of his own house (designed 1923, commenced building 1924, additions 1928 and 1949, finally completed 1968).

DE KONINCK, L-H. 'Type et procédé de construction d'une habitation rationnelle', in *La Cité*, No.1, Brussels 1930.

DE KONINCK, L-H. 'A propos du 3ème congrès international d'architecture moderne', *La Revue Documentaire*, 15 January, Brussels 1931.

DE KONINCK, L-H. 'Examen technique et calculs de l'isolation d'une toiture-terrasse', *La Cite*, No. 1, Brussels 1932.

DE KONINCK, L-H. 'Quelques considération sur l'habitation en béton armé', *L'Epoque*, No.7, Brussels 1933.

DE KONINCK, L-H. 'Pour ou contre l'ornement', *Clarté*, Nos.6 and 10, Brussels 1934.

DE KONINCK, L-H. 'Tribune Libre', *L'Emulation*, No.6, Brussels 1938.

DE KONINCK, L-H. 'L'habitation et le civisme', *La Maison*, No.5, Brussels 1945.

DE KONINCK, L-H. 'L'architecture devant les problèmes nouveaux', *La Maison*, No.2, Brussels 1945.

DE KONINCK, L-H. 'L'architecture moderne', *Rotary Club de Belgique*, No.12, Brussels 1945.

DE KONINCK, L-H. 'L'équipement moderne des habitations', *La Maison*, No.3, Brussels 1945.

DE KONINCK, L-H. 'La présentation belge à l'exposition de l'Urbanisme et de l'Habitation de Paris 1947', *L'Education Ménagère*, No.5–6, Paris 1948.

DE KONINCK, L-H. 'La cuisine fonctionnelle', *L'entreprise*, 31 January, Brussels 1963.

CULOT, M. and DELEVOY, R-L. *L-H. De Koninck*, Brussels 1970. Exhibition catalogue. Reissued as book, 1979.

CULOT, M. AND DELEVOY, R-L. *L-H. De Koninck: Architect*, London 1973. Catalogue of the exhibition at the Architectural Association.

HENVAUX, E. 'L-H. De Koninck: Architecte', *La Cité*, No.6, 1927.

PUTTEMANS, P. 'L-H. De Koninck'. *La Revue Architecture*, No.58, 1964. Special issue.

BERGEN, E. 'L-H. De Koninck', *Plan*, No.3, 1965.

FRANSSEN, BRAEM, WYNEN. 'La médaille d'or à L-H. De Koninck', *La Maison*, No.7, 1965. (Discussion)

SHARP, D. 'De Koninck', *Building Design*, No.148, 1973.

Arthur KORN (1891–1978)

Born Breslau, 1891. Died in old peoples' home near Vienna, 1978.
Studied in Berlin. Worked in Berlin first with Erich Mendelsohn in 1919 then in private practice with Sigfried Weitzmann from 1922. Responsible for a number of houses, factories, shops and interiors.
Korn was made Secretary of the 'Novembergruppe' in 1924. Became a

member of the Berlin 'Ring' in 1926. After attending the CIAM meeting in London with Walter Gropius in 1934 he returned in 1937 to settle in England. Chairman of the MARS Town Planning Committee, 1938. Taught at the Oxford School of Architecture 1941–5 and the AA School, 1945–65 and at the Hammersmith School. Hon. member, AA, London and *Festschrift*, 1967. Member of the Akademie der Künste, Berlin.

Korn's writings include an important essay on Analytical and Utopian Architecture, first published in Paul Westheim's 'Post-Expressionist' journal *Das Kunstblatt* in 1923 and the two well-known books *Glas im Bau* . . . (1929), *History Builds the Town* (1953). His architectural work has been featured in a number of international magazines, as well as in contemporary source books such as Gropius's Bauhaus book *Internationale Architektur* and Hajos and Zahn's *Berliner Architektur der Nachkriegszeit*.

KORN, ARTHUR. *Glas im Bau und als Gebrauchsgegenstand*, Berlin 1929. Published as '*Glass in Modern Architecture*', London, New York, 1967.

KORN, ARTHUR. *History Builds the Town*, London 1953.

KORN, A. 'Analytische und utopische Architektur', *Das Kunstblatt*, December 1923, pp.336–9. Republished in Conrads, U. (ed.). *Programme und Manifeste zur Architektur des 20. Jahrhunderts*, Berlin 1964, pp.71–2. *Programmes and Manifestoes on 20th Century Architecture*, London, Cambridge (Mass.), 1970, pp.76–7.

KORN, A. 'Arthur Korn, 1891 to the present day', *Architectural Association Journal*, Special No., December 1957, pp.114–18.

KORN, A. '55 years in the Modern Movement', *Architectural Association Journal*, *Arena*, April 1966, pp.263–5.

SHARP, D. (ed.) *Planning and Architecture*, London 1967. Essays presented to Arthur Korn by AA, London.

WESTHEIM, P. 'Hinweis auf Arthur Korn', *Das Kunstblatt*, December 1923, pp.334–5.

HOUSDEN, B. (ed.) 'Arthur Korn', *Architectural Association Journal*, Special No., December 1957. Containing a complete list of buildings and the biographical article by Korn listed above.

ROSENBERG, S. 'The Ring and Arthur Korn', *Architectural Association Journal*, February 1958, pp.170–1.

SHARP, D. *et al.* 'Arthur Korn: Tributes', *AA Quarterly*, Vol.11, no.3, 1979.

Jan KOTERA (1871–1923)

Born Brno, 1871. Died Prague, 1923.
The major influence on modern architecture in Czechoslovakia (*cf.* Berlage in Holland), Kotera studied at the Baugewerbeschule in Plzeu and later at the Academy of Fine Arts, Vienna, under Otto Wagner. Member of 'Siebener Club' in Vienna and later of 'Manes' in Prague. From 1898–1910 Professor at the School of Industrial Arts in Prague and from 1910–1923 Professor, Academy of Fine Arts in Prague. His major works: Museum Hradec Kralove, 1906–12, Water tower, Prague, 1905–16, National House, Prostejov, 1905–07, Lemberger Palais, Vienna, 1913.

KOTERA, J. *Prace me a mych zaku*, 1898–1901, Vienna 1902. Kotera on his work and pupils.

KOTERA. J. 'Delnicke kolonie (The Worker's Estates)', *Stavtel*, No.1, Prague 1921.

MADL, K.B. *Jan Kotera*, Prague 1922.

WIRTH, Z. *Jan Kotera 1871–1923*, catalogue of the exhibition, Prague 1926.

NOVOTNY, O. *Jan Kotera a jeho doba* (J.K. and his time), Prague 1958.

FUCHS, B. *In Margine umeleckeho odkazu Jana Kotery* (on the artistic heritage of J.K.), Brno 1972.

SLAPETA, V. and MAREK, P. *Narodni dum v Prostejove* (The National House in Prostejov), Prostejov 1978.

Jaromir KREJCAR (1895–1950)

Born Hundsheim, Austria, 1895. Died 1950.
Studied architecture at the Academy of Fine Arts, Prague, under Professor Jan Kotera.
In 1922 he worked in the office of Josef Gocar. In 1923 he opened a private office in Prague; from 1933–35 in the USSR. Architect in private practice in Prague in 1936–48.
Buildings include Olympic office building, Prague, 1923–6; Sanatorium Machnac Trencianske Teplice 1929–32; Czech Pavilion, Paris, 1937. From 1946–8 Professor of Architecture, Technical University, Brno. In 1948 he emigrated to England where he lectured at the AA School until his death.

KREJCAR, J. *L'Architecture contemporaine tchécoslovaque*, Prague 1928.

TEIGE, K. *Prace Jaromir Krejacara*, Prague 1933.

FREEMAN, D. 'Jaromir Krejcar', *AA Journal*, Vol.65, 1949–50, pp.89–90.

LE CORBUSIER (1887–1965)

Born Charles-Édouard Jeanneret, 1887, at La Chaux-de-Fonds, near Neuchâtel, Switzerland. Died August 1965 while swimming in the Mediterranean. Nothing can be said here in a short biography that cannot easily be found in the standard biographies and the Girsberger editions of the *Œuvre complète*. I will concentrate on the writings: Jeanneret's first written study was for the art school in his home town from which he had been sent on a tour of Germany: *Étude du mouvement d'art décoratif en Allemagne*, 1912.
After Jeanneret moved to Paris in 1917 he developed together with Ozenfant the painterly concept of 'Purism'. They published the Purist Manifesto in 1918. They edited the review *L'Esprit Nouveau* together with the poet Paul Dermée, 1920–5. Out of articles on architecture in this review Le Corbusier's passionate propagandist book, *Vers une architecture*, was formed. It owed much to Ozenfant, but that seems to have been forgotten. Other propaganda books followed on domestic design, decorative art and urbanism. During the war

Le Corbusier

years Le Corbusier was forming his ideas on the Modulor and *Modulor I* was published in France in 1950. His work is represented in a complete form by the Girsberger editions. His own book *My Work* is a useful record. Peter Blake's biography which appeared originally as a section of *The Master Builders* is still the best available. A selected bibliography on *Le Corbusier* was produced by Vance in 1979: A-117.

LE CORBUSIER. *Vers une architecture*, Paris 1923 (revised and expanded, Paris 1924, 1928). *Kommende Baukunst*, Stuttgart 1926. The first German translation of *Vers une architecture*, by H. Hildebrandt, based on the second French edition. *Towards a New Architecture*, London 1927 (1948). The first English edition, translated by Frederick Etchells and published by John Rodker (1000 copies) (2nd edn, 1931).

LE CORBUSIER. *Urbanisme*, Paris 1925. *The City of Tomorrow and its Planning*, London 1929 (1947). The English version of *Urbanisme*, translated by Etchells and published by Rodker.

LE CORBUSIER. *L'art décoratif d'aujourd'hui*, Paris 1925 (reissue, p.b. Paris 1959, with additional material).

LE CORBUSIER. *Le peinture moderne*, Paris 1925. With Ozenfant as co-author.

LE CORBUSIER. *Almanach d'architecture moderne*, Paris 1927.

LE CORBUSIER. *Une maison – un palais*, Paris 1928.

LE CORBUSIER. *Précisions: sur un état présent de l'architecture et de l'urbanisme*, Paris 1930.

LE CORBUSIER. *Croisade, ou le crépuscule des Acadèmies*, Paris 1932.

LE CORBUSIER. *La ville radieuse*, Boulogne-sur-Seine 1935.

LE CORBUSIER. *Aircraft*, London, New York, 1935.

LE CORBUSIER. *Quand les cathédrales étaient blanches*, Paris 1937. *When the Cathedrals were whites*, New York 1947.

LE CORBUSIER. *Des canons, des munitions? Merci! des logis . . . s.v.p.!* Paris 1938 (Previously monograph, 1937).

LE CORBUSIER. *Le lyrisme des temps nouveaux et l'urbanisme*, Paris 1939.

LE CORBUSIER. *Destin de Paris*, Paris 1941.

LE CORBUSIER. *Sur les quatre routes*, Paris 1941. *The Four Routes*, London 1947. English translation by Dorothy Todd.

LE CORBUSIER. *Les constructions Murondins*, Paris 1941.

LE CORBUSIER. *La maison des hommes*, Paris 1942. Main text by François de Pierrefou. *The Home of Man*, London 1948. English translation by Clive Entwistle and Gordon Holt.

LE CORBUSIER. *Entretien avec les étudiants des écoles d'architecture*, Paris 1943.

LE CORBUSIER. *Le Corbusier Talks with Students from the Schools of Architecture*, New York 1961. Translation by P.Chase.

LE CORBUSIER. *La charte d'Athènes*, Paris 1943 (2nd edn 1957). *The Athens Charter*, New York 1973.

LE CORBUSIER. *Les trois établissements humaine*, Boulogne-sur-Seine 1944.

LE CORBUSIER. *Propos d'urbanisme*, Paris 1946. *Grundfragen des Städtebaus*, Teufen 1945. First German edition. *Concerning Town Planning*, London 1947 (1971). English translation by Clive Entwistle.

LE CORBUSIER. *L'unité d'habitation de Marseille*, Special book number. *Le Point*, November 1950. *The Marseilles Block*, London 1950.

LE CORBUSIER. *Le modulor*, Boulogne 1950. *The Modulor*, London 1954 (p.b. 1961). Translated by Peter de Francia and Anna Bostock.

LE CORBUSIER. *Modulor 2*, Boulogne 1955. *Modulor 2*, London 1958.

LE CORBUSIER. *La chapelle Notre-Dame-du-Haut à Ronchamp*, Paris 1956. English version. *The Chapel at Ronchamp*, London 1957. Translated by Jacqueline Cullen.

LE CORBUSIER. *Les Plans de Paris 1956–1922*, Paris 1956.

LE CORBUSIER. *Le poème électronique*, Brussels 1958. Multi-lingual versions.

LE CORBUSIER. *My Work*, London, Stuttgart, 1960.

LE CORBUSIER. 'Twentieth-Century Living and Twentieth-Century Building', The Studio Year Book, *Decorative Art 1930*, pp.9–17. Also reprinted in Sharp, D. *The Rationalists*, London 1978.

MORANCÉ, A. (publisher). *L'œuvre complète de Le Corbusier et Jeanneret*, 7 vols., Paris, n.d. (*c.* 1933–)

BOESIGER, W. (ed.). *Le Corbusier: Œuvre complète*, Zürich, 1929–. Now also London and New York.

Part 1. 1910–29. *Le Corbusier et Pierre Jeanneret* (1929).

Part 2. 1929–34. *Le Corbusier et Pierre Jeanneret* (1935).

Part 3. 1934–8. *Le Corbusier et P. Jeanneret*. Introduction by Max Bill (1939).

Part 4. 1938–46. *Le Corbusier* (1946).

Part 5. 1946–52. *Le Corbusier* (1953).

Part 6. 1952–7. *Le Corbusier et son atelier rue de Sèvres 35* (1957).

Part 7. 1957–65. *Le Corbusier et son atelier rue de Sèvres 35* (1965).

PAPADAKI, S. *Le Corbusier: Architect, Painter, Writer*, New York 1948.

BARDI, P.M. *A Critical Review of Le Corbusier*, Brazil 1950. Published for the exhibition 'New World of Space'.

CHOAY, F. *Le Corbusier*, New York, London, 1960.

BLAKE, P. *Le Corbusier. Architecture and Form*. Harmondsworth, 1960 (Pelican p.b.) Taken from the section 'Le Corbusier and the Mastery of Form' in the author's *The Master Builders*, London 1960.

BOESIGER, W. (ed.). *Le Corbusier 1910–60*, Zürich, Stuttgart, London, 1960. A truncated version of the *Œuvres complètes*.

MOOS, S.VON. *Le Corbusier. Elemente einer Synthese*, Frauenfeld 1968. French version: *Le Corbusier. L'Architecte et son Mythe*, Paris 1971. English version: *Le Corbusier: Elements of a synthesis*, Cambridge (Mass.) 1979.

JENCKS, C. *Le Corbusier and the Tragic View of Architecture*, London, New York, 1973. An unusual view of Le Corbusier as a Nietzschian.

SERENYI, P. *Le Corbusier in Perspective*, Englewood Cliffs, New Jersey 1975. Includes reprinted material by Von Moos, Jencks, Giedion, Wittkower, Stirling, Teige, *et al*, with a useful, but limited, bibliography.

WALDEN, R. (ed.). *The Open Hand: Essays on Le Corbusier*, Cambridge (Mass.) 1977. A variety of hands at work (*cf*: Serenyi, *op. cit.*)

IZZO, A. AND GUBITOSI, C. *Le Corbusier, Designi*, Rome 1978. Catalogue of the exhibition of drawings shown in various countries; includes substantial section in colour. In three languages: Italian, French and English.

Le Corbusier's writings on painting:

Après le cubisme, Paris (Edition des Commentaires) 1918.

'Sur la plastique', *L'Esprit Nouveau* (Paris), 1, 1920, pp.38–48.

'Le Purisme' (with Ozenfant), *L'Esprit Nouveau*, 3, 1920, pp.369–86.
'Intéger' (with Ozenfant), *Création* (Paris), 2, 1921.
'Picasso et la peinture d'aujourd'hui', *L'Esprit Nouveau*, 13, 1922, pp.1489–1494.
'Esthétique et Purisme' (with Ozenfant), *L'Esprit Nouveau*, 15, 1922, pp.1704–08.
La Peinture moderne (with Ozenfant), Paris (Crès) 1925.
'Louis Soutter. L'inconnu de la soixantaine', *Minotaure* (Paris), 9, 1936, pp.62–65.
'Architecture and the Arts', *Transition* (New York, Paris), 25, 1936.
'De la Peinture', in *Le Corbusier: Œuvre plastique*, Paris (Morancé) 1938.
'Synthese des arts majeurs', *Werk* (Winterthur), 2, 1949, pp.50–51.
'Purisme', *L'Art d'Aujourd'hui* (Paris), 7/8, 1950, pp.36–37.
'Y a-t-il une crise de l'art?', *Comprendre* (Venice), 4, 1951.
L'Atelier de la recherche patiente, Paris 1960.
'Dessiner' (1965) in Jean Petit, *Le Corbusier, Dessins*, Geneva 1968.
Œuvre complète 1910–1965, 7 vols, Zürich (Artemis) 1929–1968 also contains many references to Le Corbusier's paintings.
A select list of material on Le Corbusier the artist:
RAYNAL, M. 'Ozenfant et Jeanneret', *L'Esprit Nouveau* (Paris), 7, 1921, pp.809–32.
DORMOY, MARIE. 'Le Corbusier', *L'Amour de l'Art* (Paris) II, 1930, p.213.
GIEDION, S. 'Le Corbusier', *Allgemeines Lexikon der bildenden Künste von Thieme-Becker*, 22, Leipzig 1928, pp.528–9.
BADOVICI, J. *Le Corbusier, Œuvre plastique*, Paris (Morancé) 1938.
GIEDION, S. *'Le Corbusier als Maler'*, Kunsthaus, Zürich 1938, pp.5–13. Exhibition catalogue.
RECASEUS, J.DE. 'Psicogenesis de la pintura de Le Corbusier', *Proa* (Bogota) 8, 1947, pp.1–18.
SOBY, J.T. 'Le Corbusier. The Painter', in Papadaki, S. (ed.) *Le Corbusier, Architect, Painter, Writer*. New York 1948, pp.115–132.
DEGAND, L. 'Le Corbusier peintre', *L'Art d'Aujourd'hui* (Paris) 2, 1952, p.25ff.
ZERVOS, C. 'L'exposition Le Corbusier au Musée National d'Art moderne', *Cahiers d'Art* (Paris) 1954, p.116ff.
JARDOT, M. *Le Corbusier, dessins*, Paris 1955.
SAVINA, J. 'Sculpture de Le Corbusier', *L'Art d'Aujourd'hui* 51, 1965, pp.96–101.

Ivan LEONIDOV (1902–1959)

Originally apprenticed to an ikon painter, Leonidov joined the recently created TVER artists' studios. In 1921 he went to Moscow to continue his studies at Zkhutemas in fine arts but later moved to the architecture faculty and came under the influence of A.Vesnin. In 1925 he entered a number of architectural competitions and won several prizes. In 1927 he completed his final year project for the Lenin Institute, Moscow, which was approved of by the Academy. He was appointed a lecturer at the students' request in 1928. His career really only spanned the years from 1927–1930 and his work deteriorated rapidly during the war, and after the war he worked only as an exhibition designer with architecture as a hobby.

KHAN-MAHOMEDOV, S. O. 'Ivan Leonidov', *Sovietskaia Arkhitektura*, 16, 1964, pp.103–16.

KHAN-MAHOMEDOV, S.O. *I.Leonidov*, Moscow 1973.

KHAN-MAHOMEDOV, S.O. 'I. Leonidov 1902–1959', *Architectural Design*, Feb. 1970, pp.104–7 (reprinted in Shvidkovsky, O.A. (ed.) *Building in the USSR 1917–1932*, London 1971, pp.124–29).

William Richard LETHABY (1857–1931)

Born Barnstaple, Devon, 1857. Died London, 1931.

After completing his articles with Alexander Lauder at Barnstaple he moved to London, via Derby and Leicester, to become senior assistant to Norman Shaw in 1877. In the evenings he pursued his studies at the Royal Academy Schools.

Lethaby was a generation younger than Morris and Webb, but closely connected with the 'circle'. He carried out a number of designs for the William Morris Co., and became President of the Arts and Crafts Society.

His first independent commission was the house at Avon Tyrell, near Salisbury. As a joint adviser, with George Frampton, to the Technical Education Board of the LCC he was instrumental in founding the Central School of Arts and Crafts in 1894. He became joint Principal with Frampton and remained in that position until 1911. After that he concentrated on his work at the Royal College of Art, where he had been made Professor of Design in 1900.

His literary work was extensive; *Architecture, Mysticism and Myth*, was published in 1891 and re-issued in 1892; *Architecture* in 1912 and *Form in Civilisation* in 1922. Besides numerous other historical and technical studies he contributed many articles to the press on all kinds of architectural topics (e.g. see *The Builder* from 1919 to 1931.

LETHABY, WILLIAM RICHARD. *Architecture, Mysticism and Myth*, London 1891 (1892). Later rewritten as articles for *The Builder* 1928 as *Architecture, Nature and Magic*, and later published, London 1956.

LETHABY, WILLIAM RICHARD. *Architecture: An Introduction to the History and Theory of the Art of Building*, London 1912. Reissued 1955 with an introduction by Basil Ward.

LETHABY, WILLIAM RICHARD. *Form in Civilisation*, London 1922. Collected papers on art and labour (1957).

LETHABY, WILLIAM RICHARD. *Londinium Architecture and the Crafts*, London 1923.

LETHABY, WILLIAM RICHARD. *Architecture, Nature and Magic*, London 1956. See first note. Bibliographical note by Alfred Powell.

MACLEOD, R. *Style and Society*, London 1971. See chapter 'W.R. Lethaby', pp.55–67.

ROBERTS, H. MOLESWORTH. *W.R. Lethaby: A Bibliography of his Literary Work*. List compiled for the RIBA Library, 1950, 41pp. typewritten.

ROBERTS, H.M. *William Richard Lethaby*, 1857–1931, London 1957.

POSENER, J. (ed.). *Anfänge des Funktionalismus: Von Arts and Crafts zum Deutschen*

Werkbund, Berlin 1964 (p.b.). Section devoted to the writings of Lethaby, pp.27–61.

BLOMFIELD, R. 'W.R. Lethaby – An Impression and a Tribute', *RIBA Journal*, February 1932, pp.239–312.
BRANDON-JONES, J. 'The Architect who Turned Teacher', *The Listener*, January 1948, pp.146–8.
VARIOUS. 'William Richard Lethaby 1857–1931', a symposium in honour of his centenary, *RIBA Journal*, April 1957, pp.218–24. Contributions by Brian Thomas; J.Brandon-Jones; Basil Ward; D.Talbot Rice; A.R.N.Roberts.

William Richard Lethaby

74

El LISSITZKY (1890–1941)

El (Lazar) Markovich Lissitzky was born near Smolensk, 1890. Died Moscow, 1941.
Studied at Darmstadt Technical College, 1909–14. Returned to Moscow on graduation. Closely associated with the Russian Constructivist groups immediately after the first world war.
Taught at Moscow Academy, 1921. Returned to Germany in 1922–3 and worked with Mies van der Rohe and with Van Doesburg. Member 'ABC' group (1925).
Lissitzky's book *Russland: Die Rekonstruktion der Architektur in der Sowjetunion*, published in Vienna in 1930 as the first volume of the '*Neues Bauen in der Welt*' series by Schroll, is still one of the best books available on progressive Russian architecture. Republished with additional material and in English, 1970.

LISSITZKY, EL, & ARP, H. *Die Kunstismen*, Zürich, Leipzig, Munich, 1925. An interesting chronology of the 'isms' of modern art. English text included.
LISSITZKY, EL. *Russland. Die Rekonstruktion der Architektur in der Sowjetunion*, Vienna 1930. Republication with additional material, *Russland. Architektur für eine Weltrevolution*, Berlin 1965 (p.b.). English version: *Russia: An Architecture for World Revolution*, London, Cambridge (Mass.), 1970.

J.B. van LOGHEM (1881–1940)

Born Haarlem, 1881. Died 1940.
Van Loghem originally started as a building engineer before setting up practice in Haarlem.
From 1920–26 he ran his practice as a co-operative. Worked from 1926–28 in the Soviet Union. On his return he set up a one-man office in Rotterdam.
Although his buildings were mainly in the Dutch Functionalist style, Van Loghem's contributions to the Modern Movement in architecture consist mainly of his writings which were 'purist' in content. From 1919–21 he was active on the editional board for *Wendingen* magazine and had served previously on the editorial board of the magazine *Bouwkundig Weekblad*. Later, in the 1930s, he contributed many articles to *De 8 en Opbouw*, and in 1932 he produced his important book in four languages called *Bouwen*.

VAN LOGHEM, J.B. *Bouwen, Bauen, Building, Bâtir*, Amsterdam 1932.

VAN DE BEEK, J. and SMIENK, G. *J.B. Van Loghem: Dutch Architecture 1881–1940*, Delft 1972. Typewritten exhibition catalogue. A typewritten English version of this catalogue was edited by D. Sharp with translations by R. Vickery, London 1973.

Adolf Loos

Adolf LOOS (1870–1933)

Born Brno, 1870. Died Vienna, 1933.

Studied architecture at Dresden Polytechnic. His trip to England and the United States (where he stayed for three-and-a-half years) immediately after graduation coloured his whole attitude to architecture and living. In England he saw the simplicity of domestic architecture, in the United States the simplicity of modern dress.

On his return to Vienna he poured out his ideas as a journalist, from 1897 to 1900, in the *Neue Freie Presse*. He became the master of the architectural maxim. His articles, later collected into a volume called *Ins Leere Gesprochen* and published in Paris in 1921, attacked the established principles of the Sezession and clearly presented Loos's own ideas. They found an immediate public in the Viennese *avant-garde* circles, which included such associates as Oskar Kokoschka, Arnold Schoenberg, Karl Kraus and Peter Altenberg.

In 1908 he published the famous 'Ornament and Crime' essay, while two years earlier he had founded a Free School of Architecture. His architectural work began with the Café Museum, Vienna, 1899. He was in charge of housing in Vienna from 1920 to 1922. In 1922 he moved to Paris and into the Jeanneret-Ozenfant and the Dadaist circles. He built a house for Tristan Tzara, Paris, 1926. The books by Kulka (1931) and Münz and Künstler contain all his work except the writings which appear in two separate volumes, published by Herold (Vol. 1, 1962).

LOOS, ADOLF. *Ins Leere Gesprochen*, Paris 1921 (2nd edn Innsbruck 1932). Articles written between 1897 and 1900.
LOOS, ADOLF. *Trotzdem, 1900–1930*, Innsbruck 1931. Articles and essays written between 1903 and 1930. Includes 'Ornament und Verbrechen'. See also next item in this list, *Sämtliche Schriften 1*.
LOOS, ADOLF. *Sämtliche Schriften*, 2 vols. Vol.1: 'Ins Leere Gesprochen 1897–1900' and 'Trotzdem 1900–30', Vienna 1962. Edited by Franz Glück. Selected maxims from 'Ins Leere Gesprochen' and 'Trotzdem', *Architectural Review*, October 1934, p.151. Translated by P.Morton Shand.

MARILAUN, A. *Adolf Loos*, Vienna 1922.
VARIOUS CONTRIBUTIONS. *Adolf Loos, zum 60. Geburtstag, am 10. Dezember 1930*, Vienna 1930. A Festschrift with contributions from Berg, Taut, Oud, Schoenberg, etc.
GLÜCK, F. *Adolf Loos*, Paris 1931. (Collection: 'Les Artistes Nouveaux'). p.b.
KULKA, H. *Adolf Loos, das Werk des Architekten*, Vienna 1931. In the series *'Neues Bauen in der Welt'*.
MARKALAUS, B. *Adolf Loos*, Vienna 1931.
MÜNZ, L. *Adolf Loos*, Milan 1956.
MÜNZ, L., & KÜNSTLER, G. *Adolf Loos: Pioneer of Modern Architecture*, London 1966. Intro. by Nikolaus Pevsner.
CZECH, H. & MISTELBAUER, W. *Das Looshaus*, Vienna 1977.

SHAND, P.M. 'Loos', *Architectural Review*, October 1934. pp.134–7.
MISC. 'Numero dedicato ad Adolf Loos', Special No. *Casabella*, No.233.
BANHAM, R. 'Ornament and Crime, the decisive contribution of Adolf Loos', *Architectural Review*, February 1957, pp.85–8.

Berthold LUBETKIN   (1901–   )

Born Tiflis (Georgia), 1901. Lives in Bristol.
Studied in Moscow, Warsaw and in Paris in the Atelier Perret and at various Parisian architectural schools.
He quickly established an international reputation, winning the competition for the Urals Polytechnic, USSR, in 1925. Site architect for Melnikov's pavilion at 1925 Paris Exposition. He was also among the prizewinners for the Palace of Soviets competition, Moscow 1931. Arrived in England from France in 1930.
In England Lubetkin carried out important work through the partnership Tecton, that had been formed in 1932 between himself and six graduates of the Architectural Association School. Tecton put English modern architecture on the world map, with of all things, zoo buildings. These buildings, as R.F.Jordan points out in his useful *Architectural Review* article, 'were a curtain raiser to Highpoint'. Highpoint I was built in 1934, to be followed by Highpoint II in 1937.
After producing the plan for the New Town of Peterlee (1955) Lubetkin gradually retired from practice.

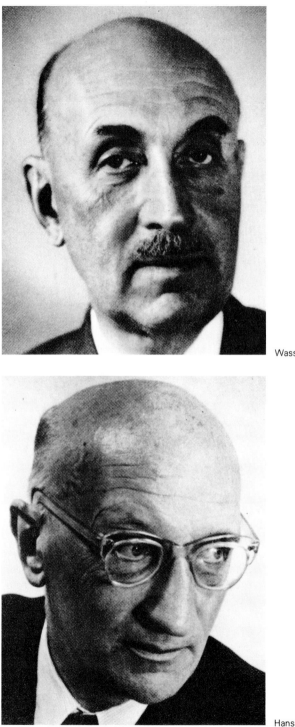

Wassili Luckhardt

Hans Luckhardt

LUBETKIN, BERTHOLD. 'The Builders', article in Special No. on Russia, *Architectural Review*, May 1932, pp.201–14.
LUBETKIN, BERTHOLD. 'Modern Architecture in England', *American Architect and Architecture*, February 1937, pp.29–42.
LUBETKIN, BERTHOLD. 'Soviet Architecture. Notes on Developments from 1917 to 1932', *Architectural Association Journal*, May 1956, pp.260–4.
LUBETKIN, BERTHOLD. 'Soviet Architecture. Notes on Developments from 1932 to 1955', *Architectural Association Journal*, September–October 1956, pp.85–9.

JORDAN, R.F. 'Lubetkin', *Architectural Review*, July 1955, pp.36–44. Republished in D.Sharp (ed.). *The Rationalists*, London 1978.

Wassili LUCKHARDT (1889–1972) and Hans LUCKHARDT (1890–1954)

Wassili Luckhardt was born in Berlin 1889. Died in Berlin 1972.
Studied in Charlottenburg, Munich and Dresden. After the first world war he set up practice with his brother in association with Alfons Anker in Berlin.
Hans Luckhardt was born in Berlin, 1890. Died Bad Wiessee, 1954. Studied at Karlsruhe.
Both brothers were signatories to the Architectural Programme issued by the *Arbeitsrat für Kunst* in 1919 and both contributed sketches and letters to Bruno Taut's 'Utopian Correspondence'. After the period of fantasy was over the Luckhardts turned to a very controlled rectilinear architecture, and to extremely precise detailing.
Many of the early sketches were included in *Frühlicht*. The work of the brothers is covered in the book edited by Udo Kultermann.

LUCKHARDT, HANS. Letters in *Die Gläserne Kette*, Berlin 1963. Exhibition catalogue. A number of sketches and the letters are included in this catalogue.

KULTERMANN, U. (ed.). *Wassili und Hans Luckhardt; Bauten und Entwürfe*, Tübingen 1958. The standard collection of work.

Charles Rennie MACKINTOSH (1868–1928)

Born Glasgow, 1868. Died of cancer, London, 1928.
He studied by taking evening classes at Glasgow School of Art and at the same time working as an articled pupil of John Hutchison. He won a scholarship that enabled him to travel abroad in 1891. Joined the firm of Honeyman and Keppie in 1889.
The first articles on the Glasgow group of designers appeared in *The Studio* in 1897. 'The Four' had come together from different disciplines, the Macdonald sisters from painting and Mackintosh and McNair from an architectural background. The result of this was not only a fusion of styles, they also married – McNair to Frances and Mackintosh to Margaret.
In 1896 the firm of Honeyman and Keppie won the competition for the new Glasgow School of Art – it had been designed by Mackintosh. In the years

1900–2 'The Four' established a European reputation. Mackintosh left the firm of Honeyman and Keppie in 1913. He and his wife moved south to Suffolk in 1914. Very little else emerged from his hand after his move to London in 1915.

Thomas Howarth's study is still the most complete available, adequately supplemented by Macleod. The pamphlet produced by the School of Art, Glasgow in 1961 is photographically very good. See also Vance Bibliography: A-250 *Charles Rennie Mackintosh, Architect and designer*.

KOCH, A. (publisher). *C.R.Mackintosh, Hans eines Kunstfreundes*, Darmstadt 1902, in the series '*Meister der Innen-Kunst*', Introduction by Hermann Muthesius.

PEVSNER, N. *Ch. R.Mackintosh*, Milan 1950.

HOWARTH, T. *Charles Rennie Mackintosh and the Modern Movement*, London 1952 (1978).

BLISS, D.P. (ed.). *Charles Rennie Mackintosh and the Glasgow School of Art*, Glasgow 1961 (p.b.).

YOUNG, A.H. *Charles Rennie Mackintosh (1868–1928): Architecture, Design and Painting*, Edinburgh 1968. Exhibition catalogue.

MACLEOD, R. *Charles Rennie Mackintosh*, London 1968. An important contribution to the theory behind Mackintosh's work.

DOAK, A. (ed.). *Architectural Jottings by Charles Rennie Mackintosh*, (selected by A.H.Young), Glasgow 1968.

ALISON, F. *Charles Rennie Mackintosh as a designer of chairs*. Milan, New York, 1973.

BILLCLIFFE, R. *Architectural sketches and flower drawings by Charles Rennie Mackintosh*, London 1977.

COOPER, J. (ed.). *Mackintosh Architecture: The Complete Buildings and Selected Projects*, London 1978. Useful for its illustrations.

HOWARTH, T. 'C.R.Mackintosh 1868–1928', *RIBA Journal*, Nov. 1950, pp.15–19.

WALKER, D. 'The early work of Charles Rennie Mackintosh', *Architectural Review*, Nov. 1968. (reprinted Richards, J.M. and Pevsner, N. (eds). *The Anti-Rationalists*, London 1973, pp.116–135.

SEKLER, E.F. 'Mackintosh and Vienna', *Architectural Review*, Dec. 1968 (reprinted Richards, J.M. and Pevsner, N. (eds). *The Anti-Rationalists*, London 1973, pp.136–142.)

Sven MARKELIUS (1889–1972)

Born Stockholm, 1889. Died 1972.

Sven Markelius, who was both architect and town planner, studied at Stockholm Technical College and the Academy of Fine Arts. He commenced his career in the office of Östberg at the time he was working on Stockholm Town Hall. Nonetheless Markelius was a great admirer of Le Corbusier and, it is recorded, was 'the first Swedish architect to design in the international style of the 30s'. His chief works include villa designs for the Stockholm Exhibition (1930; Concert Hall, Halsingborg 1932; 'Collective house', Stockholm 1935,

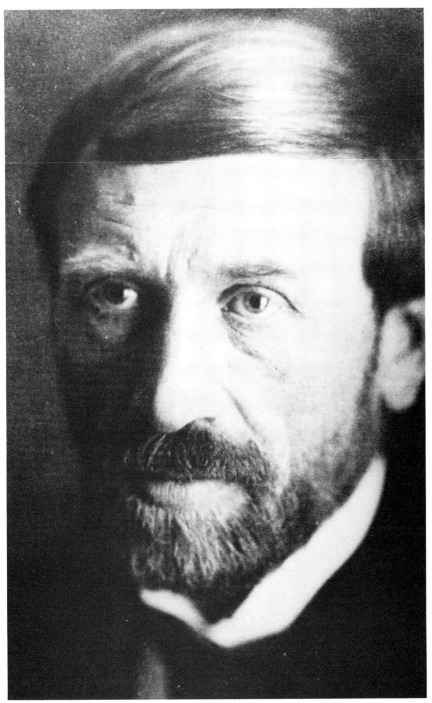

Charles Rennie Mackintosh

and the Swedish Pavilion at New York World Fair 1939). His own house at Kevinge became the prototype for similar houses all over the world. He also designed numerous blocks of flats and offices in and around Stockholm. He was appointed Director of City Planning, Stockholm, 1944–54 and prepared the regional plan for Stockholm. He designed the satellite town of Vallingby in 1955. He taught in Stockholm and was visiting professor at Yale. In 1962 he was awarded RIBA Gold Medal. Good bibliography on Markelius in Stefano Ray's book.

MARKELIUS, S. *Vallingby, Stockholm. The new self-supporting neighbourhood,* Stockholm 1955.
MARKELIUS, S. In C.E.Kidder Smith, *Sweden Builds*, London 1957.
MARKELIUS, S. with SIDENBLADH, G. 'Town Planning in Stockholm – Housing and Traffic' in *Ten Lectures on Swedish Architecture* (ed. Jacobson), Stockholm 1949. English translation.

RAY, S. *Il Contributo svedere all'architettura contemporanea e l'opera di Sven Markelius,* Rome 1969.

HAMLIN, T.F. 'Sven Markelius', *Pencil Points,* June 1939, pp.357–66.

ANON. 'The New Empiricism – Sweden's latest style house at Kevinge', *Architectural Review,* June 1947, pp.199–201.
ROSENTHAL, R. 'Vallingby Town Centre Stockholm', *Architectural Design,* Oct. 1956, p.312ff. See also *Architect and Building News*, 14 July 1955, pp.47–54.
RICHARDS, J.M. 'Stockholm's new commercial centre', *Architectural Review,* Aug. 1961.
ANON. 'Redevelopment in Stockholm', *Architect and Building News*, 24 Jan. 1962.
MARKELIUS, S. 'Architecture in a social context. The work of Sven Markelius', *Architectural Record*, April 1964, pp.153–64.

Ernst MAY (1886–1970)

Born Frankfurt-Main, 1886. Died Hamburg, 1970.
Educated at the Munich Technical High School under Tiersch and Fischer where even as an architectural student he knew he wanted to become a town planner. Completed his studies in England in order to see work of Ebenezer Howard. Worked for a time in Unwin's office in London and also in Theodor Fischer's in Munich. In 1925 became city architect, Frankfurt, where he produced his celebrated schemes for the new Frankfurt. Produced the influential magazine *Das Neue Frankfurt* 1926/27–1931.
In 1930 invited to USSR to act as town-planning adviser. There for three years with twenty architects and planners. Worked on the new towns in the Urals, W. Siberia and Armenia plus satellite towns around Moscow. His most famous project Magnitogorsk. In East Africa from 1934 as planning adviser to Ugandan Government, also worked in Kenya and Tanganyika. After war became consultant to *Neue Heimat* for whom he planned Kranichstein near Darmstadt.

Ernst May

MAY, E. *Die Wohnung für Existenzminimum*, CIAM, Frankfurt 1930.

BUECKSCHMITT, J. *Ernst May: Bauten und Planungen*, Stuttgart 1963.
BORNGRÄBER, C. *et al.*, various articles on May and Das Neue Frankfurt in *AA Quarterly* special issue 'Social Housing in the Weimar Republic', Vol.11, No.1, 1979.

Konstantin MELNIKOV   (1890–1974)

Born Moscow, 1890. Died Moscow, 1974.
Studied painting at Moscow School under Miliutin. In 1914 transferred to Architecture Department, graduating in 1917. Melnikov became teacher in the Vkhutemas. One of the twelve disciples of I.V.Zholtooskii in 1922. In 1924 Melnikof was firmly established as leader of the new *avant garde*; designed sarcophagus for Lenin. In 1925 his Soviet Pavilion was erected by Lubetkin in Paris. His own circular house was designed in 1927. From 1927–29 he designed seven clubs in and around Moscow of which six were built. Heavily criticised in early 1930s, denounced in 1936, after which he returned to painting. Continued to design architectural projects but all were abortive. Full bibliography in S.Frederick Starr's monograph.

STARR, S.F. *Melnikov: Solo Architect in a Mass Society*, Princeton 1978.
Also articles by Starr in *Lotus International*, No.10, 1977, pp.13–18; *Architectural Design*, July 1969, pp.367–73; and (On Stalinist architecture), in *AA Quarterly*, Vol.11, No.2, pp.49–55.

Eric MENDELSOHN (1887–1953)

Born Allenstein, East Prussia, 1887. Died San Francisco, 1953.
Studied at Charlottenburg and Munich under Theodor Fischer, 1907–11.
Practised as designer and architect, Munich, 1911–14.
During the first world war, a productive period in the establishment of his theoretical position and for the early sketches, he served on the German front in Russia with the Engineers. After the war he returned to Berlin to set up practice. In 1919 his sketches were shown at Paul Cassirer's Berlin galleries under the exhibition title, 'Architecture in Concrete and Steel'.
Mendelsohn's building for Professor Albert Einstein, the Observatory, Potsdam was erected in 1920–1. This was followed by a number of important commissions including the Hat Factory, Luckenwalde, 1921 (destroyed by fire, 1925); Textile Factory, Leningrad, 1925; important store buildings in various German towns; and the 'Queen' of cinema buildings, the Universum, Berlin, 1926–29.
Mendelsohn left Germany in 1933. Came to England in the same year and joined Serge Chermayeff in partnership. Became an English subject in 1938 and dropped the 'h' in Erich. In 1941 emigrated to the USA. Started practice in California in 1945. The Berlin period is well recorded in the Mosse publication of complete works that appeared in 1930.
Whittick's biography and Banham's article in the *Architectural Review* are invaluable. An edited version of his letters to his wife were published in German in 1961. A complete record of his sketches are to be found in successive copies of *L'Architettura*, Nos.79ff; now available in book form edited by Zevi.

MENDELSOHN, ERICH. *Erich Mendelsohn: Structures and Sketches*, translated by H.G.Scheffauer, London 1924. (Reprinted from *Wasmuth Monatshefte für Baukunst* article 'Erich Mendelsohn; Bauten und Skizzen', Year 8, 1924, pp.1–66.)
MENDELSOHN, ERICH. *Amerika: Bilderbuch eines Architekten*, Berlin 1926.
MENDELSOHN, ERICH. *Russland, Europa, Amerika – ein Architektonischer Querschnitt*, Berlin 1929.
MENDELSOHN, ERICH. *Erich Mendelsohn. Das Gesamtschaffen des Architekten. Skizzen, Entwürfe, Bauten*, Berlin 1930.
MENDELSOHN, ERICH. *Der Schöpferische Sinn der Krise*, Lecture given in Zürich, May 1932, Berlin 1932.
MENDELSOHN, ERICH. *Neues Haus – Neue Welt*, Berlin 1932.
MENDELSOHN, ERICH. *Three Lectures on Architecture*, Berkeley and Los Angeles (University of California), 1944.
MENDELSOHN, ERICH. *Briefe eines Architekten*, Munich 1961. The collected (edited) letters to his wife. (English trans., New York 1966).

MENDELSOHN, ERICH. 'Architecture of our own Times', *Architectural Association Journal*, June 1930, pp.5–18.
MENDELSOHN, ERIC. 'Background to Design', *Architectural Forum*, April 1953, pp.105–8.
MENDELSOHN, ERIC. 'The 3-Dimensions of Architecture – Their Symbolic Significance', *Symbols and Values*, New York 1954 (Ch.XVII, pp. 235–54).

WHITTICK, A. *Eric Mendelsohn*, London 1940 (3rd edn 1965).
ROGGERO, M.F. *Il contributo di Mendelsohn alla evoluzione dell'architettura moderna*, Milan 1952.
ECKARDT, W.VON. *Eric Mendelsohn*, New York, London, 1960.
ZEVI, B. *Erich Mendelsohn: Opera Completa, Architetture e Immagini Architettoniche*, Milan 1970. A magnificent production including the magazine articles referred to in *L'Architettura* (see entry below).
BEYER, O. 'Architectuur in Ijzer en Beton', special issue, *Wendingen*, No.10, 1920.
SCHEFFAUER, H.G. 'Erich Mendelsohn', *Architectural Review*, May 1923, pp.156–9.

Erich Mendelsohn

DUSSELL, K.K. 'Drei Kaufhäuser Schocken in Nürnberg, Stuttgart, und Chemnitz von Erich Mendelsohn', *Moderne Bauformen*, November 1930, pp.461–84.

HUXLEY, A. 'Puritanism in Art', *The Studio*, March 1930, pp.200–2. An interesting comment by Aldous Huxley on Mendelsohn's work.

MISC. 'Eric Mendelsohn', *Architectural Form*, April 1953, pp.105–21. Including the article 'Background to Design' by Mendelsohn.

ZEVI, B. 'Eric Mendelsohn', *Metron*, Nos.49–50, Rome 1954.

BANHAM, R. 'Mendelsohn', *Architectural Review*, August 1954, pp.84–93.

SCHILLER, H. 'The Last Work of a Great Architect', *Architectural Forum*, February 1955, pp.106–17.

MISC. 'Disegni di Eric Mendelsohn', *L'Architettura*, Nos.79–.
The complete publication of Mendelsohn's sketches began in issue No.79.

ZEVI, B. (ed.). 'Eric Mendelsohn: an -ism for a man', a special issue of *L'Architettura*, No.95, Milan, September 1963, dedicated to the work of Eric Mendelsohn. Includes a review of his work, ten years after his death, with biographical notes by Louise Mendelsohn.

Hannes MEYER (1889–1954)

Born Basel, 1889. Died Lugano, 1954.
The son of an architect, he studied at the Technical School, Basel, and followed this as an apprentice to a firm of architects and builders, 1905–9. Went to Berlin in 1909 where he worked as an architect and continued his studies. From 1912 to 1913 he studied in England. In 1919 he began in private practice in Basel and in 1926 joined Hans Wittwer in partnership. His move to the Dessau Bauhaus came in 1927 when he became Master of Architecture. This was followed in 1928 by his appointment as successor to Walter Gropius as Director. He organized the Bauhaus architectural course on scientific principles. He left Dessau in 1930. From 1930 to 1936 Meyer was in Russia. In 1936 he returned to Switzerland. After 1939 he spent most of his time working in Mexico. Meyer contributed to a number of periodicals throughout his career and towards the end of his life he was made an honorary technical director of a Mexican publishing house. From 1928 to 1929 he published the periodical *Bauhaus* (eight issues in all). A full bibliography is available (selected by Hannes and Lena Meyer) in Claude Schnaidt's monograph which is the best publication available on Meyer.

MEYER, HANNES. 'Die neue Welt', *Das Werk*, Special No.7, 1926, reproduced in Schnaidt, see below.

MEYER, HANNES. 'Bauhaus und Gesellschaft', *Bauhaus*, No.1, 1929.

MEYER, HANNES. 'Mein Hinauswurf aus dem Bauhaus', *Das Tagebuch*, Berlin, August 1930.

SCHNAIDT, C. *Hannes Meyer: Buildings, Projects and Writings*, London 1965. Two-language edition (German and English) with introduction by Maldonaldo. Important. Biographical and bibliographical information, and the writings on Meyer's Bauhaus experience are included.

ANON. 'Hannes Meyer Arquitecto, Urbanista', *Arquitectura y Decoracion*, Special No., 12 October 1938. An early monograph.

MÜNZ, W. 'Werk und Wirken des Architekten und Städtebauers Hannes Meyer 1889–1954', *Deutsche Bauzeitung*, No.3, 1961.

Ludwig MIES VAN DER ROHE (1886–1969)

Born Aachen, 1886. Died Chicago, 1969.
After attending the Cathedral School at Aachen he moved to Berlin in 1905. In Berlin he became apprenticed to Bruno Paul, 1905–7. Began practice on his own account in 1907 but joined the office of Peter Behrens where he stayed from 1908–11. From 1912 to the outbreak of war he worked on a number of house commissions as an independent architect. Returning from the war he again set up practice in Berlin. In these years he was caught up with the revolutionary groups and directed the architectural sections of the 'Novembergruppe'. In 1925 he founded the famous Berlin 'Ring of Ten'. He became increasingly associated with the new spirit in the Werkbund, firstly as Vice-president in 1926 and then as Director of the 1927 Stuttgart exhibition at the Weissenhof. He designed the German Pavilion for the International Exhibition at Barcelona, 1929. From 1930 to 1933 he was Director of the Bauhaus at Dessau and later at Berlin.
He emigrated finally to the USA in 1938 and became an American citizen in 1944. In the USA he found great success. Philip Johnson published the first collection of his works in 1947 on the occasion of the exhibition of Mies van der Rohe's work at the Museum of Modern Art. Mies himself was commissioned to carry out major schemes in Chicago and later in New York. All the time Mies continued to teach and it is impossible to assess the influence this has had, through example and pupils, on modern architecture.

MIES VAN DER ROHE, LUDWIG. 'Arbeitsthesen', *Programme und Manifeste zur Architektur des 20. Jahrhunderts*, Berlin 1964, p.70. *Programmes and Manifestoes on 20th Century Architecture*, London, Cambridge (Mass.), 1970, p.74.

MIES VAN DER ROHE, LUDWIG. 'Über die Form in der Architektur', *op. cit.*, p.96. English edition, p.102.

MIES VAN DER ROHE, LUDWIG. 'Die neue Zeit', *op. cit.*, p.114. English edition, p.123.

MIES VAN DER ROHE, LUDWIG. 'Technik und Architektur', *op. cit.*, p.146. English edition, p.154.

JOHNSON, P. *Mies van der Rohe*, New York 1947 (2nd edn, revised, 1953). Contains translations of the writings of Mies. Bibliography and biography (updated re-issue, London and New York, 1978).

BILL, M. *Mies van der Rohe*, Milan 1955.

HILBERSEIMER, L. *Mies van der Rohe*, Chicago 1956.

DREXLER, A. *Ludwig Mies van der Rohe*, New York 1960; London 1961.

BLAKE, P. *The Master Builders*, New York, London, 1960. See chapter: 'Mies van der Rohe and the Mastery of Structure', pp.129–204. Also reprinted as p.b.

Ludwig Mies van der Rohe

Mies van der Rohe – Architecture and Structure, Harmondsworth 1963.
BLACKWELL, J.F.F. *Mies van der Rohe*. A prize-winning bibliography submitted in part requirement for University of London Diploma in Librarianship, August 1964. Typescript in RIBA Library.
BLASER, W. *Mies van der Rohe, the Art of Structure*, London 1965.
GLAESER, L. *Ludwig Mies van der Rohe: Drawings in the Collection of the Museum of Modern Art*, New York 1969.
CARTER, P. *Mies van der Rohe and his work*, London 1974.
BONTA, J.P. *Mies van der Rohe, Barcelona 1929*, Barcelona 1975. Text in Spanish, French, English and Russian.

CADBURY-BROWN, H.T. 'Ludwig Mies van der Rohe', *Architectural Association Journal*, Special No., July–August 1959.
CARTER, P. 'Mies van der Rohe', An appreciation on the occasion of his 75th birthday. *Architectural Design*, Special No., March 1961.
BONTA, J.P. *Mies van der Rohe, Barcelona 1929: An anatomy of architectural interpretation*, Barcelona 1975. Quadrilingual. An excellent semiotic review of the criticisms of the pavilion.
CARTER, P. 'Mies van der Rohe', in SHARP, D.(ed.). *The Rationalists*, London 1978, pp.58–71.

Ladislas (Laszlo) MOHOLY-NAGY (1895–1946)

Born Bácseborsod, South Hungary, 1895. Died Chicago, 1946.
Studied law at Budapest University. Served at the Russian front in the Austrian–Hungarian army, 1914–18, and was severely wounded. Before going to Berlin in 1920 he had become interested in the Constructivists, Malevich and El Lissitzky in Russia. In 1922 he joined the staff of the Bauhaus. He was also responsible for the production of the Bauhaus Books. Left the Bauhaus with Gropius in 1928. Became an active painter and developed his interests in documentary film techniques, photography and the theatre. Met Kassak in Vienna in 1920 and became German correspondent to his magazine *MA* in 1921.
Worked in Amsterdam in 1934 and in London from 1935 before moving to the USA to take up an appointment as Director of the New Bauhaus in Chicago in 1937. This venture was not a success and was replaced later by an Institute of Design.
His writing covers all aspects of visual design: film, stage, painting and architecture. His book *The New Vision* has become a classic and this was followed by the posthumous publication of *Vision in Motion* in 1947. The Moholy-Nagy Archives are in The Smithsonian Institution, Washington.

MOHOLY-NAGY, LASZLO. *Horizont*, Vienna 1921.
MOHOLY-NAGY, LASZLO. *Buch neuer Künstler*, Vienna 1922. With L.Kassák. (Facsimile edn, Budapest 1977).
MOHOLY-NAGY, LASZLO. *Malerei, Photographie, Film*, Munich 1925. 2nd edn, Munich 1927. *Painting, Photography, Film*, London, Cambridge (Mass.), 1969.
MOHOLY-NAGY, LASZLO. *Von Material zu Architektur*, Munich 1929. English

translation: *The New Vision: from Material to Architecture*, London, New York, 1939. Enlarged and revised version, *The New Vision, and Abstract of an Artist*, New York 1944 (3rd edn). (Reprinted 1961).
MOHOLY-NAGY, LASZLO. *Telehor*, Brno 1936.
MOHOLY-NAGY, LASZLO. *Vision in Motion*, Chicago 1947. (Reprinted 1965).

MOHOLY-NAGY, S. *Moholy-Nagy, Experiment in Totality*, New York 1950. (1969).
KOSTELANETZ, R. (ed.). *Moholy-Nagy*, London 1971.

Hermann MUTHESIUS   (1861–1927)

Born Thüringen, 1861. Died in a tram accident, 1927.
Studied architecture at the Technical High School, Berlin. After a period of private practice, service in government departments and extensive travel abroad, Muthesius was sent to London by the Prussian Ministry of Finance in 1896.
In London he assumed the position of 'attaché for architecture' and studied in perceptive detail the English domestic architectural situation. His comprehensive account of English domestic design is contained in the influential three-volume work, *Das englische Haus*, 1904–5. Prolific writer and editor.
Before returning to Germany in 1904 he visited the St Louis World Fair. In October 1907 Muthesius helped found the Deutscher Werkbund against a lot of bitter opposition. Inside the Werkbund Muthesius also met conflict – this came to a head at the 1914 Congress at Cologne when Van de Velde's views clashed with his own. His Werkbund speech *Wo stehen wir?* – given at the 1911 Dresden Congress – has now been reprinted in the book edited by Julius Posener and noted below. Muthesius wrote numerous books – large and small – on individual and estate housing. He also wrote introductions to the *Meister der Innen-Kunst*, Vols.1 and 2, on M.H.Baillie Scott and Charles Rennie Mackintosh.

MUTHESIUS, HERMANN. *Die englische Baukunst der Gegenwart*, Leipzig 1900.
MUTHESIUS, HERMANN. *Stilarchitektur und Baukunst*, Mülheim-Ruhr 1902.
MUTHESIUS, HERMANN. *M.H.Baillie Scott, Haus eines Kunstfreundes*, Vol.1 in the series *Meister der Innen-Kunst* Darmstadt, London, 1902. Introduction by Muthesius.
MUTHESIUS, HERMANN. *Charles Rennie Mackintosh, Glasgow Haus eines Kunstfreundes*, Darmstadt, London, 1902. Introduction by Muthesius.
MUTHESIUS, HERMANN. *Das englische Haus*, 3 vols. Berlin 1904–5 (2nd edn 1908–12). 1: Entwicklung; 2: Anlage und Aufbau; 3: Der Innenraum.
Re-issued in English language: Sharp, D. (ed.). *The English House*, London, New York, 1979. (Translated by Janet Seligman).
MUTHESIUS, HERMANN. *Landhaus und Garten*, Munich 1967.
MUTHESIUS, HERMANN. *Landhäuser*, Munich 1912.

POSENER, J. (ed.). *Anfänge des Funktionalismus. Von Arts and Crafts zum Deutschen Werkbund*, Berlin, etc. 1964 (p.b.). In the series, *Ullstein Bauwelt Fundamente*. A

90

major part of this book is devoted to the writings of Hermann Muthesius. It includes *Stilarchitektur und Baukunst, Wo stehen wir?* and the record of the Werkbund speeches at Cologne 1914. Muthesius's writings are side by side with those of Lethaby, Ashbee and Voysey.

POSENER, J. 'Hermann Muthesius', *Architects' Year Book, No.10*, 1962, pp.45–61.
POSENER, J. and GÜNTHER, S. (eds). *Hermann Muthesius 1861–1927*, Berlin 1977. Catalogue of the Akademie der Künste Exhibition.
SHARP, D. (ed.). *Hermann Muthesius 1861–1927*, London 1979. Catalogue of AA Exhibition with contributions from Eckart Muthesius and Julius Posener.

Pier Luigi NERVI   (1891–1979)

Born Sondrio, Lombardy, 1891. Died Rome, 1979.
Studied engineering at Bologna University. After gaining experience with a concrete contractor in Bologna he set up his own firm in 1923. Nervi epitomized the architect/engineer. His skill as a constructor was matched by his sensitivity as the artist of *ferro-cemento*.
He was Professor of Technology and Technique of Construction in the Architecture Department of Rome University.
Honoured by architectural societies and academies throughout the world he was elected RIBA Royal Gold Medallist in 1960. One of his earliest works was the Municipal Stadium at Florence, won in competition in 1927, and erected

Pier Luigi Nervi

in 1930–2. Later he designed and built the Exhibition Hall, Turin, 1948–9; Palazzetto dello Sport, Rome, 1956–7. He collaborated with Breuer and Zehrfuss on the UNESCO buildings, Paris, 1953–7; he also collaborated with Gio Ponti on the Pirelli Tower, Milan, 1955–8.

Nervi has contributed to many technical journals and to the architectural press. *The Works of Pier Luigi Nervi*, published by the Architectural Press and Gerd Hatje in 1957, is still the best general introduction to his work.

NERVI, PIER LUIGI. *Arte o scienza del costruire?*, Rome 1954.
NERVI, PIER LUIGI. *Costruire correttamente*, Milan 1955. English translation. *Structures*, New York 1956.
NERVI, PIER LUIGI. *The Works of Pier Luigi Nervi*, Stuttgart, London, 1957. Introduction by Ernesto Rogers. Translated by Ernst Priefert.
NERVI, PIER LUIGI. *New Structures*, London, Stuttgart, 1963.
NERVI, PIER LUIGI. *Aesthetics and Technology in Building*, Cambridge (Mass.), London, 1965.

ARGAN, G.C. *Pier Luigi Nervi*, Milan 1955.
HUXTABLE, A.L. *Pier Luigi Nervi*, London, New York, 1960; Ravensburg 1961.

Richard NEUTRA (1892–1970)

Born Vienna, 1892. Died in USA, 1970.

Trained at the Technical High School, Vienna; graduated with honours in 1917. Developed an early interest in the United States and in the buildings of Frank Lloyd Wright and the Chicago school. Met Sullivan in 1923 and Frank Lloyd Wright a year later at Sullivan's funeral. Set up practice in California in 1925–6 with Schindler. Earlier, he became acquainted with the work of Erich Mendelsohn while working in Luckenwalde. Won first prize with Mendelsohn for a Business Centre in Haifa (Arthur Korn came second). His Lovell House, Los Angeles, 1927–9, was one of the finest houses to emerge from the early Modern Movement. His reputation grew as an architect for whom the site had as much meaning as the structure.

In 1949 Neutra went into partnership with Robert Alexander. His books fully represent his philosophy of a truly modern architecture, unornamented – according to the laws of Loos – and sympathetic to social and environmental needs.

NEUTRA, RICHARD. *Wie Baut Amerika?*, Stuttgart 1927.
NEUTRA, RICHARD. *Amerika*, Vienna 1930. In the *Neues Bauen in der Welt* (No.2) series.
NEUTRA, RICHARD. *Architecture of Social Concern in Regions of Mild Climate*, São Paulo 1948.
NEUTRA, RICHARD. *Mystery and Realities of the Site*, New York 1951.
NEUTRA, RICHARD. *Survival through Design*, New York, London, 1954 (also p.b.).
NEUTRA, RICHARD. *Life and Human Habitat. Mensch und Wohnen*, Stuttgart 1956.
NEUTRA, RICHARD. *Auftrag für Morgen*, Hamburg 1962.

Richard Neutra

NEUTRA, RICHARD. 'Human Setting in an Industrial Civilisation', *Zodiac 2*, Milan 1957, pp.68–75.

NEUTRA, R. *Building with Nature*, Stuttgart 1970.

NEUTRA, R. *Kaufmann Desert House, etc.*, Tokyo 1971. Japanese and English text.

NEUTRA, R. and NEUTRA, D. *Pflanzen, Wasser, Steine, Licht*, Berlin 1974.

NEUTRA, R. 'Epoch – Richard Neutra describes his early years and contacts with members of the Bauhaus', *Canadian Architect*, May 1970, pp.57–66.

NEUTRA, R. 'Task for tomorrow: vitality and future', *Sport & Badebauten*, Düsseldorf, Oct. 1970, pp.465–80. Abstract in English of talk given by RN to 1970 Aquatic World Congress.

BOESIGER, W. (ed.). *Richard J.Neutra: Bauten und Projekte*, 3 vols. (Vol.1, 1927–50, Zürich, 1951; London, 1965; Vol.2, 1950–60, Zürich, 1959; London, 1965; Vol.3, 1961–66, London, New York, 1966).

ZEVI, B. *Richard Neutra*, Milan 1954.

MCCOY, E. *Richard Neutra*, London 1960.

PAWLEY, M. *Richard Neutra*, London 1971. Photos by Yukio Futagawa.

SPADE, R. *Richard Neutra*, London 1971. Photos by Yukio Futagawa.

HARRISON, H.R. 'Richard J. Neutra, A Center of Architectural Stimulation', *Pencil Points*, July 1937, pp.410–38.

MISC. 'Deux œuvres nouvelles de Richard J.Neutra', *L'Architecture d'Aujourd'hui*, June 1948, pp.38–47.

MISC. 'Richard Neutra and his work', *Arquitectura* (Madrid), Special No. Sept. 1965, pp.3–60.

MISC. 'Richard Neutra'. *L'Architettura*, Special No., 181, Nov. 1970.

Oscar NIEMEYER (1901–   )

Born Rio de Janeiro, 1901.
Studied at the National School of Fine Arts, Rio de Janeiro, graduating in 1934. Influenced early in his career by Le Corbusier, with whom he worked on the Ministry of Education and Health Building for a short time in the mid-thirties, Niemeyer has become Brazil's best known architect. His buildings have about them an authority and dignity quite different from European 'functionalist' buildings. Niemeyer has added to the functionalist tenets a new one, that of visual excitement in form and structure. In 1950 he began his designs for the great public buildings for the new capital of Brasilia. A number of these were completed within the decade. During this period his own practice flourished and he produced buildings for São Paulo, Berlin and Rio. His work is well represented in the books by Papadaki and in South and North American and European magazines; see in particular *Modulo*.

NIEMEYER, OSCAR. *Minha Experiencia em Brasilia*, Rio de Janeiro 1961.

PAPADAKI, S. *The work of Oscar Niemeyer*, New York 1950.

PAPADAKI, S. *Oscar Niemeyer: Works in Progress*, New York 1956.

PAPADAKI, S. *Oscar Niemeyer*, Ravensburg 1962.

Juan O'GORMAN   (1905–   )

Born Mexico City, 1905.
Educated in Jesuit schools, graduating in architecture from the National
University of Mexico 1927 where he was taught by Jose Villagran Garcia who
introduced modern architecture into Mexico. O'Gorman's work was very
much influenced by Le Corbusier. Between 1928–37 he built twelve
'functional' private houses including house and studio for the painter Diego
Rivera. Became chief architect of Government's Department of School
Construction erecting many Corbusier-influenced buildings. Became
attracted to the Frank Lloyd Wright ideas from America and rejected
International Style and sought to design a style-less architecture to meet needs
of exploding population demands for mass housing. Associated strongly with
the decoration movement in Mexico in the 1950s and responsible for the mural
mosaic screen for the Museum of Ancient Mexican Sculpture, the Library of
the National Autonomous University, Mexico, 1950–52. Attempted to mix
what he called a truly organic with a truly Mexican architecture. Some of his
later work could be called trendy Baroque Goff, although no direct reference is
intended.

MYERS, I.E. *Mexico's Modern Architecture*, New York 1952. For context of
O'Gorman's work.

SMITH, C.B. *Buildings in the Sun: Five Mexican Architects*, New York 1957,
pp.15–50.

Josef Maria OLBRICH   (1867–1908)

Born Troppau, 1867. Died Düsseldorf, 1908.
Studied architecture as a pupil of Otto Wagner after starting his career as a
book illustrator. One of the founders of the Austrian Sezession, he designed,
with Klimt, Sezession House that opened in 1898. In 1900 he moved to
Darmstadt at the invitation of the Grand Duke Ernst Ludwig of Hessen. There
he designed Ernst Ludwig House (1901) and a number of houses for his
colleagues. Olbrich continued to work in Darmstadt – the Jugendstil annexe –
and designed the impressive Hochzeitsturm for the 1908 exhibition. That year
Olbrich died.
Useful accounts of the work of Olbrich are given in Madsen, S.T., *Sources of Art
Nouveau* (New York 1957) and Howarth, T., *Charles Rennie Mackintosh and the
Modern Movement* (London, New York, 1952).
For an account of the Olbrich work at Darmstadt the five catalogues *Ein
Dokument Deutscher Kunst 1901–1976*, Darmstadt 1976, are indispensable. See
also *Künstlerkolonie Mathildenhöhe Darmstadt 1899–1914* (formerly Catalogue
No.5) now issued as separate publication.

OLBRICH, JOSEF MARIA. *Ideen*, Vienna 1900.
OLBRICH, JOSEF MARIA. *Architekten von Prof. J.M. Olbrich*, 3 vols., Berlin 1903–7.
LUX, J.A. *Josef Maria Olbrich*, Vienna 1919.

VERONESI, G. *Josef M. Olbrich*, Milan 1948.

ROETHEL, J. 'Josef Maria Olbrich', *Der Architekt*, No.7, 1958, pp.291–318.

Ragnar ÖSTBERG   (1866–1945)

Born Vaxholm, Sweden, 1866. Died 1945.
Östberg's parents were both on the stage and later he became a noted stage designer, as well as draughtsman, painter and etcher. He travelled in England as student, sketching cathedrals, churches, villages, etc. and worked in office of J.G.Clason. He visited America in 1893 and Europe in 1896–9. He became the main leader of Swedish 'National' architecture – 'eclectic but homegrown'. His best known work is the romantic Stockholm Town Hall designed 1909 but built between 1911–23. He also designed the Ostermalm School 1910, Royal Patent Office 1921, Marine Historical Museum 1934, all in Stockholm, and the Varmland National House, Uppsala 1930, Kalmar Secondary School, Halsingborg 1933, Crematorium (1935) and Zoorn Museum, Mora (1939) as well as several private houses. He received the RIBA Gold Medal in 1926.
His work, together with that of Asplund, is undergoing a revival of interest particularly insofar as it relates to the decorative elements of his designs.

ÖSTBERG, R. *Stockholm Town Hall*, Stockholm 1929. The book of the Town Hall in English; to my knowledge Östberg's only publication.

AHLBERG, H. *Swedish Architecture of the Twentieth Century*, London 1925. This excellent survey places Östberg's work in context.

ANON. 'The Stadshus at Stockholm', *Architectural Review*, Jan. 1924, pp.1–6, good photos by F.R.Yerbury with plans.
ROBERTSON, HOWARD. 'Ragnar Östberg', *RIBA Journal*, 6 Nov. 1926, pp.15–23.
ANON. 'Crematorium Halsingborg', *Architect and Building News*, 8 Jan. 1932, pp.44–46.
ANON. 'Naval Museum, Stockholm', *Architect and Building News*, 17 Jan. 1936.

Frei OTTO   (1925–   )

Born Siegmar, Saxony, 1925. Lives in Stuttgart where he heads Institute of Lightweight Structures. Began career designing aircraft.
Studied architecture in Berlin Technological University 1948–52.
He is well known for his work on suspended structures, inflatable and temporary buildings. Study tour in USA, 1950. Numerous executed works in Germany 1955 to date. Founded Institute of Lightweight Structures, TU, Stuttgart 1964.
His work on pneumatic structures from 1953–67 has been systematically analyzed in Conrad Roland's book and in the *Architectural Design* article by the same writer. See the IL publications for latest developments and Philip Drew's book.

OTTO, FREI. *Das hängende Dach: Gestalt und Struktur*, Berlin 1954. Published doctoral thesis: 'The Suspended Roof'.

OTTO, FREI. *Über zugbeanspruchte Konstruktion*, 2 vols, 1962.

OTTO, FREI. 'Les toitures suspendues et les voilures', *L'Architecture d'Aujourd'hui*, March 1956, pp.56–63.

OTTO, FREI. 'Contribution à l'architecture pneumatique', *L'Architecture d'Aujourd'hui*, June 1962, pp.89–93.

OTTO, FREI. Information of the Institute of Lightweight Structures, 21 volumes (to date), 1971–9, Stuttgart.

OTTO, FREI. *Tensile Structures*, 2 vols., Cambridge (Mass.), London, 1969.

ROLAND, C. *Frei Otto – Spannweiten, Ideen und Versuche zum Leichtbau*, Berlin, etc. 1965.

ROLAND, C. *Frei Otto: Structures*, London 1970. Translated by C.V.Amerongen.

GLAESER, L. *The Work of Frei Otto*, New York 1972. MOMA Exhibition catalogue, p.b.

DREW, P. *Frei Otto: Form and Structure*, London 1976.

ROLAND, C. 'Frei Otto's Pneumatic Structures', *Architectural Design*, July 1966, pp.341–60.

J.J.P. OUD   (1890–1963)

Jacobus Johannes Pieter Oud was born at Purmerend, North Holland, 1890. Died Wassenaar, 1963.

Educated at the Quellinus Arts and Crafts School, Amsterdam. Studied architecture at the Rijksnormaal school, Amsterdam and at the Technical University, Delft. Worked for a short time with Theodor Fischer in Munich. Moved to Leiden in 1913 and met Theo Van Doesburg in 1915–16. Through this meeting he was brought into contact with the Elementarists and with the formation of the Stijl group in 1917. He relates his position in the group in his last book, *Mein Weg in 'de Stijl'* written in 1957–8.

Oud was made Municipal Architect – in charge of housing – of Rotterdam in 1918, but early in the thirties he had to retire due to poor health. Independent architect from 1933.

His best known works are the housing schemes at Spangen (1918–19), Oud-Mathenese (1922), Hook of Holland (1926–7), the row-houses at the Weissenhof, Stuttgart (1927) and the Kiefhoek development, Rotterdam (1928–9).

Oud wrote one of the Bauhaus books in 1926 on Dutch architecture and was also responsible for articles on contemporary architecture in *The Studio*.

OUD, J.J.P. *Holländische Architektur*, Munich 1926, Bauhaus Book No.10 (2nd edn 1929).

OUD, J.J.P. *Mein Weg in 'de Stijl'*, The Hague and Rotterdam, n.d. (1960).

OUD J.J.P. 'Architecture and the Future', *The Studio*, December 1928, pp.401–6.

OUD, J.J.P. 'European Movement Towards a New Architecture', *The Studio*, April 1933, pp.249–56.

J.J.P.Oud

OUD, J.J.P. 'J.J.P. Oud', *Forum*, 5–6, Special No., Amsterdam 1951, pp.114–48.

HITCHCOCK, H-R. *J.J.P. Oud*, Paris 1931 (p.b.).

BARR, A., HITCHCOCK, H-R., JOHNSON, P., & MUMFORD, L. *Modern Architects*, New York 1932. The catalogue of the exhibition at the Museum of Modern Art, New York. Article on Oud, pp.91–109.

VERONESI, G. *J.J.P. Oud*, Milan 1953.

MISC. *J.J.P. Oud. Bauten 1906–1963*, Munich 1965. Exhibition catalogue.

WIEKART, R. *J.J.P. Oud*, Amsterdam, 1965, (p.b.).

WIESSING, H.P.L. 'J.J.P. Oud', *Building*, July 1938, pp.274–8.

Amedée OZENFANT   (1886–1966)

Born Saint-Quentin, 1886. Died 1966.
Studied in Spain and at Saint-Quentin. In 1915 he began publishing his magazine *L'Élan* and through this laid down the principles of Purism. After meeting Charles-Édouard Jeanneret (Le Corbusier) in 1917 in Paris a marriage of ideas on painting took place and they jointly published the manifesto of Purism, *Après le cubisme*, in 1918. From 1920 to 1925 they edited the review *L'Esprit nouveau*, with Paul Dermée the poet. In 1928 Ozenfant published his book *Art*, which has become a classic. It is divided into two

Giuseppe Pagano

sections – 1: The Balance Sheet of Modern Arts; 2: The Structure of the New Spirit. He moved to New York in 1938 where he founded the Ozenfant School of Fine Arts.

OZENFANT, AMEDÉE, & JEANNERET, C-E. *Après le cubisme*, Paris 1918. The Purist manifesto.
OZENFANT, AMEDÉE, & JEANNERET, C-E. *La peinture moderne*, Paris 1925. Another work of collaboration between Ozenfant and Le Corbusier.
OZENFANT, AMEDÉE. *Art*, Paris 1928. English translation *Foundations of Modern Art*, London 1931 (New York 1952, p.b.)
OZENFANT, AMEDÉE. 'Colour and Method', *Architectural Review*, February 1937, pp.89–92.
Other articles by Ozenfant on colour appeared in the *Architectural Review*, January, April, May, July, 1937.

NIERENDORF, K. *Amedée Ozenfant*, Berlin 1931.

Giuseppe PAGANO   (1896–1945)

Born Parenzo, 1896. Died Mauthausen, 1945.
Studied architecture at the Polytechnic, Turin, graduating in 1924. He became closely associated with the Rational Movement in Italian architecture

through his friendship with the critic Persico in Turin in the late twenties. Originally staunch fascist he joined the resistance in the second world war. During the 1930s he edited *Casabella*, which, with the Milan Triennale, became centre of the Italian Modern Movement. His writings brought to a head the then current argument about architecture and politics. Pagano's beliefs eventually led to his arrest for anti-fascist views and subsequently to his death in the concentration camp at Mauthausen.

PAGANO, G. 'Tre anni di architettura in Italia', *Casabella*, Feb. 1937.
POGATSCHNIG, G.P. *Giuseppe Pagano Pogatschnig: Architetturi e scritti*, Milan 1947.

VERONESI, G. *Difficoltà politiche dell'architettura in Italia, 1920–1940*, Milan 1953. See chapter on Pagano, pp.44–79.
MELOGRANI, C. *Giuseppe Pagano*, Milan 1955. In *Il Balcone* series (p.b.)

Auguste PERRET (1874–1964)

Born in Brussels of French parents, 1874. Died Paris, 1954.
Studied at the École des Beaux-Arts, Paris, 1891–5. He left the École and entered his father's building firm as a designer, without completing his architectural studies. He was responsible for the erection of a number of buildings for this firm on a speculative basis. The now famous apartment block in the rue Franklin, Passy, was also a speculation by the family firm, and here reinforced concrete was used for the first time by Perret. It proved to be the opening of the reinforced concrete era. Perret was to refine its use, develop its possibilities and pass on the knowledge of its use to pupils such as Le Corbusier. Rooted in the works on Viollet-le-Duc, via Gaudet, Perret continued the line of French rationalism into the twentieth century. Had his own atelier, Le Palais de Bois, Paris 1926. In 1932 he joined his friend H. Proust on the staff of the École speciale d'architecture in Paris. Taught at the École des Beaux-Arts from 1940. The story of his devotion to an 'honest' architecture and his skill in construction is told in Peter Collins's book *Concrete: The Vision of a New Architecture*. Perret's own philosophy is outlined in the little book, *Contribution to a Theory of Architecture*; it consists largely of maxims.

PERRET, AUGUSTE. *Contribution à une théorie de l'architecture*, Paris 1952.
PERRET, AUGUSTE. 'Architecture: science et poésie', *La Construction Moderne*, 48, October 1932.

JAMOT, P. *A. et G. Perret et l'architecture du béton armé*, Paris, Brussels, 1927.
DONNÉ, A. LE. *L'Architecte dans la cité*, Paris 1945.
PETTENGILL, G.E. (compiler). *Auguste Perret: A Partial Bibliography*, AIA Library (USA), 1952. Typewritten.
ROGERS, E. *Auguste Perret*, Milan 1955.
CHAMPIGNEULLE, B. *Auguste Perret*, Paris 1959.
COLLINS, P. *Concrete: The Vision of a New Architecture*, London 1959. An excellent, scholarly study of the work of Perret and the Parisian constructors.

Hans Poelzig

DORMOY, M. 'Auguste und Gustav Perret', *Das Kunstblatt*, No.7, October 1923, pp.302–4.
BADOVICI, J. 'A. et G. Perret', *L'Architecture Vivante*, Summer 1925, pp.17–23; 25–8.
COLLINS, P. 'The Doctrine of Auguste Perret', *Architectural Review*, August 1953, pp.90–8. Republished in D.Sharp (ed.) *The Rationalists*, London 1978, pp.16–25.

Hans POELZIG (1869–1936)

Born Berlin 1869, Died Berlin, 1936.
The son of an Englishman, G.A.Ames, and the Countess Clara Henrietta Poelzig. They were divorced in 1870.
Studied at the Technical High School, Charlottenburg, 1888–95. Also Berlin Technische Hoschschule under Karl Schäfer. Later he became a professor at the School.
In 1899 moved to Breslau to take up a teaching position at Breslau School of Arts and Crafts (later called 'Breslau Academy'), and became Head of the Academy 1911–16. He lived in Dresden 1916–19 returning to Berlin in that year. From 1920 in Berlin as teacher and practitioner.
His position as the Master of many of the younger Berlin 'visionary' architects is well known.

His influential buildings include an office block in Breslau, 1911; Chemical Factory, Luban, 1911–12; work with Max Berg on the Centenary Exhibition, Breslau, 1913; the reconstruction of Reinhardt's Schumann Circus, Berlin, as the Grosses Schauspielhaus, 1919, and the imaginative schemes for the proposed Festival Hall, Salzburg.

His work is well represented in the books by his biographer, the late President of the Federal Republic, Theodor Heuss. H.G.Scheffauer wrote an excellent article on Poelzig for the *Architectural Review* in 1923.

POELZIG, HANS. *Der Architekt*, Stuttgart 1931 (1955) (36 pp.)

POELZIG, HANS. 'Rede Gehouden ter Gelegenheid van de Herleving van de "Werkbund"', *Wendingen*, No.11, 1919, pp.4–14.

HEUSS, T.H. *Hans Poelzig: Bauten und Entwürfe*, Berlin 1939.

HEUSS, T.H. *Hans Poelzig: Lebensbild eines Baumeisters*, Tübingen 1948 (1955). Revised edition of 1939 book.

POSENER, J. *Hans Poelzig: Gesammelte Schriften und Werke*, Berlin 1970. The definitive work with good bibliography.

SCHEFFAUER, H.G. 'Hans Poelzig', *Architectural Review*, October 1923, pp.122–7.

DRESDNER, A. 'Modern Tendencies in Architecture – the Work of Hans Poelzig', *The Studio*, May 1931, pp.367–71.

POSENER, J. 'Poelzig', *Architectural Review*, June 1963, pp.401–5. Republished in J.M.Richards and N.Pevsner (eds) *The Anti-Rationalists*, London 1973, pp.193–202.

Antoine POMPE   (1873–1980)

Born Brussels, 1873. Until his death in 1980 the oldest living architect.

Entered the Académie Royale des Beaux-Arts (Brussels) in 1886, at the age of 13, and in 1893 the Kunstgewerbeschule in Munich. In 1910 he designed an orthopaedic clinic for his friend Dr Maurice Van Neck, which was both his first major work and one of his most successful designs. From 1912 to 1921 he was in partnership with Fernand Bodson, during which time they were both very concerned with prefabrication, especially in relation to housing. Both men were very influenced by Baillie Scott, Frank Lloyd Wright and Berlage. Throughout his long career, he concentrated on housing, both in the form of individual houses and apartment buildings, but he also designed some shops, offices and industrial buildings. Between 1922–26 he was working on the design and building of 124 houses as an area of the garden city of Kapelleveld.

POMPE, A. 'Un architecte en Allemagne', *Tekhné*, 31/8 and 7/9, 1912.

POMPE, A. 'L'art moderne et la tradition', *Tekhné*, Nos. 101, 102, 103, 1913.

POMPE, A. 'L'architecture moderne en Belgique', *Le Document*, 1924, pp.90–92.

POMPE, A. 'L'architecture moderne: Petite histoire retrospective', *L'Emulation*, 1924, pp.90–92.

POMPE, A. 'Propos d'un nebuleux', *L'Emulation*, 1925, pp.39–43.

Antoine Pompe

POMPE, A. 'Les propos d'un pseudo-moderniste', *L'Emulation*, No.3, 1929.

POMPE, A. 'La terrasse et l'ornement dans l'architecture moderne', *Clarté*, Nos. 1 and 2, 1931.

POMPE, A. 'L'architecture du beton et du beton armé', *L'Emulation*, 1931, pp.103–111.

POMPE, A. 'Ou va l'architecture en Belgique', *Structure*, No.8, 1938.

POMPE, A. 'Pour comprendre l'architecture', essay of about 50pp, 1940–45 (not published).

POMPE, A. 'Le super homme ou l'homme de demain', 154p., 1941 (not published). A pamphlet attacking modern functionalist architecture.

POMPE, A. 'L'architecture est un art: La construction est une science', *Rythme*, No.41, 1965.

CULOT, M. & TERLINDEN, F. *Antoine Pompe et l'effort moderne en Belgique*, 1890–1940, Brussels 1969. Catalogue of exhibition at Ixelles Museum.

CULOT, M. & DELEVOY, R-L. *Antoine Pompe: Or the architecture of the sentiment*, Brussels 1973. Catalogue of exhibition at Ixelles Museum.

BLEYENBERG, C. van. 'Antoine Pompe', *Bâtir*, 1933, pp.176–7.

BLEYENBERG, C. van. 'L'architecte Antoine Pompe', *Savoir et Beauté*, No.7/8, 1936.

MISC. 'Antoine Pompe', *FAB*, No.6, 1963–64.

MISC. 'Antoine Pompe', *Rythme*, No.41, 1965. Special issue on the architect.

Gio Ponti

MISC. 'Antoine Pompe', *Architecture, Mouvement, Continuité*, No.173, 1969.
BARDESCHI, M.D. 'Antoine Pompe e il movimento moderno in Belgio', *Necropoli*, Vol.II, 1970.
SHARP, D. 'Pompe and circumstance', *Building Design*, No.51, 18 May 1973, pp.24–25.

Gio PONTI (1891–1979)

Born Milan, 1891. Died 1979.
Graduated from Polytechnic, Milan in 1922. Although aware of the Italian Rationalist Movement in architecture he did not join in the controversies that raged.
In 1928 he founded the magazine *Domus*, and during the following years became closely associated with the Milan Triennale. His own practice flourished. In 1936 he was appointed Lecturer in Architecture at the Polytechnic, Milan. Afterwards, taught in many foreign universities. He became president of the newly formed International Museum of Modern Art, Milan in 1961. Ponti's greatest contribution has been in drawing architecture, the arts and industry closer together. He has written many articles on these subjects and his book *In Praise of Architecture* has shown how perceptive his criticism can be.

PONTI, GIO. *In Praise of Architecture*, New York 1960. Originally: *Amate l'architettura*, Milan 1957.

PONTI, GIO. 'Esperienze d'architetto', *Pirelli* (Rivista d'informazione e di technica), No.6, November–December 1951, pp.10–11.

PLAUT, J.S. *Espressione di Gio Ponti*, Milan 1954.

PERSICO, E. 'Giovanni Ponti', *L'Italia Letteraria*, No.29, April 1934.

GENNARINI, P.E. 'Gio Ponti: dell'architettura al disegno per l'industria', *Pirelli*, No.6, November–December 1951, pp.8–9.

Jean PROUVÉ (1901–1966)

Born Nancy, 1901, the son of Victor Prouvé, a leading member of the Nancy School of designers. Died 1966.

Prouvé pioneered industrialized building methods in France. His initial training as an art metal worker and his connection with the Nancy School led to a marriage of craft with modern techniques. He employed young architects from the École des Beaux-Arts in his factory who quickly adapted themselves to designing for production.

His work led him inevitably into experiments in structure and form – his projects include complete factory-made houses, curtain walling systems and mass-produced community buildings.

PROUVÉ, J. 'Jean Prouvé', Special No., *Architecture* (Brussels), Nos.11/12, 1954.

PROUVÉ, J. 'L'habitation de notre époque', *AA Journal*, December 1965, pp.128–9. A report edited by Colin Davidson.

GASSIOT-TALABOT, G. 'Jean Prouvé', *Cimaise* (Paris), No.54, 1961.

Antonin RAYMOND (1888–1976)

Born Kladno, Bohemia, in 1888 of Czech parentage. Worked in Japan and USA. Died Japan, 1976.

Studied at University of Prague. Emigrated to the USA in 1910. Joined Frank Lloyd Wright at Taliesin in 1916 after having lived in Rome. After the war he went to Japan with Wright to supervise the erection of the Imperial Hotel. He left Wright's employ in 1920 and chose to remain in Japan where he set up an independent practice 'American Architect-Engineers'. His office expanded after the Tokyo earthquake and among his assistant architects were Junzo Yoshimura and Kunio Maekawa.

After leaving Japan in 1937 the Raymond family returned to the USA via India. He started an office in New York City in 1938 and held an exhibition of work in the Rockefeller Center. In 1948 he reopened his Tokyo office. The AIA awarded him their Medal of Honour in 1956. Other awards followed.

Raymond published his first book in 1935, a bilingual book (Japanese and English) that outlined his work from 1920 to 1935. This was followed in 1937 by the publication *Architectural Details*. 'The Work of Antonin Raymond' published as a special issue of the *AA Journal*, August 1962, is an excellent survey of the architect's work.

RAYMOND, A. *Raymond's House*, Tokyo 1931. Preface by Paul Claudel.
RAYMOND, A. *Antonin Raymond, His Work in Japan 1920–1935*, Tokyo 1935. Edited by K.Nakamura. Preface by Elie Faure.
RAYMOND, A. *Architectural Details*, Tokyo 1937. Republished New York 1947.
RAYMOND, A. *Autobiography*, Rutland (Vermont), Tokyo, 1973.

KILLICK, J. (ed.). 'Antonin Raymond, Architect', Special No. *Architectural Association Journal*, August 1962.

H.H. RICHARDSON (1838–1886)

Henry Hobson Richardson was born in the parish of St James, Louisiana, 1838. Died Boston, 1886.
Brought up in New Orleans. In 1856 went to Harvard from where he graduated in 1859. He never returned to the south. Travelled to Paris via England in 1860 where he continued his studies at the École des Beaux-Arts. Returned to New York in 1865 where he ran a partnership from 1867–1878. After 1878 he practised on his own and also worked in collaboration with Olmsted, the leading landscape architect of the day. In 1878 he moved his practice to Boston and there made his reputation as an extremely original architect. His style was heavy but his buildings brought him fame, as Louis Sullivan has said, as the 'sole giant of his day'. His career was a short one but most effective in that it laid the foundation on which architects such as Louis Sullivan and Frank Lloyd Wright built their own architecture. See *Henry Hobson Richardson, Boston Architect* in Vance bibliographies, A-40.

VAN RENSSELAER, M.G. *H.H.Richardson and his Works*, Boston 1888. Reprinted in p.b. New York, 1969.
HITCHCOCK, H-R. *The Architecture of H.H.Richardson and his Times*, New York, London, 1936 (2nd revised edn; Hamden, Conn., 1961).
GIEDION, S. *The Architecture of H.H.Richardson and his times*, New York 1936.
DOUMATO, L. *Henry Hobson Richardson*, Vance Bibliography A.40. 1979.

ICKEUS, R.L. 'H.H.Richardson and Basic Form Concepts in Modern Architecture', *Art Quarterly*, No.3, 1940, pp.273–91.
SCHEYER, E. 'Henry Adams and Henry Hobson Richardson', *Journal of the Society of Arch. Historians* (USA), Vol.XII, No.1, pp.7–12.

Gerrit Thomas RIETVELD   (1888–1964)

Born Utrecht, 1888. Died Utrecht, 1964.
Worked for his father as an apprentice cabinet-maker, 1899–1906. Studied
architecture on a part-time basis under P.J.Klaarhamer at Utrecht, 1911–15
whilst working as independent cabinet maker (1911–19). During this time he
opened his own business in Utrecht while studying. From 1921–31 he
collaborated with Mrs Schroeder-Schrader. In 1923 he worked briefly with
Van Doesburg and Van Eesteren on two architectural projects.
In 1918 he became acquainted with the architect Rob van 't Hoff and members
of the newly formed de Stijl group. He became a member of de Stijl in 1919
(until 1931), the year in which he opened an architectural office in Utrecht. He
was one of the founder members of CIAM, and one of the Dutch delegates at the
2nd CIAM Congress at Frankfurt in 1929. He received commissions and carried
out work in many countries and taught architectural and industrial design in
The Hague, Rotterdam, Amsterdam and Arnhem.
The standard biography on Rietveld by T.M.Brown covers all the major
works executed by this architect and also includes a complete bibliography.

RIETVELD, G. *Nieuwe Zakelijkheid in der Nederlandsche Architektuur*, Amsterdam
1932.
RIETVELD, GERRIT. *Rietveld, 1924, Schröder Huis*, Amsterdam 1963. *Quadrat* Print.
Private circulation. A study in colour of the Schröder house.

BROWN, T.M. *The Work of G. Rietveld, Architect*, Utrecht 1958. A complete
bibliography, pp.188–95. This includes articles written by Rietveld himself
and references to his work in book and periodicals.
MISC. *Rietveld*, Amsterdam 1959. Exhibition catalogue.
SCHAAFSMAH, G. *Rietveld: Bouwmeester van een Nieuwetigd*, Utrecht 1959.
BUFFINGA, A. *G.Th.Rietveld*, Amsterdam 1971.
MISC. *G.Rietveld, Architect*, London 1972. Catalogue for the Hayward Gallery
exhibition. Based on the original Dutch version.
WILSON, C.S. 'Gerrit Rietveld, 1888–1964', *Architectural Review*, Vol. 136, 1964,
pp.399–402.
BROWN, T.M. 'Rietveld's egocentric vision', *Journal of Society of Architectural
Historians* (USA), Vol.24, No.4, 1965, pp.292–6.
MISC. 'Gerrit Thomas Rietveld, 1888–1964', *Bauen und Wohnen*, Vol.19, No.11,
1965.

Ernesto ROGERS   (1909–1969)

Born Trieste, 1909. Died 1969.
Studied architecture at Milan Polytechnic, graduating in 1932. A member of
the Italian architectural firm of BBPR, he is equally well known as the
publisher of *Domus* and as the editor of *Casabella Continuità* from 1954 to 1965.
He wrote numerous articles for these and other magazines on Italian and
international architecture and was looked upon – at least among English
architects – as the spokesman for the Modern Movement in Italy. His

monographs and articles on various architects have contributed to a new understanding of the cultural and social forces at work within the architectural profession.

ROGERS, ERNESTO. *Auguste Perret*, Milan 1955.
ROGERS, ERNESTO. *Experienza dell'architettura*, Turin 1958.
ROGERS, ERNESTO. *The Works of Pier Luigi Nervi*, London 1958. Introduction by Rogers.

Kamil ROSKOT (1886–1945)

Born Vlasim, 1886. Died Paris, 1945.
This key, but little known Czech architect, studied at the German and Czech Polytechnical University, Prague, philosophy and history of art at Charles University in Prague, painting under Prof. Max Svabinsky at the Academy of Fine Arts, architecture under Prof. Jan Kotera at the Academy of Fine Arts, Prague, 1919–1922. Architect in Prague, Member of Sdruzeni Architektu, Member of Artists Club 'Manes', President of the Association of Academic Architects in Prague.

CERNY, F.M. & STEPANEK, J. *K.Roskot*, Zivotni dib. 1979.

Alfred ROTH (1903–)

Born Wangen a. A., Bern, 1903. Lives in Zürich.
Studied at the Technical High School, Zürich. Worked initially with Professor K. Moser in Zürich and with Le Corbusier in Paris on the houses for the Werkbund Exhibition, Stuttgart, 1927. From 1928 to 1930 he worked with Ingrid Wallberg in Sweden designing a number of small houses.
In 1932 he set up practice in Zürich and has been responsible for many important modern buildings in and around the city. He designed the well known Doldertal flats with Marcel Breuer and his cousin Emil Roth in 1935. With Emil Roth he has also been responsible for planning schemes and work in various countries in Europe. In 1943 he became editor of the Swiss review, *Werk*. He has also edited and published numerous books, the best known of which is *The New Architecture*.

ROTH, ALFRED. *Zwei Wohnhäuser von Le Corbusier und P. Jeanneret*, Stuttgart 1927.
ROTH, ALFRED. *Architecture: Contemporary Problems; Contemporary Solutions*, Zürich 1937.
ROTH, ALFRED. *The New Architecture*, Zürich, 1940. 4th edn 1948. Trilingual edition.
ROTH, ALFRED. *Neugeburt der Stadt*, Zürich 1946.
ROTH, ALFRED. *The New School*, Zürich 1950 (1966). Trilingual edition.
ROTH, ALFRED. *A Decade of Contemporary Architecture*, Zürich 1951.

Alfred Roth

Paul Rudolph

Paul RUDOLPH (1918–)

Born Elkton, Kentucky, 1918. Lives in New Haven, Connecticut.
Studied architecture at Alabama Polytechnic Institute and Harvard. Fellow
in Architecture at Harvard, 1941–2. Began in practice with Twitchell,
1947–51, but now practises under his own name. He has carried out buildings
of many types and his work is difficult to categorize. His principal buildings
include the Riverview High School, Sarasota, Florida, 1957; Jewett Arts
Center, Wellesley College, Mass., 1958 and student accommodation at Yale.
He was Dean of the Department of Architecture, Yale University from 1958.
Select bibliography in Vance series: *The work of Paul Rudolph* (A-33).

RUDOLPH, PAUL. 'Changing Philosophy of Architecture', *AIA Journal*, August
1954, pp.65–70.
RUDOLPH, PAUL. 'Six Determinants of Architectural Form', *Architectural Record*,
October 1956, pp.183–90. Also *Architectural Design*, May 1957, pp.149–50.
RUDOLPH, PAUL. 'Architectural Eucation in USA', *Zodiac 8*, pp.162–5.
RUDOLPH, PAUL. 'What is Quality?', *AIA Journal*, July 1963, pp.38–43.
RUDOLPH, PAUL. Special issue *Architecture & Urbanism*, Tokyo, No.80, 1977.

MOHOLY-NAGY, S. *The Architecture of Paul Rudolph*, New York 1970.

VERONESI, G. 'Paul Rudolph', *Zodiac 8*, pp.148–61.
COLLINS, P. 'Whither Paul Rudolph?', *Progressive Architecture*, August 1961,
pp.130–3.
MOHOLY-NAGY, S. 'Beau Geste of Paul Rudolph', *Perspecta* (Yale University
Journal) No.7, 1961, pp.71–3.
EHRMANN, J. 'Paul Rudolph', *L'Œil* (Lausanne), February 1965, pp.20–9.

Eero SAARINEN (1910–1961)

Born Kirkkonummi, Finland, 1910. Died, Ann Arbor, USA, 1961.
Son of Eliel Saarinen, he left Finland for the USA in 1923 when his father went
to Cranbrook Academy. Studied at Yale, receiving his degree in 1934. He
worked with his father from 1925 onwards. His first major work was the
General Motors Technical Center at Warren, Michigan (completed 1955)
built very much under the influence of the work of Mies van der Rohe.
Gradually his views on architectural expression changed over the next few
years and his later buildings provide a complete contrast to the Miesian ideas
implicit in the GM work. The Yale Hockey Rink, completed in 1958, a giant
multi-curved shell, and the TWA Terminal, Kennedy Airport – with its
bird-like form – are dramatic structures that make Saarinen's work impossible
to classify. He died at the height of his career.
Alan Temko's book on Saarinen is a short but useful introduction to this
architect's work and includes biographical and bibliographical information.
All his major buildings have been covered extensively in the world
architectural press. *Architecture USA* (London, 1959) by Ian McCallum puts his
work in its American context. See pp.141–52.

SAARINEN, EERO. *Eero Saarinen on his Work 1947–1964*, New York 1962. Edited by
Aline B.Saarinen. Covering projects of the period 1947–1964.
SAARINEN, EERO. 'Function, Structure and Beauty', *Architectural Association
Journal*, July–August 1957, pp.40–51.

TEMKO, A. *Eero Saarinen*, New York, London, 1962.

DORFLES, G. 'Eero Saarinen: The TWA Terminal and the American Embassy,
London', *Zodiac 8*, 1961, pp.84–9.
MCQUADE, N. 'Eero Saarinen, a complete architect', *Architectural Forum*, 116,
April 1962, pp.102–19. A well illustrated survey.

Eliel SAARINEN (1873–1950)

Born Rantasalmi, Finland, 1873. Died Michigan, USA, 1950.
Studied painting at Helsinki University and architecture at the Helsinki
Polytechnic.
He was in partnership with Gesellius and Lindegren in Helsinki from
1896–1907. Their work established the school of architecture known as the
'National Romantic' which had some similarity to Continental *art nouveau*. The
masterpiece of this trend was undoubtedly the competition design by Saarinen
for the main station at Helsinki of 1904, which was erected between 1910 and
1916. He produced a project plan for Canberra. In 1922 Saarinen was
awarded the second prize in the Chicago Tribune Tower Competition. He
moved to the USA in 1923. In 1925 he was made Director of the Cranbrook
Academy of Art, Michigan. In 1937 he formed a partnership with his son Eero.
His book *Search for Form* was published in 1948. It is a confused but
heart-searching examination of creativity.

Eliel Saarinen

SAARINEN, ELIEL. *Munkkiniemi-Haaga ja suur-Helsinki*, Helsinki 1915 (p.b.). The Helsinki plan.

SAARINEN, ELIEL. *The City: Its Growth, its Decay, its Future*, New York 1943.

SAARINEN, ELIEL. *Search for Form, a Fundamental Approach to Art*, New York 1948.

CHRIST-JANER, A. *Eliel Saarinen*, Chicago 1948. Includes list of buildings and bibliography. Foreword by Alvar Aalto. Reissued 1979.

REID, K. 'Eliel Saarinen. Master of Design', *Pencil Points*, September 1936, pp.465–94.

Antonio SANT'ELIA (1888–1916)

Born Como, 1888. Killed in action, Monfalcone, 1916.
Studied at Milan and Bologna. He completed his studies in 1912 and set up practice that year in Milan. Sant'Elia became closely involved with Marinetti's Futurists and in 1914 he published his *Manifesto of Futurist Architecture*. His drawings for a 'Città Futurista' were exhibited in Milan in 1914. His *Messagio* prefaced the catalogue for this exhibition organized by the Nuove Tendenze Group.
The best available introduction to the work of Sant'Elia is to be found in the catalogue of the permanent exhibition at Como prepared by Caramel and

Longatti. It includes – as does the much earlier *Dopo Sant'Elia* (1935) – the Futurist Manifesto. English translations can be found in the article by Reyner Banham and in the book on Futurism by Carrieri.

SANT'ELIA, ANTONIO. 'Architettura Futurista', Manifesto, 1914. Included in Argan, G.C., *et al. Dopo Sant'Elia*, Milan 1935. English translation in Carrieri, R., *Futurism*, Milan 1963, pp.150–1.

SARTORIS, A. *L'Architetto Antonio Sant'Elia*, Milan 1930.
DOTORRI, G. *Sant'Elia e la nuova architettura*, Rome 1933.
ARGAN, G.C., *et al. Dopo Sant'Elia*, Milan 1935.
APOLLONIO, U. *Antonio Sant'Elia*, Milan 1958. In *Il Balcone* series.
CARAMEL, L., & LONGATTI, A. *Antonio Sant'Elia*, Como 1962. Catalogue of the permanent collection of Sant'Elia's work. Includes biographical and bibliographical sections.

ARGAN, G.C. 'Il pensiero critico di Antonio Sant'Elia', *L'arte* (Rome), September 1930.
TENTORI, F. 'Le origini Liberty di Antonio Sant'Elia', *L'Architettura*, No.2, July–August 1955, pp.206–8.
MARIANI, L. 'Disegni inediti di Sant'Elia', as above, pp.210–15.
BANHAM, R. 'Sant'Elia', *Architectural Review*, May 1955, pp.295–301.

Carlo SCARPA (1906–1978)

Born Venice, 1906. Died in a building accident in Japan, 1978. Graduated in architecture from the Academy of Fine Arts, Venice in 1926. Always an individualist, Scarpa was a dedicated architect-builder who because of his devotion to Wright's organic architecture (which he 'rediscovered' after the war through Zevi's *Metron* magazine) has been somewhat overlooked by architectural historians. Also influenced by Mondrian and De Stijl. Designed many projects in 1930s: 1941 consultant for Biennale. Taught at Venice University; became Director in 1972. In the fifties his practice took off and he was responsible for numerous exhibitions, museum conversions, etc. His Olivetti Shop in Venice dates from 1957–8, the conversion of the Castelvecchio, Verona from 1964. The superb design for the Galleria Querini Stampalia, Venice, with its witty Wrightian details dates from 1961–3. Louis I. Kahn wrote: 'In the work of Carlo Scarpa/'Beauty'/the first sense/Art/the first word/Then wonder . . .' Scarpa himself wrote very little. His work appeared in the main Italian journals.

LOS, S. *Carlo Scarpa Architetto Poeta*, Venice 1967.
CANTACUZINO, S. (Intro.). *Carlo Scarpa: architetto poeta*, London 1974. RIBA exhibition catalogue; small p.b.
MAZZARIOL, G. 'Opera dell'architetto Carlo Scarpa', *l'Architettura*, No.3, 1955.
TENTORI, F. 'Progetti de Carlo Scarpa', *Casabella*, 222, 1958.
BETTINI, S. 'L'architettura di Carlo Scarpa', *Zodiac* 6, 1960, pp.140–187. A major review of Scarpa's work.
BRUSATIN, M. 'Carlo Scarpa Architetto Veneziano', *Controspazio*, 3–4, 1972.

Hans Scharoun

Hans SCHAROUN (1893–1972)

Born Bremen, 1893. Died West Berlin, 1972.
Studied at the Technical High School, Charlottenburg, 1912–14. During the first world war he was involved in reconstruction schemes in East Prussia. At the end of the war he set up in practice in East Prussia. He became an active member of the Bruno Taut circle and a corresponding member of the 'Glass Chain'. In 1925 he became a professor at the Breslau Academy of Arts and Crafts, holding the post until 1932. He also became actively engaged in the activities of the newly formed 'Ring' in Berlin. During this time he built many blocks of flats in Berlin and worked on town-planning projects. In 1932 he set up his office in Berlin. Little was heard of Scharoun under the Nazis. In 1945 he was appointed Head of the Department for Building and Housing, Berlin and set up planning group called the Berliner Kollectiv which produced revolutionary plan for rebuilding Berlin in 1946 influenced by the ideas of Miliutin. From 1947–50 Head of Building Institute at Germany Academy of Science. From 1946 to 1958 he lectured at the Berlin Technical University. Scharoun is probably best known for his competition entries; for years he seems to have taken second prize (which of course is usually reserved for the most adventurous schemes) but more recently he won first awards and buildings like the Philharmonic, Berlin, have been the result.
He received many international and national honours including a UIA award for architecture and also served as President of the Berlin Academy. For a

description of the work of the Breslau Academy see *Poelzig, Endell, Moll und die Breslauer Kunstakademie 1911–32*, Berlin 1965 (Akademie der Künste catalogue); foreword by Hans Scharoun.

SCHAROUN, HANS. 'Struktur in Raum und Zeit', *Handbuch Moderner Architektur*, Berlin 1957, pp.13–21.
SCHAROUN, HANS. 'Raum und Milieu der Schule', *Bauen und Wohnen*, No.4. 1961, pp.4–8.
PFANKUCH, P. (ed.) *Hans Scharoun*, Berlin 1967. Catalogue of the exhibition at the Akademie der Künste, Berlin.
JONES, P.B. *Hans Scharoun, a monograph*, London 1978.

STABER, M. 'Hans Scharoun. Ein Beitrag zum organischen Bauen', *Zodiac 10*, 1962, pp.52–93. An important article on Scharoun's contribution to organic building. English translation, pp.195–200.
FRAMPTON, K. 'Genesis of the Philharmonie', *Architectural Design*, March 1965, pp.111–12. Followed by a description of the building, pp.113–28.
MISC. 'Hans Scharoun', *L'Architecture d'Aujourd'hui*, No.57/58, Oct. 1967, pp.8–61.

Paul SCHEERBART (1863–1915)

Born Danzig, 1863. Died 1915.
Freelance writer, *phantastischer* novelist and poet in Berlin from 1887.
Published his first book through his own publishing house, Verlag der Phantasten. Published 26 books.
Scheerbart was the grandfather of astral fantasies and *Glaspapa* of modern architecture. Closely associated with Herwarth Walden's *Sturm* group in pre-war Berlin. His last propagandist publication on glass architecture was published by Walden in 1914. It was dedicated to his close friend Bruno Taut. Taut's little Glass Pavilion at the 1914 Werkbund Exhibition was in its turn a monument to Scheerbart's ideas. Taut published some of Scheerbart's writings posthumously in his Berlin copies of *Frühlicht* in 1920. Many of his writings have recently been reissued in German.

SCHEERBART, PAUL. *Immer Mutig!* Minden 1902, 2 vols, 'A fantastic hippopotamus novel'!
SCHEERBART, PAUL. *Glasarchitektur*, Berlin 1914 (reissued, Munich 1971). A slim volume published by *Der Sturm*. A word picture of the new glass culture. English translation: D.Sharp, *Glass Architecture and Alpine Architecture*, London, New York, 1972.
SCHEERBART, PAUL. 'Glashausbriefe', *Frühlicht*, Supplement 3, Berlin 1920. In Taut, B. *Frühlicht 1920–22*, Berlin 1963, pp.18–23.
SCHEERBART, PAUL. 'Der Architektenkongress', *Frühlicht*, Magdeburg, autumn 1921. In: Taut, B., *op. cit.*, pp.94–6.

BANHAM, R. 'The Glass Paradise', *Architectural Review*, February 1959, pp.87–9. A discussion of the Taut and Scheerbart connections.

Paul Scheerbart

Rudolf M. SCHINDLER (1887–1953)

Born Vienna, 1887. Died Los Angeles, 1953.
Studied in the Technical College, Vienna, 1906–11, and the Vienna Academy
of Fine Arts 1910–13, under Otto Wagner. Also from 1911–13 worked in the
office of Mayr and Mayer. Designed an actors' club in 1913, from 1914–1915
travelled to the USA, worked in Chicago and made extensive tour of the South
West. Planned to return to Vienna to work with Loos but was prevented by
war. Instead took up unpaid employment with Frank Lloyd Wright. Wright
sent him to California to supervise Barnsdell house construction in 1920. 1921
saw him in practice on his own account. In 1925 Richard Neutra came to Los
Angeles and opened office in Schindler's studio. They collaborated on a
number of projects. Schindler was a prolific designer and produced
typography and furniture.

SCHINDLER, R.M. *Modern Architecture: A Programme*, Vienna 1912 (unpublished
manuscript).
SCHINDLER, R.M. 'A Manifesto 1912', in Benton, T. & C. and Sharp, D. (eds)
Form and Function, London 1975, pp.113–114. Further reference pp.44–46.

MCCOY, E. *Five Californian Architects*, New York 1960, pp.149–193.
GEBHARD, D. *R.M.Schindler: An Exhibition of the Architecture of R.M.Schindler
(1887–1953)*, Santa Barbara 1967. Exhibition catalogue.

GEBHARD, D. *Schindler*, London, New York, 1971. Preface by H.-R.Hitchcock.

HERTZBERGER, H. 'Dedicato a Schindler' *Domus*, No.465, Sept. 1967, pp.2–7.
MCCOY, E. 'R.M.Schindler', *Lotus*, No.5, 1968, pp.92–105.

José Luis SERT   (1902–   )

Born Barcelona, 1902. Works in Cambridge, Mass.
Studied at the School of Architecture, Barcelona. Worked in the office of Le
Corbusier and Pierre Jeanneret, 1929–30. From 1929 to 1938 he ran his own
office in Barcelona.
In 1939 he emigrated to the United States and has remained there ever since.
Sert was an active member of CIAM, compiling the volume *Can our Cities Survive?*
for the Group in 1942. He was President of CIAM from 1947 to 1956.
Now an equally active member of the International Union of Architects (UIA).
He was appointed Dean of Faculty and Professor of Architecture at the
Harvard Graduate School of Design in 1953. Partner in the firm Sert, Jackson,
Gourley and Associates. His work includes a number of important American
town-planning schemes and university buildings as well as buildings in
Europe e.g. Micro Foundation, Barcelona.

SERT, JOSÉ LUIS. *Can our Cities Survive? An ABC of Urban Problems, their Analysis,
their Solutions*, Cambridge (Mass.), London, 1942 (3rd edn 1947). The CIAM
publication.
SERT, J.L., TYRWHITT, J., & ROGERS, E.N. *The Heart of the City. Towards the
Humanisation of Urban Life*, London, New York, 1952. The theme of the 8th
CIAM Congress.
SERT, J.L. & SWEENEY, J.J. *Antoni Gaudí*, London, New York, 1960.
SERT, J.L. 'The Human Scale in City Planning' in Zucker, P. *New Architecture
and City Planning*, New York 1944, pp.392–412.

BASTLUND, K. *José Luis Sert: 1927–1965*, Zürich 1966. Text in German, English,
French.
BASTLUND, K. (ed.) *J.L.Sert: Architecture, City Planning, Urban Design*, New York
1966.
BORAS, M. *Sert: Mediterranean Architecture*, New York 1976.

ANDERSON, S. 'Sert's Concept of Living', *Architectural Design*, August 1965,
p.376. This brief article is followed by a description of recent work by Sert,
Jackson and Gourley: the married student housing, Harvard and the
University Campus, Boston.

José Luis Sert

P. Morton SHAND (1888–1960)

Born Kensington, London, 1888. Died Lyon, 1960.
Shand's inclusion in this Bibliography is due to the fact that he was largely responsible for introducing the English to the modern architecture of the Continent. He was not an architect but he was a founder member of the English MARS Group. He was educated at Eton, King's College, Cambridge, and later at the Sorbonne and in Germany.
Well known for his gastronomic interests he is the author of classic books on French wines and food. His book on 'the architecture of pleasure', *Modern Theatres and Cinemas* (1930), has also become a classic work. Shand was responsible for the first publication and the translation of *The New Architecture and the Bauhaus* by Walter Gropius. His main contributions to a real understanding of the Modern Movement are to be found in the articles published in the *Architectural Review* under the title 'Scenario for a Human Drama'. These and other writings are included in the *AA Journal* monograph.

MORTON SHAND, P. *Modern Theatres and Cinemas*, London 1930.
MORTON SHAND, P. 'Scenario for a Human Drama' Articles in *Architectural Review:*
I. 'Forward', July 1934, p.9.
II. 'Immediate Background', August 1934, pp.39–42.
III. 'Peter Behrens', September 1934, pp.83–6.

IV. 'Van de Velde to Wagner', October 1934, pp.x31–4.
V. 'Glasgow Interlude', January 1935, pp.23–6.
VI. 'La machine-à-habiter to the House of Character', February 1935, pp.61–4.
VII. 'Looping the Loop' (Voysey, Webb, Morris and Soane), March 1935, pp.99–104.
MORTON SHAND, P. 'Van de Velde: Memoirs 1891–1901', *Architectural Review*, September 1952, pp.143–55.

HOUSDEN, B. (ed.) Special No. *Architectural Association Journal*, January 1959. Devoted to the writings of P.Morton Shand.

R.Norman SHAW   (1831–1912)

Born Edinburgh, 1831. Died Hampstead, London, 1912.
Educated in Edinburgh. He was articled for some time to the Edinburgh architect William Burn, who had his office in London. He also attended the Royal Academy Schools. He gained there the Gold Medal for Architecture. In 1858 he joined G.E.Street as an assistant. In 1863 he began his own practice, with an old colleague from Burn's office, W.E.Nesfield, as a partner.
Although it is to Shaw's private houses that most architects and historians of the Modern Movement refer it should be remembered that he was one of the most important of the Victorian 'commercial' architects. He built New Zealand Chambers, Leadenhall Street, 1872; the offices for the Allied Assurance, St James's, 1882; the White Star Offices, Liverpool, 1896. His finest work he considered to be New Scotland Yard.
In 1877 he became a full member of the Royal Academy.
Shaw's work is discussed at length in Hitchcock's *Architecture Nineteenth and Twentieth Centuries* (Pelican History of Art) and in two articles that appeared in the *AA Journal* in 1955 by John Brandon-Jones.

SHAW, R.NORMAN, & ADAMS, M.B. *Sketches for Cottages*, London 1878.
SHAW, R.NORMAN, & JACKSON, T.G. (eds.). *Architecture, a Profession or an Art?* London 1892. A collection of thirteen essays on the profession of architecture by various authors.

BLOMFIELD, R. *Richard Norman Shaw, R.A.*, London 1940.
SAINT, A. *Richard Norman Shaw*, New Haven, London, 1976 (p.b. 1977).

PEVSNER, N. 'Richard Norman Shaw: 1831–1912', *Architectural Review*, March 1941, pp.41–6.
BRANDON-JONES, J. 'The Work of Philip Webb and Norman Shaw', *Architectural Association Journal*, June 1955, pp.9–21; July–August 1955, pp.40–7.

R. Norman Shaw

Peter SMITHSON (1923–) and Alison SMITHSON (1928–)

Peter Denham Smithson was born at Stockton-on-Tees, 1923.
Educated at Stockton. Studied architecture at University of Durham,
Newcastle upon Tyne, 1939–42, 1945–8. A year at the Royal Academy
School, London, 1948–9. Worked for LCC Schools Division, 1949–50.
Hunstanton school was designed (privately) during this period. He began
teaching at the AA School, London, in 1955 – resigned in 1960. Smithson has
contributed a great deal to Team 10, being one of the signatories of the Doorn
Manifesto in 1954. Much of the Smithsons' theoretical work and many of the
projects of the following years were for various scales of community for Team
10. Almost accidentally, it would seem, the word *Brutalism* was dropped.
Banham and Summerson caught it, shaped it like a medal and presented it
back to the Smithsons. It has stuck.
Alison Margaret Smithson (née Gill) was born in Sheffield, 1928. Studied
architecture at University of Durham, 1944–9. Met her future husband.
Worked with him later in LCC Schools Division. The major work produced by
the couple has been done in collaboration, including most of the writing. The
Smithsons specialize in the architectural epithet – a sketch and a pithy note.
Their many contributions have appeared in the major English periodicals,
Architectural Design, Architectural Review and the *Architects' Year Book* as well as in
foreign journals. A chronological survey of their work (including articles and
short biographies) appeared in the Architectural Association Journal *Arena*,

119

Peter Smithson

Alison Smithson

February 1966. See also *Uppercase 3* (London), now out of print and virtually unobtainable.

SMITHSON, A., & P. *Urban Structuring*, London, New York, 1967. Studio Paperback series.
SMITHSON, A., & P. *Ordinariness and Light: Urban Theories 1952–1960 and their application in a building project 1963–1970*, London 1970. Includes most of the major magazine articles on urbanism.
SMITHSON, A., & P. *Without Rhetoric: An Architectural Aesthetic 1955–72*, London 1973.
SMITHSON, A., & P. 'The Themes of Team 10', *Architects' Year Book*, No.7, pp.28–31.
SMITHSON, A., & P. 'Aesthetics of Change', *Architects' Year Book*, No.8, pp.14–22.
SMITHSON, A., & P. 'The Rebirth of Japanese Architecture', Special No. *Architectural Design*, February 1961.
SMITHSON, A. 'Team 10 Primer 1953–62', Special No. *Architectural Design*, December 1962. Reprinted as separate publication *Team 10 Primer*, London 1965, with additional reprints from other editions showing the work of members of Team 10. Important.
SMITHSON, A., & P. 'The Pavilion and the Route', *Architectural Design*, March 1965, pp.143–6.
SMITHSON, A., & P. 'The Heroic Period of Modern Architecture', Special No. *Architectural Design*, December 1965. A comprehensive photographic record of the Modern Movement, 1917–37.

BAKER, J. (ed.). 'A Smithson File', Special No. *Architectural Association Journal*, *Arena*, February 1966.

Paolo SOLERI (1919–)

Born Turin, 1919. Lives in Scottsdale, Phoenix, Arizona. Studied at Turin Polytechnic School of Architecture, graduating in 1946. On scholarship to USA where he was apprenticed to Wright, 1947–8. In 1949 returned to Italy. In 1953 he built ceramics studio, Vietri-sul-mare. Returned to USA in 1955 settling at Scottsdale where he has since built up the Cosanti Foundation from origins as a workshop base prior to work starting on Arcosanti, Cordes Junction in 1961. Initial ideas for Mesa City led to development of Arcological concepts. Culminated in vast Corcoran Gallery, Washington exhibition and publication of large book – dedicated to miniaturisation – on the city in the image of man (1969). Followed two years later by the *Sketchbooks* publication. Earlier had contributed bridge designs for publications. Soleri lectures widely throughout world on his new city ideas which now incorporate notions about the consumption and conservation of energy developed with interdisciplinary teams of experts (see articles on 2-suns arcologies). Holds Hon. Professorship in Architecture, Arizona State University, Tempe where his Archive is held. For detailed bibliography see below; selected bibliography in Vance Architecture series, no. A-200.

Paolo Soleri

SOLERI, P. *Arcology: The City in the Image of Man*, Cambridge (Mass.) 1969. Large format p.b. (reissued as smaller p.b.).

SOLERI, P. *The Bridge between Matter and Spirit is Matter becoming Spirit: The Arcology of Paolo Soleri*, New York 1973 (p.b.). Soleri's philosophy, 1961–72.

SOLERI, P. 'A prospective of Environment and Building', *Image*, No.1, 1965, pp.4–7.

SOLERI, P. 'Two Suns Arcology', *AA Quarterly*, Vol.7, No.2, 1975, pp. 33–41.

WALL, D. *Visionary Cities: The Arcology of Paolo Soleri*, New York 1971.

BLAKE, P. 'The Fantastic World of Paolo Soleri', *Architectural Forum*, February 1960, pp. 104–9.

COOK, J. 'Paolo Soleri', *AA Quarterly*, Vol.1, No.1, pp. 16–23.

SKOLIMOWSKI, H. 'Paolo Soleri: The Philosophy of Urban Life', *AA Quarterly*, Vol.3, No.1, 1970, pp.34–42.

SHARP, D. 'Paolo Soleri', *Building*, 10, November 1972, pp. 75–82.

MOHOLY-NAGY, S. 'The Arcology of Paolo Soleri', *Architectural Forum*, May 1970, pp.70–5

MISC. 'Arcosanti', *L'Architecture d'Aujourd'hui*, No.167, May 1973, p.48ff.

WILCOXEN, R. *Paolo Soleri: A Bibliography*, Monticello (CPL), 1969.

Mart STAM (1899–)
Mart (Martinus Adrianus) Stam was born in Purmerend, 1899.
Attended the State School for Draughtsmanship 1917–19. During vacations
worked for J.M.Van der Mey. From 1919–22 he acted as draughtsman for
various architects in Rotterdam and elsewhere. Travelled to Berlin 1922 and
made contact with the Tauts and El Lissitzky. In 1926 after participating in
Bauhaus exhibition went to Switzerland where he worked with Werner Moser
in Zürich. Worked as architect in Thur 1924–5 but during this and subsequent
years edited *ABC* in Zürich for Hans Schmidt and Emil Orth. Returned to
Holland in 1925 via Paris when he became assistant architect to Brinkman and
Van der Vlugt. Member of 'Opbouw' 1925–28. In 1927 he worked for Mies at
Stuttgart Werkbund exhibition before setting up practice in Frankfurt where
he worked closely with Ernst May and also lectured at Dessau Bauhaus.
1930–4 worked in Russia with Ernst May returning to Amsterdam in 1934.
Five years later he became Director of the Institute of Applied Art,
Amsterdam, until 1948. Still active in the post-war years, from 1948–50
became Director of Academy for Fine and Applied Arts, Dresden, 1950–52
Director, College of Fine and Applied Arts, East Berlin. He resumed practice
in Amsterdam 1953–66 after which he went into seclusion in Switzerland.

STAM, MART. 'Modernes Bauen' published in three parts in *ABC* 1, 2 and 3/4,
Zürich 1924. Reissues of this magazine were produced by the Architecture
Department of Delft for an early exhibition on Mart Stam's work shown in
Delft, Eindhoven and other centres.

MISC. 'Mart Stam', special issue of *Bouwkundig Weekblad*, Vol.87, No.25, 23 Dec.
69. English version *Mart Stam*, London 1970. A full bibliography exists in
English, but referring to Dutch source material, in this publication edited by
D.Sharp *et al*.

Rudolf STEINER (1861–1925)

Born Kraljevec, Southern Austria, 1861. Died Dornach, Switzerland, 1925.
Studied at the Technical High School, Vienna.
Steiner was not a trained architect. He worked for six years in Weimar at the
Goethe Archive, 1890–6. Edited Goethe's writings on natural sciences for the
well-known publication Kürschner's *National Literatur*. In 1892 he published
his book *The Philosophy of Spiritual Activity*, a work important in that it set a
foundation for his later anthroposophical works. He became aware of the
principle of metamorphosis in nature and related it to a concept of man and
man's relation to the spiritual world.
In 1912 an Anthroposophical Society was founded by Steiner's followers. In
1913 the first Goetheanum at Dornach was erected. This was burnt down on
New Year's Eve, 1922–3. The second Goetheanum was built on the same site
as the first and officially opened (although incomplete) in 1928. A great deal
has been written recently about Steiner's approach to architecture. A useful
introduction is Kenneth Bayes's article 'Architecture in Accord with Man'.
But books by Raab, Zimmer, etc. now supersede.

STEINER, RUDOLF. *Architectural Forms considered as the Thoughts of Culture and World Perception*, London 1919.

STEINER, RUDOLF. *The Story of my Life*, London 1928.

STEINER, RUDOLF. *Ways to a New Style in Architecture*, London, New York, 1927. German original edition: *Wege zu einem neuen Baustil*, Dornach 1926.

STEINER, RUDOLF. *Der Baugedanke des Goetheanum*, Stuttgart 1932 (1958).

HARWOOD, A.C. (ed.) *The Faithful Thinker*, London 1961 (see essay by Bayes, K. 'Architecture in Accord with Man', pp.163–78). Centenary Essays.

ANON. *The Goetheanum*, Dornach 1961 (pamphlet).

RAAB, R. KLINGBORG, A., & FANT, A. *Eloquent Concrete*, Dornach, London, 1979. Previously published in German as *Sprechender Beton: Wie Rudolf Steiner den Stahlbeton verwendete*, Dornach 1972.

ZIMMER, E. *Rudolf Steiner als Architekt von Wohn- und Zweckbauten*, Stuttgart 1971.

KEMPER, C. *Der Bau: Studien zur Architektur und Plastik des Ersten Goetheanum*, Stuttgart 1955.

CARLGREN, F. *Education Towards Freedom*, East Grinstead 1972. English edition edited by Joan and Siegfried Rudel on Steiner's ideas on education including section on 'environmental studies'.

BIESANTZ, H., KLINGBORG, A., & RAAB, R. *Rudolf Steiner 1861–1925*, London, Dornach, 1978–9. The well illustrated comprehensive catalogue produced for the 50th anniversary exhibition held in Dornach in 1978.

Rudolf Steiner

ROBERTSON, H., & YERBURY, F.R. 'The Goetheanum at Dornach', *Architect and Building News*, 15 March 1929, pp.359–62, 365.

ANON. 'Il primo Goetheanum a Dornach (1913)', *L'Architettura*, No.55, pp.58–63.

ANON. 'Il secondo Goetheanum a Dornach', *L'Architettura*, No.56, pp.130–5.

ANON. 'Edifici minori a Dornach', *L'Architettura*, No.57, pp.202–7, and No.58, pp.276–9.

SHARP, D. 'Rudolf Steiner and the Way to a New Style in Architecture', *Architectural Association Journal*, June 1963, pp.371–83.

RAAB, R. 'Rudolf Steiner und die Baukunst', *Bauwelt*, No.7, 1964.

SHARP, D. 'Love in a concrete climate', *The Guardian*, July 31, 1971.

Louis SULLIVAN (1856–1924)

Born Boston, 1856. Died Chicago, 1924.

Studied for a time at MIT before working for Frank Furness in Philadelphia. In 1874 he went to Paris to study for a short time at the École des Beaux-Arts. In 1881, after being in the employment of Dankmar Adler, he became a partner of the firm.

Sullivan's Wainwright Building, St Louis was erected in 1890–1. The ornamentation of the top storey is typical of the kind of decoration in which

Louis Sullivan

Sullivan excelled. His philosophy of architecture is contained in his writings, which appeared in collected form after his death: *Kindergarten Chats* were written for the *Interstate Architect and Builder* in 1901–2; *The Autobiography of an Idea*, written in 1922–3, was published in 1924, the year of his death, with a Foreword by Claude Bragdon. It is in this Foreword that Bragdon couples Sullivan with the great giants of the New World, Whitman and Lincoln. This has led to a number of rather pedantic studies of Sullivan in defence of American culture.

SULLIVAN, LOUIS. *Kindergarten Chats*, serialized in *Interstate Architect and Builder*, 1901–2. Revised 1918. Limited edn, Kansas 1934; enlarged edn, New York, 1947 (p.b. 1955).
SULLIVAN, LOUIS. *The Autobiography of an Idea*, New York 1924. Reprinted 1934 (p.b. 1956).

MORRISON, H. *Louis Sullivan, Prophet of Modern Architecture*, New York 1952.
KAUFMANN, JR., E. (ed.) *Louis Sullivan and the Architecture of Free Enterprise*, Chicago 1956 (p.b.).
SZARKOWSKI, J. *The Idea of Louis Sullivan*, Minneapolis 1956.
CONNELY, W. *Louis Sullivan as he lived*, New York 1960.
BUSH-BROWN, A. *Louis Sullivan*, New York, London, 1960.
PAUL, S. *Louis Sullivan. An Architect in American Thought*, Englewood Cliffs, N.J., 1962.

DORFLES, G. 'Sullivan: decorazione e funzione', *Domus*, May 1951.
HITCHCOCK, H-R. 'Sullivan and the Skyscraper', *RIBA Journal*, July 1953, pp.353–61.
MANSON, G. 'Sullivan and Wright: an uneasy union of Celts', *Architectural Review*, November 1955, pp.297–300.

Kenzo TANGE (1913–   )

Born Imabari, Ehime Prefecture, Japan, 1913. Lives in Tokyo.
Studied architecture at Tokyo University, 1935–8. Graduate course in architecture, Tokyo University, 1942–5. Then worked for Kunio Maekawa through whom he joined Japanese Werkbund.
In 1949 he won the Hiroshima Peace Museum Competition. He followed this up in 1952 by winning the competition for Tokyo Town Hall.
Tange has become the most important post-war figure in Japanese architecture and planning. He joined the group known as the Metabolists in 1960 and has since become, in one critic's view, the 'catalytic leader'. In 1960 he also produced, in collaboration with his team of designers, the Tokyo Bay Project.
He was Visiting Professor at MIT, 1959–60. He is at present Professor at Tokyo University. He was awarded the Royal Gold Medal of the RIBA in 1965.
His major publication so far is *Katsura: Tradition and Creation in Japanese Architecture* produced at the suggestion of Walter Gropius, who also contributed an introduction.

His recent work is well represented in European periodicals, particularly in the British magazine *Architectural Design*. Boyd's book is a very useful study – but already dated.

TANGE, KENZO (with GROPIUS, W., & ISHIMOTO, Y.) *Katsura – Tradition and Creation in Japanese Architecture*, Tokyo, New Haven, 1960.

TANGE, KENZO. *A Plan for Tokyo, 1960*, Tokyo 1960. Produced by the Kenzo Tange Team.

TANGE, KENZO (with KAWAZOE, N., & WATANABE, Y.) *Ise – Prototype of Japanese Architecture*, Tokyo 1961.

TANGE, KENZO. 'Creation in Present-Day Architecture and the Japanese Architectural Tradition', *Shinkenchiku* (now *The Japan Architect*), June 1956, pp.25–33. Reprinted in Boyd, R., *Kenzo Tange*, see below.

TANGE, KENZO. 'Architecture and Urbanism' and other articles in *The Japan Architect*, October 1960, pp.8–16.

TANGE, KENZO. 'Kenzo Tange, Tokyo, Japan' section in *CIAM 1959 in Otterlo*, Stuttgart, 1961 (ed. Oscar Newman), pp.170–85. Includes speeches by Tange.

BOYD, R. *Kenzo Tange*, New York, London 1962. Includes a useful biographical and bibliographical section.

KULTERMANN, U. (ed.). *Kenzo Tange 1946–69: Architecture and Urban Design*, London, New York, 1972.

KULTERMANN, U. 'Kenzo Tange', *Das Kunstwerk*, November–December 1960, pp.39–50.

SMITHSON, P. 'Reflection on Kenzo Tange's Tokyo Bay Plan', *Architectural Design*, October 1964, pp.479–80. The plan itself is featured on pp.501 ff.

HOZUMI, N., & DODD, J. (compilers). 'Junzo Sakakura, Kunio Maekawa and Kenzo Tange', *Architectural Design*, May 1965, pp.222–56. Tange article pp.238–56. A very good summary of their work.

Bruno TAUT (1880–1938)

Born Königsberg, 1880. Died Istanbul, 1938.
Studied in Stuttgart under Theodor Fischer. Returned to Berlin in 1908. He opened office with Franz Hoffmann in 1909. Was later joined in practice by brother Max (*q.v.*). Bruno Taut became the virtual leader of the Berlin *avant-garde* 'Utopian' groups immediately after the first world war. His inventiveness before the war is shown in the two exhibition buildings he designed in association with Franz Hoffmann, the Steel Industries Pavilion, Leipzig Fair, 1913 and the Glass Pavilion for the 1914 Werkbund exhibition, Cologne.
Taut became chairman of the 'Arbeitsrat für Kunst' in 1918 and was responsible for the first pamphlet, an 'Architectural Programme'. During the war years Taut had prepared drawings of his Utopia; these were published in 1919 under the title of *Alpine Architektur*. Edited *Frühlicht* 1920–22.
Moved to Magdeburg in 1921 to become City Architect; moved back to Berlin

Bruno Taut

in 1923 to join with his brother Max Taut and Hoffmann in practice.
In all Taut's writing during his Utopian phase, the spirit of the older
Expressionist poet Paul Scheerbart (1863–1915) obtrudes: see *Die Gläserne
Kette* (Berlin, n.d.).
Visited Russia in 1931. In 1932 he left Germany for good to go to Japan. In
1936 settled in Turkey where he also died.

TAUT, BRUNO. *Architektur-Programme*, Berlin 1918 (1919). First published by the
Arbeitsrat für Kunst as a pamphlet, Christmas 1918. Reproduced in Conrads, U.
(ed.), *Programme und Manifeste zur Architektur des 20. Jahrhunderts*, Berlin 1964.
Programmes and Manifestoes on 20th Century Architecture, London, Cambridge
(Mass.), 1970, pp.41–43.
TAUT, BRUNO. *Alpine Architektur*, Hagen 1919. English version in Sharp, D.
(ed.). *Glass Architecture*, London, New York 1972.
TAUT, BRUNO. *Die Stadtkrone*, Jena 1919. Includes contributions from
Scheerbart, Baron and Behne.
TAUT, BRUNO. *Der Weltbaumeister. Architekturschauspiel für symphonische Musik*,
Hagen 1920.
TAUT, BRUNO. *Organisation des Bauwesens*, Berlin 1920.
TAUT, BRUNO. *Die Auflösung der Städte, oder die Erde eine gute Wohnung*, Hagen 1920.
TAUT, BRUNO. *Frühlicht*, Magdeburg, 1921–2. Four issues. The earlier issues of
the magazine appeared as supplements to *Stadtbaukunst Alter und Neuer Zeit*,
Berlin 1920–1. Taut was co-editor. Taut, B., see, *Frühlicht: Eine Folge für die*

Verwirklichung des neuen Baugedankens, Berlin 1963 (p.b.).

TAUT, BRUNO. *Die neue Wohnung*, Leipzig 1924 (4th edn 1926).

TAUT, BRUNO. *Bauen: Der neue Wohnbau*, Leipzig 1927.

TAUT, BRUNO. *Ein Wohnhaus*, Stuttgart 1927.

TAUT, BRUNO. *Modern Architecture*, London 1929.

TAUT, BRUNO. *Die neue Baukunst in Europa und Amerika*, Berlin 1929.

TAUT, BRUNO. *Grundlinen der Architektur Japans*, Tokyo 1936. English version *Fundamentals of Japanese Architecture*, Tokyo 1937.

TAUT, BRUNO. 'Für die neue Baukunst!' *Das Kunstblatt 1*, 1919, p.20 ff.

TAUT, BRUNO. 'The Nature and Aims of Architecture', *The Studio*, March 1929, pp.170–4.

JUNGHANNS, K. *Bruno Taut 1880–1938*, Berlin (DDR) 1970.

SCHEFFAUER, H.G. 'Bruno Taut: A Visionary in Practice', *Architectural Review*, December 1922, pp.155–9. An important early article on Bruno Taut.

CONRADS, U. 'Bruno Taut e la rivista "Frühlicht"', *Edilizia Moderna*, No.86, 1965, pp.37–45.

MIHARA, T. (ed.) 'Bruno Taut', Special issue *S.D.* (Tokyo), December 1978. With articles by H. Taut, K. Jughauns, etc. in Japanese. Short English summary.

Max TAUT   (1884–1967)

Born Königsberg, 1884. Died Berlin, 1967.

After studying at the *Baugewerbschule* he began his architectural career working in 1905 at Rixdorf, together with Mies van der Rohe. From 1906 to 1911 he worked in Karlsruhe under Hermann Billing. Before the war he worked on his own in Berlin. After the war he carried out work in association with Franz Hoffmann and his brother Bruno Taut. Contributed to *Frühlicht*. The office closed when Hoffmann died in 1950.

Whilst his brother, the leader of the Berlin Circle, was noted for the fantasy of his early designs, Max Taut was the practical architect and although caught up in the revolutionary atmosphere of post-war Berlin he remained a straight-line functionalist all his life. His buildings include schools, apartment and estate housing and offices. From 1945 to 1954 he was appointed Professor at the High School for Fine Arts, Berlin. In 1955 he became Director of the Architecture Section of the Academy of Arts, Berlin.

His early work was published in 1927 with an essay by Adolf Behne. An exhibition of his life's work was shown at the Academy in 1964.

TAUT, MAX. *Bauten und Pläne*, Berlin 1927. Introduction by Adolf Behne.

TAUT, MAX. *Berlin in Aufbau*, Berlin 1946.

TAUT, MAX. *Max Taut*. Exhibition catalogue, Akademie der Künste, Berlin 1964. Introduction by Julius Posener.

Max Taut

Giuseppe Terragni

Giuseppe TERRAGNI (1904–1943)

Born Meda, near Milan, 1904. Died Como, 1943 as a result of wounds on the Russian front.
Studied at the Milan Polytechnic until 1926. During most of his short career he collaborated with Pietro Lingeri and on occasions with Cattaneo. Terragni practised from Como, the centre of modern architecture in Italy in the twenties and thirties. He was one of the founders of the 'Comasco' M.I.A.R. – the movement for rational architecture – and also a member of Group 7. His Casa del Popolo (originally Casa del Fascio) has been referred to as 'one of the canonical works of Italian rationalist architecture' – it still stands today having been rescued for posterity by Terragni's brother who was at one time Mayor of Como. His other work included houses, monuments, a series of important architectural projects (many for competitions) and a number of town planning schemes.
His working career lasted only from graduation in 1926 to call up in 1939.
His position in Italy at the time is summed up in Giulia Veronesi's book, which sets out the political and social problems that beset the architect in Fascist Italy. The special issue of *Architectural Design* (March 1963) contains many of Terragni's projects.

LABÒ, G. *Giuseppe Terragni*, Milan 1947.
VERONESI, G. *Difficoltà politiche dell'architettura in Italia, 1920–1940*, Milan 1953. See chapter on Terragni, pp.80–93.
MANTERO, E.G. *Terragni a la città razionalisma italiana*, Bari 1969.
EISENMAN, P. *Giuseppe Terragni*, Cambridge (Mass.) 1978.

PODESTA, A. 'Omaggio a Terragni', *Emporium*, Vol.CVII, No.640, April 1948.
KOULERMOS, P. (ed.). 'The Work of Terragni and Lingeri', *Architectural Design*, Special No. March 1963. See article 'The Work of Terragni, Lingeri and Italian Rationalism', pp.108–9.
MISC. 'Omaggio a Terragni', special issue of *Arte e architettura*, No.153, July 1968.
EISENMAN, P. 'From Object to Relationship II: Giuseppe Terragni. Casa Giuliano Frigeno, Casa del Fascio.' *Perspecta*, 13/14, 1971.

Heinrich TESSENOW (1876–1950)

Born Rostock, 1876. Died Berlin, 1950.
Served as carpenter's apprentice to his father's building firm before studying at the School of Building, Leipzig, 1896–8, and the Technical High School, Munich, 1899–1901.
Tessenow is best known for his work as an architectural teacher. In 1913 he was made a Professor at the State Art School, Vienna; in 1920, Head of the Department of Architecture, Academy of Fine Arts, Dresden; in 1926, Ordinarius in Building Design, Technical High School, Berlin; in 1936, Head of the Architecture Department of the Academy of Fine Arts, Berlin. He

retired in 1941 but he was invited back to teaching at the Technical University in Berlin after the war.

For his best known planning work, the Garden City at Hellerau, he also acted as chief architect.

His writing was largely about small houses and craft influence on architecture. A number of catalogues issued on him; Hamburg exhibition 1957.

TESSENOW, HEINRICH. *Der Wohnhausbau*, Munich 1909 (1927).
TESSENOW, HEINRICH. *Hausbau und dergleichen*, Berlin 1917 (1929). This volume reissued, Baden-Baden 1953 (4th edn). Illustrated by Tessenow's characteristic line drawings.
TESSENOW, HEINRICH. *Handwerk und Kleinstadt*, Berlin 1919.
TESSENOW, HEINRICH. *Land in der Mitte*, Dresden-Hellerau 1920.

WANGERIN, G. and WEISS, G. *Heinrich Tessenow: ein Baumeister 1876–1950*, Essen 1976. Full bibliography.

POSENER, J. 'Two Masters, Hans Poelzig and Heinrich Tessenow at the Technische Hochschule, Berlin-Charlottenburg', *Lotus International*, No.16, 1977, pp.20–25.

Eduardo TORROJA (1899–1961)

Born Madrid, 1899. Died 1961.

He studied civil engineering in Madrid. He held a number of important positions during his lifetime, being President of the International Federation of Prestressing, the International Association of Shell Structures, Director of the Spanish Technical Institute for Construction and Concrete, etc. Another great master engineer-architect, Torroja has explained his ideas on the philosophy of structures in the book of that name. His work in Agericas (market hall, 1933); Basel (market hall, 1929); Madrid (Hippodrome, 1935) and the churches at Sant Esperit and Pont de Suert (c.1952) are examples that depend as much on aesthetic considerations as mathematical skill

TORROJA, EDUARDO. *Philosophy of Structures*, Los Angeles 1958.
TORROJA, EDUARDO. *The Structures of Eduardo Torroja. An Autobiography of Engineering Accomplishment*, New York 1958.
TORROJA, EDUARDO. *Logik der Form*, Munich 1961.
TORROJA, EDUARDO. 'Influence of the Structural Form in Architecture', *Architectural Association Journal*, February 1961, pp.198–213. Important.

JOEDICKE, J. 'Eduardo Torroja Miret', *Bauen und Wohnen*, No.11, 1960, pp.111/1.

Henry VAN DE VELDE (1863–1957)

Born Antwerp, 1863. Died Zürich, 1957.
Started his career as a painter. In the last decade of the nineteenth century he began designing furniture and interiors. Van de Velde has been described as the 'Father of Modern Architecture' and the 'ardent protagonist' of the *art nouveau*. Bing and Meier-Graefe visited him in Uccle in the mid-nineties. It was the start along the road to international fame, first with Bing's shop in Paris, *L'Art Nouveau*, for which Van de Velde designed four rooms; then with Meier-Graefe's introduction to the Berlin *Pan* circle.
In 1902 he completed the decoration of the Folkwang Museum at Hagen. His commissions in Germany multiplied; he made his name there. His friendship with the Grand Duke of Saxe-Weimar (for whom he acted as artistic adviser) led to his founding the Weimar School of Applied Arts. He designed the school buildings, 1905. The first world war changed Van de Velde's life. He moved to Switzerland in 1917 and later back to Belgium. He held the Chair of Architecture at Ghent from 1926 to 1936 and at the same time founded the school that became the École Nationale Supérieure d'Architecture et des Arts Décoratifs. He moved to Switzerland in 1947.
The legacy that Van de Velde has left is the vast collection of writings on art, architecture, design, education and aesthetics, many of which are now just beginning to be reissued and translated. his autobiography is itself one of the most important commentaries on the architecture and aesthetic thinking of our age.

VAN DE VELDE, HENRY. *Déblaiement d'art*, Brussels 1894.

VAN DE VELDE, HENRY. *La Future*, Brussels 1895.

VAN DE VELDE, HENRY. *Aperçue en vue d'une synthèse d'art*, Brussels 1895.

VAN DE VELDE, HENRY. *Die Renaissance in modernen Kunstgewerbe*, Berlin 1901.

VAN DE VELDE, HENRY. *Kunstgewerbliche Laienpredigten*, Leipzig 1902.

VAN DE VELDE, HENRY. *Der neue Stil*, Weimar 1906.

VAN DE VELDE, HENRY. *Vom neuen Stil*, Leipzig 1907.

VAN DE VELDE, HENRY. *Vernunftsgemässe Schönheit*, Weimar 1909.

VAN DE VELDE, HENRY. *Amo*, Leipzig 1909 (2nd edn 1912).

VAN DE VELDE, HENRY. *Essays*, Leipzig 1910.

VAN DE VELDE, HENRY. *Les formules de la beauté architectonique moderne*, Weimar 1916–17 (2nd edn Brussels 1923).

VAN DE VELDE, HENRY. *Die drei Sünden wider die Schönheit*, Zürich 1918.

VAN DE VELDE, HENRY. *Le théâtre de l'exposition du 'Werkbund' à Cologne 1914, et la scène tripartite*, Antwerp 1925.

VAN DE VELDE, HENRY. *Der neue Stil in Frankreich*, Berlin 1925.

VAN DE VELDE, HENRY. *Le Style Moderne, contribution de France*, Paris 1925. Introduction by Van de Velde.

VAN DE VELDE, HENRY. *Le Nouveau. Son apport à l'architecture et aux industries d'art*, Brussels 1929.

VAN DE VELDE, HENRY. *Deux rapports*, Brussels 1931.

VAN DE VELDE, HENRY. *Les formules d'une esthétique moderne*, Brussels 1932.

VAN DE VELDE, HENRY. *Le Voie Sacrée*, Brussels 1933.

Henry Van de Velde

VAN DE VELDE, HENRY. *Les fondements du style moderne*, Brussels 1933.

VAN DE VELDE, HENRY. *Pages des doctrines*, Brabant 1942.

VAN DE VELDE, HENRY. *Geschichte meines Lebens*, Munich 1962. Edited with introduction by Hans Curjel.

OSTHAUS, K.E. *Van de Velde, Leben und Schaffen des Künstlers*, Hagen 1920.

CASTEELS, M. *Henry van de Velde*, Brussels 1932.

CURJEL, H. *Henry van de Velde, zum neuen Stil*, Munich 1955.

CATALOGUE. *Henry van de Velde 1863–1957*, Rijksmuseum Kröller-Müller, Otterlo, 21 March–24 May 1964. An important source document containing a comprehensive bibliography, including contributions to journals, pp.91–9.

HAMMACHER, A.M. *Le monde de Henri van de Velde*, Antwerp 1967.

MISC. 1971 *Guimard, Horta, Van der Velde*, Paris 1971. Exhibition catalogue, pp.67–121.

SHARP, D. and CULOT, M. (eds) *Henri van de Velde: Theatre Designs, 1904–1914*, London, Brussels, 1974. Bilingual text.

SHAND, P.M. 'Van de Velde to Wagner' *Architectural Review*, October 1934, pp.131–4.

SHAND, P.M. 'Van de Velde, Extracts from Memoirs 1891–1901' *Architectural Review*, September 1952, pp.143–55.

MISC. 'Van de Velde', *Casabella*, No.237, Special issue, March 1960.

MISC. 'Henri van de Velde', a special issue of *La Cité*, Nos.5–6, Brussels 1933.

Robert VENTURI (1925–)   and Denise SCOTT BROWN (1931–)

Robert Venturi was born in 1925 in Philadelphia, where he lives now and works in partnership with wife Denise Scott Brown (born in Northern Rhodesia 1931) and John Rauch. Venturi is probably the most important of the younger generation of architect/theorists. His book *Complexity and Contradiction in Architecture* published as the first of a proposed series of monographs on modern architecture by MOMA, New York in 1968. Hailed by Scully as the 'most important writing on the making of architecture since Le Corbusier's *Vers une Architecture . . .*' which as Scully confesses in the most recent edition was an outrageous proposition but nonetheless entirely accurate. The same cannot be said for the later *Learning from Las Vegas*. Consistently controversial work has kept him and his ideas in the public eye. Studied under Louis Kahn. Taught at Yale and the University of Pennsylvania. Architect in Residence, American Academy, Rome.
See Vance Bibliography No.A-25.

VENTURI, R. *Complexity and Contradiction in Architecture*, New York 1966 (p.b.). Introduction by Vincent Scully. Second edition (also p.b.) New York, London, 1977.
VENTURI, R., BROWN, D.S., IZENOUR, S. *Learning from Las Vegas*, Cambridge (Mass.), London, 1972. Now p.b.
VENTURI, R. and BROWN, D.S. 'A significance for A & P Parking lots or learning from Las Vegas', *Architectural Forum*, March 1968, pp.36–43. Also in *Lotus*, 5, 1968, pp.70–91.
VENTURI, R. 'Focus: The Recent Nine Works by Venturi and Rauch', *Architecture and Urbanism*, January 1978, pp.16–18.

COOK, J.W. and KLOTZ, H. *Conversations with Architects*, New York, London, 1973. See chapter: 'Robert Venturi & Denise Scott Brown', pp.247–66.
DUNSTER, D. (ed.) *Venturi and Rauch: Public Buildings*, London, New York, 1977 (p.b.). Essays by Robert Maxwell and Robert Stern. 'Architectural Monographs' series No.1.

COLQUHOUN, A. 'Robert Venturi', *Architectural Design*, August 1967, p.362.
HUXTABLE, A.L. 'The Case for Chaos', *New York Times*, Section 2, 1 October 1971, p.32. See also her book *Kicked a Building Lately?* New York 1976, pp.43–47.

C.F.A.VOYSEY (1857–1941)

Born Hessle, Yorks, 1857. Died Winchester, 1941.
At the age of 14 he came to London where after a brief spell at Dulwich he was educated by a private tutor. In 1874 he entered the office of J.P.Seddon as a pupil. He joined the staff of George Devey in 1880. It was two years later that he set up his own practice in London. During the early years of his practice he designed wallpapers, textiles and carpets.
After this initial success as an interior decorator he turned, with an increase in commissions, to domestic architectural design. These houses (often quite

C. F. A. Voysey

small) became very well known both in England and on the Continent through their publication in the journals. *The Architect* began publishing his work in 1888. *The British Architect* between 1889 and 1918 published almost every building he designed.

In 1940 he was nominated as the Royal Gold Medallist of the RIBA. His work has always fascinated Pevsner and it is to his articles and standard books on the Modern Movement that one must turn for information. This information is well supplemented by the article by John Brandon-Jones in the *AA Journal*, May 1957.

VOYSEY, C.F.A. *Reason as a Basis of Art*, London 1906 (pamphlet).
VOYSEY, C.F.A. *Individuality*, London 1915 (not illustrated).
VOYSEY, C.F.A. 'An interview with Mr C.F.A.Voysey', *The Studio*, Vol.1, 1893, pp.231–7.

BRANDON-JONES, J., *et al. C.F.A.Voysey: Architect and Designer 1857–1941*, London 1978.
SIMPSON, D. *C.F.A.Voysey: An Architect of Individuality*, London 1979.

MISC. 'C.F.Annesley Voysey: The Man and his Work', *Architect and Building News*, Vol.CXVII, 21 January; 4 February; 11 February (incl. a number of writings); 18 February 1927.
BETJEMAN, J. 'C.F.A.Voysey', *Architectural Review*, October 1931, pp.93–6.

Konrad Wachsmann

SUMMERSON, J. 'Mr Voysey: Veteran Gold Medallist', *The Listener*, 7 March 1940, pp.479–80.

RICHARDS, J.C. 'C.F.A.Voysey' (obituary notice), *Architectural Review*, March 1941, pp.59–60.

PEVSNER, N. 'C.F.A. Voysey 1858–1941', *Architectural Review*, May 1941, pp.112–13.

BANHAM, R. 'The Voysey Inheritance', *Architectural Review*, December 1952, pp.367–71.

BRANDON-JONES, J. 'C.F.A.Voysey', *Architectural Association Journal*, May 1957, pp.238–62.

Konrad WACHSMANN (1901–   )

Born Frankfurt/Oder, 1901. Practice in Europe and the USA.
Studied at the Arts and Crafts Schools in Berlin and Dresden, under Tessenow, and at the Academy, Berlin, under Poelzig, 1922–5. From 1926 to 1929 he worked for a timber prefabrication firm as their chief architect. He wrote an early book on timber technology, *Holzhausbau, Technik und Gestaltung* (1930).
In 1929 he began a practice in Berlin and built among other things a house for Albert Einstein. In 1932 after winning the *Prix de Rome* of the German Academy in Rome he set up practice in that city. He emigrated to France in

137

1938 and went to the USA in 1941. He became an American citizen in 1947. His practice in the USA was shared by Walter Gropius from 1941 to 1948. During this time he invented the first of his 'Mobile Structures' in tubular steel. Appointed Professor at IIT, Chicago in 1950 and researches into the design of junctions, universal elements and modulor structures. His own book *Turning Point of Building* is a significant contribution to a concept of architecture that is founded on engineering principles and a 'true technology'. With Buckminster Fuller he is one of the real visionaries of the age.

WACHSMANN, KONRAD. *Holzhausbau. Technik und Gestaltung*, Berlin 1930.
WACHSMANN, KONRAD. *Wendepunkt im Bauen*, Wiesbaden 1959. English trans. *The Turning Point of Building*, New York 1960.
WACHSMANN, KONRAD. *Aspekte*, Wiesbaden 1961.
WACHSMANN, KONRAD. 'Building in our Time', *Architectural Association Journal*, April 1957, pp.224–33.
WACHSMANN, KONRAD. 'Concetti di architettura', *Casabella*, No.244, pp.38–43.
WACHSMANN, KONRAD. 'Konrad Wachsmann', Special No., *Bauen und Wohnen*, No.10, 1960, pp.351–84.

ARGAN, G.C. 'La sintassi spaziale di Konrad Wachsmann', *Casabella*, No.244, p.37.

Otto WAGNER   (1841–1918)

Born Penzing, near Vienna, 1841. Died Vienna, 1918.
Educated in Vienna. Studied architecture at the Polytechnic Institute, Vienna (1857–9), at the Royal Academy of Building, Berlin (1860–1) and finally completed his studies at the Vienna Academy (1861–3). He was later appointed professor of a special class in architecture at the Academy in 1894. In 1895 his now famous book *Moderne Architektur* was published. Its title was generic.
Otto Wagner was the father of the 'Vienna School' of architects, bringing his deep understanding of Renaissance architecture to bear on the problem of creating a new architecture, relevant to its age and free in its formation. His mission was helped by his brilliant followers and pupils, men such as J.M.Olbrich and Josef Hoffmann who saw (and built) an architecture with roofs like table-tops and an honest structural expression.
Wagner was caught up in the contemporary *Sezession Stil*, but he did not get lost in the frills and fancies of this *fin de siècle* movement – as designs for the Wiener Stadtbahn show. These are reproduced with all the major schemes in Heinz Geretsegger and Max Peintner's beautiful but confused book *Otto Wagner 1841–1918*. A comprehensive bibliography is also included.

WAGNER, OTTO. *Einige Skizzen, Projekte und Ausgeführte Bauwerke*, Vol.1, Vienna 1890; Vol.2, Vienna 1897; Vol.3, Vienna 1906; Vol.4, Vienna 1922.
WAGNER, OTTO. *Moderne Architektur*, Vienna 1895; 2nd edn, Vienna 1899; 3rd edn, 1902. The 4th edn, retitled: *Die Baukunst unserer Zeit*, Vienna 1914. US edition (1902?) exists, but untraceable.

Otto Wagner

WAGNER, OTTO. *Die Grosstadt. Eine Studie über diese*, Vienna 1911.
WAGNER, OTTO. *Die Qualität des Baukünstlers*, Leipzig, Vienna, 1912. An
expansion of the article appearing under the same title in *Der Architekt*, 1912.

LUX, J.A. *Otto Wagner*, Vienna 1914. Lux also wrote a number of articles on
Wagner in contemporary magazines. See list in Geretsegger and Peintner.
TIETZE, H. *Otto Wagner*, Vienna, Berlin, Munich, Leipzig, 1922.
GERETSEGGER, H., & PEINTNER, M. *Otto Wagner 1841–1918*, Salzburg 1964.
Introduction by Richard J. Neutra. Important monograph now in English,
London 1970 (p.b. 1979). Full bibliography.

Philip WEBB (1831–1915)

Born Oxford, 1831. Died Worth, Sussex, 1915.
Educated at Aynho, Northants. After a period as an articled pupil for a firm in
Reading he moved to London to work for G.E.Street. In 1856 he set up his own
practice in London and in 1859 he built the Red House, Bexleyheath for
William Morris. This was followed by many important house commissions
including Rounton Grange, Yorks (1875, now demolished); Smeaton Manor,
Yorks (1877); Clouds House, Wilts (1881–6), etc.
Webb was by no means a 'modern' but he did develop a house style that no
longer resorted to slavish copying of past ideas. His importance lies not only in

Frank Lloyd Wright

the fact that he was actively involved in the English revival of arts and craftsmanship, but also because his work pre-dates Lutyens by nearly thirty years.

His work was well represented in *Country Life* at the time; John Brandon-Jones's lectures (see *AA Journal*) are intensely interesting accounts of his work and provide starting points for examination of his work in depth. For reference see also *The English House*, by Hermann Muthesius.

LETHABY, W.R. *Philip Webb and his Work*, London 1935.

LETHABY, W.R. 'Philip Webb', *The Builder*, 9 January 1925, p.42.
BRANDON-JONES, J. 'The Work of Philip Webb and Norman Shaw', *Architectural Association Journal*, June 1955, pp.9–21; July–August 1955, pp.40–7.

Frank Lloyd WRIGHT (1867–1959)

Born Richland Center, Wisconsin, 1867. Died, Taliesin West, Arizona, 1959. In 1885 entered University of Wisconsin for 2 terms. In 1887 he went to Chicago where he worked for a short time with Silsbee before joining Sullivan's staff in 1888. He stayed until 1893. After this his practice developed. In 1900, as Hitchcock has remarked, 'he came to maturity'. The prairie house period began. People in America were beginning to take notice of his writings, lectures and buildings. During the next decade Europe became aware of the work of this remarkable architect. Berlage and Van 't Hoff saw his work in the United States; Wasmuth, the Berlin publisher, issued a large portfolio of his work and projects. In 1925 the Dutch magazine *Wendingen* featured his work in seven special issues.

In the 1930s the house 'Falling Water' at Bear Run was erected for Kaufmann and the Johnson administrative building completed at Racine. Frank Lloyd Wright's work needs no explanation here; his entire output is recorded with loving care by his disciples and biographers and what they leave out Wright's own writing adequately covers.

The enterprising Prairie School Press, Illinois (publishers of *Prairie School Review*) have consistently re-issued rare – even previously unknown – Wright material over the past decade.

In a recent survey (1979) Wright's 'Falling Water' was shown to be the 'most depicted' building of the twentieth century in books and magazines.

In 1979 Robert L.Sweeney's invaluable annotated bibliography (over 2,000 items) was also produced; Vance bibliography A-19 also useful.

WRIGHT, FRANK LLOYD. *Ausgeführte Bauten und Entwürfe von Frank Lloyd Wright*, Berlin 1910. The first Wasmuth portfolio on Wright in German. (Re-issued, New York 1963 as *Buildings, Plans and Designs*.)
WRIGHT, FRANK LLOYD. *Frank Lloyd Wright. Ausgeführte Bauten*, Berlin 1911. The second smaller edition of the Wasmuth book with an introduction by C.R.Ashbee.
WRIGHT, FRANK LLOYD. *The Life Work of the American Architect, Frank Lloyd Wright*,

Sandport, Holland, 1925 (re-issued, New York 1965). H.T.Wijdeveld's edited version of the special issues of *Wendingen* that appeared on Wright's work in 1925.

WRIGHT, FRANK LLOYD. *Two Lectures on Architecture*, Chicago 1931.

WRIGHT, FRANK LLOYD. *Modern Architecture*, Princeton 1931. The Kahn Lectures for 1930 at Princeton University.

WRIGHT, FRANK LLOYD. *An Autobiography*, New York 1932 (London 1945). Re-issued with additions, London, New York, 1979.

WRIGHT, FRANK LLOYD. *An Organic Architecture: The Architecture of Democracy*, London 1939 (Reprint London, Cambridge (Mass.), 1970).

WRIGHT, FRANK LLOYD. *Frank Lloyd Wright on Architecture, Selected Writings 1894–1940*, New York 1941 (p.b.). Edited by Frederick Gutheim.

WRIGHT, FRANK LLOYD. *The Natural House*, New York 1954 (p.b. 1963).

WRIGHT, FRANK LLOYD. *The Future of Architecture*, New York 1953; London 1955 (p.b. 1963). The above three books were issued in a uniform p.b. series.

WRIGHT, FRANK LLOYD. *A Testament*, New York, London, 1957.

WRIGHT, FRANK LLOYD. *An American Architecture*, New York 1955. Edited by Edgar Kaufmann.

WRIGHT, FRANK LLOYD. *The Living City*, New York 1958.

WRIGHT, FRANK LLOYD. *Drawings for a Living Architecture*, New York 1959. A collection of Wright's drawings; many coloured.

WRIGHT, FRANK LLOYD. *Frank Lloyd Wright: Writings and Buildings*, New York 1960. Selected by E.Kaufmann and Ben Raeburn. Includes list of buildings 1893–1959.

WRIGHT, FRANK LLOYD. 'In the Cause of Architecture', *Architectural Record*, March 1908, pp.155–221.

WRIGHT, FRANK LLOYD. 'In the Cause of Architecture: Second Paper', *Architectural Record*, May 1914, pp.405–13.

FRIES, H.DE, *Frank Lloyd Wright*, Berlin 1926.

HITCHCOCK, H-R. *In the Nature of Materials*, New York 1942. Reprinted many times this book is still the best available on Wright from 1887 to 1941.

ZEVI, B. *Frank Lloyd Wright*, Milan 1947.

KAUFMANN, E. *Taliesin Drawings: Recent Architecture of Frank Lloyd Wright*, New York 1952.

MANSON, G.C. *Frank Lloyd Wright to 1910, The First Golden Age*, New York 1958.

SCULLY, JR., V. *Frank Lloyd Wright*, London, New York, 1960. In the 'Masters of World Architecture' series.

BLAKE, P. *Frank Lloyd Wright. Architecture and Space*, Harmondsworth 1963. The Pelican reprint taken from Blake, P., *The Master Builders*, London, New York, 1960.

BROOKS, H.ALAN. *The Prairie School: Frank Lloyd Wright and his midwest contemporaries*, Toronto 1977. A well researched book showing Wright in a new light.

STOVER, W.A. *The Architecture of Frank Lloyd Wright*, Cambridge (Mass.) 1974. A catalogue of his buildings.

SERGEANT, J. *Frank Lloyd Wright's Usonian Houses; The case for Organic Architecture*, New York 1976.

HOFFMANN, D. *Frank Lloyd Wright's Falling Water: The House and its History*, New York 1978 (p.b.) Introduction by E. Kaufmann.

TWOMBLY, R.C. *Frank Lloyd Wright: His Life and Architecture*, New York 1971 (re-issued, New York, Chichester, 1979). Well documented bibliography included.

TAFEL, E. *Apprentice to Genius*, New York 1979. Edgar Tafel was Wright's assistant in the 1930s responsible for erection of Johnson Wax building and 'Falling Water'.

HANKS, D.A. *The Decorative Designs of Frank Lloyd Wright*, New York, London, 1979 (p.b.).

SWEENEY, R.L. *Frank Lloyd Wright: An annotated bibliography*, Los Angeles 1979.

IZZO, A. and GUBITOSI, C. *Frank Lloyd Wright Designi, 1887–1959*, Florence 1976. English version: *FLW Drawings*, London 1978.

BERLAGE, H.P. 'Frank Lloyd Wright'; *Wendingen*, Special No., No.11, 1921.

MISC. 'Frank Lloyd Wright', *Architectural Forum*, Special Nos., January 1938, January 1948. 'Special Portfolio', June 1959.

PEVSNER, N. 'Frank Lloyd Wright's Peaceful Penetration of Europe', *Architects's Journal*, Vol.89, 1939, pp.731–4. Reprinted in D.Sharp, *The Rationalists*, London 1978.

MISC. 'Frank Lloyd Wright', *Architectural Forum*, Special No., January 1948.

F.R.S. YORKE (1906–1962)

Francis Reginald Stevens Yorke was born in Stratford-upon-Avon, 1906. Died, 1962, at the early age of 55.
Studied at the Birmingham School of Architecture and Town Planning at Birmingham University. A founder member and Secretary of the MARS Group. Private practice with Marcel Breuer (1935–7); Eugene Rosenberg and Cyril Mardall, from 1944 to the time of his death. A prolific writer, his articles appeared mainly in the *Architectural Review* and the *AJ*.
Well known for his own early modern houses, Yorke is probably best-known for his books written in the thirties on domestic architecture. These books provided the spearhead for the Modern Movement in England. They included examples drawn from many countries. All his books have gone through many editions, having been constantly revised and reset.
He was editor of *Specification*, the annual Architectural Press publication, which assumed almost biblical importance for private practitioners in England during his 'reign'.

YORKE, F.R.S. *The Modern House*, London 1934.

YORKE, F.R.S. *The Modern House in England*, London 1937.

YORKE, F.R.S. *The Modern Flat*, London 1937. With Frederick Gibberd as co-author.

YORKE, F.R.S. *A Key to Modern Architecture*, London 1939. With Colin Penn as co-author.

YORKE, F.R.S. *Specification*, London, Yearly. Yorke was editor from 1935 until the time of his death in 1962.

FRY, M. 'F.R.S.Yorke: A memoir', in *Architectural Review*, July 1962.

Subject bibliography

This section of the bibliography is devoted to books that do not fit easily into either the Biographical or National sections. As a subject list it covers various aspects of architectural theory, general publications on modern architecture as well as specialized sources such as the *Bauhausbücher* and Art Nouveau. Further detailed information can be found in the standard and up-to-date catalogues of various libraries that specialize in architecture and town planning. The more important of these sources include:

United Kingdom: *RIBA Library Bulletin* (superseded by the *Annual Review of Architectural Periodicals*), London, published quarterly by the British Architectural Library. This important publication contains a review of periodicals and accession to the Library arranged in UDC order.

United States: *Catalogue of the Avery Memorial Architectural Library*, Columbia University, 12 vols., G.K.Hall, Boston 1958; *Avery Index to Architectural Periodicals*, 12 vols., G.K.Hall, Boston 1963; *Avery Obituary Index of Architects and Artists*, G.K.Hall, Boston 1963.

Germany: *Architekten des XX. Jahrhunderts: Literatur-verzeichnis*, Berlin Zentralbibliothek and Amerika-Gedenkbibliothek 1964. Also of great value is *Wasmuths Lexikon der Baukunst*, 5 vols., Berlin 1929–37.

IDEALS·IN·ART:
PAPERS·THEORETICAL·PRACTICAL·CRITICAL·
BY·WALTER·CRANE·Author·of·"Line·&·Form"·&

LONDON:GEORGE·BELL·&·SONS:1905

Title page from W. Crane *Ideals in Art* (see page 157)

Modern architecture: General studies

BANHAM, R. *Theory and Design in the First Machine Age*, London 1960.

BANHAM, R. *Guide to Modern Architecture*, London 1962; later, *Age of the Masters. A Personal View of Modern Architecture*, London, New York, 1975.

BANHAM, R. *The New Brutalism*, Stuttgart, London, New York, 1966.

BARGELLINI, P., & FREYNIE, E. *Nascita e vita dell'architettura moderna*, Florence 1947.

BEHRENDT, C. *Modern Building*, London 1937 (Reprint 1978).

BENEVOLO, L. *Storia dell'architettura moderna*, 2 vols., Bari 1960. English version, *History of Modern Architecture*, London, New York, 1972.

BLAKE, P. *The Master Builders*, London 1960. (The work of Le Corbusier, Mies van der Rohe and Frank Lloyd Wright.) Each part published separately by Penguin books (p.b.).

BLAKE, P. *Form follows Fiasco: Why Modern Architecture hasn't worked*, New York 1977. Developed from author's *Atlantic Monthly* article attacking the hand that had fed him. Probably the best of the pessimistic writings.

CHAMPIGNEULLE, B., & ACHE, J. *L'architecture du XXe siècle*, Paris 1962.

CHENEY, S. *The New World Architecture*, London 1930 (Reprint 1970).

CONDER, N. *An Introduction to Modern Architecture*, London 1949.

CONRADS, U. *Programmes and Manifestoes on 20th Century Architecture*, London, Cambridge (Mass.), 1970.

CONRADS, U., & SPERLICH, H.G. *Fantastic Architecture*, London 1963 (translated by G. and C. Collins). Original version: *Phantastiche Architektur*, Stuttgart 1960.

CROSBY, T. *Architecture: City Sense*, London, New York, 1965.

DONAT, J. (ed.). *World Architecture One*, London 1964. *World Architecture Two*, London 1965.

DORFLES, G. *L'architettura moderna*, Milan 1954.

GIEDION, S. *Space, Time and Architecture*, Cambridge (Mass.), London, 1941 (4th edn 1963).

GIEDION, S. *A Decade of New Architecture*, Zürich, New York, 1951.

GIFFORD, D. *The Literature of Architecture: The Evolution of Architectural Theory and Practice in 19th Century America*, New York 1966.

HAMLIN, T. *Architecture, an Art for all Men*, New York 1947.

HAMLIN, T. *Forms and Functions of Twentieth Century Architecture*, 4 vols, New York 1952.

HITCHCOCK, H-R. *Modern Architecture: Romanticism and Reintegration*, New York 1929.

HITCHCOCK, H-R. *Architecture: Nineteenth and Twentieth Centuries*, Harmondsworth 1958 (2nd edn, 1963, also New York).

HITCHCOCK, H-R., & JOHNSON, P. *The International Style: Architecture since 1922*, New York 1932 (now p.b.).

HOWARTH, T. *Charles Rennie Mackintosh and the Modern Movement*, London 1952.

JENCKS, C. *Modern Movements in Architecture*, London, New York, 1973 (p.b.).

JENCKS, C. & BAIRD, G. *Meaning in Architecture*, London, New York, 1969.

JOEDICKE, J. *A History of Modern Architecture*, New York, London, 1959.

JOEDICKE, J. *Architecture since 1946*, London, New York, 1972.

JOHANSSON, G. *Funktionalismen I Verkligheten*, Stockholm 1931.

JONES, C. *Architecture Today and Tomorrow*, New York, London, 1961.

KAUFMANN, E. *Von Ledoux bis Le Corbusier*, Leipzig 1933.

KULTERMANN, U. *Architecture of Today: A Survey of New Buildings throughout the World*, London 1958.

LEITNER, B. *Architecture of Ludwig Wittgenstein*, New York, London, 1974. An interesting view of Wittgenstein House and contemporary Vienna.

LINDNER, W., & STEINMETZ, G. *Die Ingenieurbauten und ihre Entwicklung*, Leipzig 1923.

MARCHI, V. *Architettura Futurista*, Foligno 1924. Written 1919.

McGRATH, R. *Twentieth Century Houses*, London 1934.

MEYER, P. *Modern Architektur u. Tradition*, Zürich 1928.

NEWMAN, O. *CIAM'59 in Otterlo, themes, buildings, projects*, London 1961.

PEHNT, W. (ed.). *Encyclopaedia of Modern Architecture*, London 1963.

PEHNT, W. *Expressionist Architecture*, London, New York, 1973.

PETER, J. (ed.). *Masters of Modern Architecture*, London 1958.

PEVSNER, N. *Pioneers of Modern Design*, Harmondsworth 1960 (p.b.). Original edition: *Pioneers of the Modern Movement from William Morris to Walter Gropius*, London 1936.

PICA, A. *Nuova Architettura nel mondo*, Milan 1936.

PLATZ, G. *Die Baukunst der neuesten Zeit*, Berlin 1927 (1930).

POSENER, J. *Anfänge des Funktionalismus: Von Arts and Crafts zum Deutschen Werkbund*, Berlin 1964 (p.b.).

POSENER, J. *From Schinkel to the Bauhaus*, London, New York, 1971. Introduction by D. Sharp. AA Paper No. 5.

RIBA (Catalogue) *International Architecture 1924–34* (Centenary Exhibition), London 1934.

RICHARDS, J.M. *An Introduction to Modern Architecture*, Harmondsworth 1940 (p.b.). See latest edition.

ROTH. A. *The New Architecture*, Zürich 1948. (Buildings of the 1930s.)

ROTH, A. *A Decade of Contemporary Architecture*, Zürich 1951. (Buildings of the period 1937–47.)

SARTORIS, A. *Gli elementi dell'architettura funzionale*, Milan 1932 (2nd edn 1935).

SARTORIS, A. *Introduzione all'architettura moderna*, Milan 1949.

SCULLY, JR. V. *Modern Architecture*, New York 1974 (p.b.).

SFAELLOS, C. *Le fonctionalisme dans l'architecture contemporaine*, Paris 1952.

SHARP, D. *Modern Architecture and Expressionism*, London 1966.

SHARP, DENNIS. *A Visual History of Twentieth Century Architecture*, London, New York, 1972 (1979, p.b.). Covering the period 1900–1970.

SIEGEL, C. *Structure and Form in Modern Architecture*, New York 1975 (reprint of 1962 edn).

SMITHSON, A. & P. *Without Rhetoric. An Architectural Aesthetic 1955–1972*, London, New York, 1974.

TAFURI, M. and F. DAL CO. *Architettura Contemporanea*, 2 vols, Milan 1976 (p.b.). English version: *Modern Architecture*, New York, London, 1980.

TAUT, B. *Modern Architecture*, London 1929. German edition: *Die neue Baukunst in Europa und Amerika*, Stuttgart 1929.

WHITTICK, A. *European Architecture in the Twentieth Century*, 2 vols., London 1950–3. (Vol.1 to 1924; London 1950. Vol.2 to 1933; London 1953). Reissued as one volume (1974).

YORKE, F.R.S., & PENN, C. *A Key to Modern Architecture*, London 1939.

VRIEND, J.J. *Nieuwe Architectuur*, Bussum 1957.

ZEVI, B. *Towards an Organic Architecture*, London and Hollywood, Florida, 1950.

ZEVI, B. *Storia dell'architettura moderna*, Turin 1950 (3rd edn 1955).

148

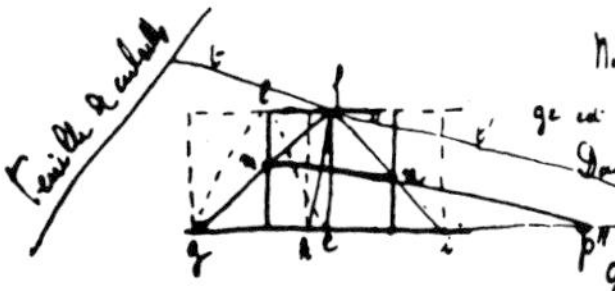

Nous prenons comme unité le côté du carré initial
ge est égal à el, c'est-à-dire à $\sqrt{1^2+\frac{1}{2}^2} = \frac{\sqrt5}{2}$
Dans le triangle rectangle gfi où fe est hauteur, on a
$ge \times ei = ef^2$ c'est-à-dire $\frac{\sqrt5}{2} \times ei = 1$ d'où $ei = \frac{2}{\sqrt5}$
$gi = ge + ei = \frac{\sqrt5}{2} + \frac{2}{\sqrt5} = \frac{5+4}{2\sqrt5} = \frac{9}{2\sqrt5} = \frac{9\sqrt5}{10}$ # 2,0125

Donc k étant le milieu de gi $gk = ki = 1{,}0062$

Les rectangles construits sur gk et ki et de hauteur 1 ne sont donc qu'approximativement des carrés car leur base = 1,0062

Le cercle passant par les 3 points g f i donc contenant l'angle droit en f comme angle inscrit a pour centre k

$ke = ge - gk = \frac{\sqrt5}{2} - \frac{9\sqrt5}{20} = \frac{\sqrt5}{20}$

$\frac{ke}{ef} = \frac{\frac{\sqrt5}{20}}{1} = \frac{\sqrt5}{20}$ $kf = kg = ki = \frac{9\sqrt5}{20}$ = rayon du cercle

La tangente en f à ce cercle est perpendiculaire à kf
donc fait avec l'horizontale le même angle que kf fait avec fe
Cette tangente coupe l'horizontale de base en p' tel que les deux triangles fke et fep' sont semblables (Sa pente est $-\frac{\sqrt5}{20}$)

$ep' = ef \times \frac{ef}{ke} = 1 \times \frac{1}{\frac{\sqrt5}{20}} = \frac{20}{\sqrt5} = \frac{20\sqrt5}{5} = 4\sqrt5$ # 8,94 = 10 ei

La droite mn est déterminée par les points m et n.

La droite gf: $\frac{x}{-\frac{\sqrt5}{2}} + \frac{y}{1} = 1$ ou $-\frac{2x}{\sqrt5} + y = 1$

Le point m a pour abscisse $-\frac{1}{2}$ et pour ordonnée $\frac{1}{\sqrt5} + y = 1$ $y = 1 - \frac{1}{\sqrt5} = \frac{\sqrt5-1}{\sqrt5}$

La droite fi perpendiculaire à fg a pour équation $y = -\frac{\sqrt5}{2}x + 1$

Le point n a pour abscisse $\frac{1}{2}$ et pour ordonnée $y = -\frac{\sqrt5}{2} \cdot \frac{1}{2} + 1 = \frac{4-\sqrt5}{4}$

$m\left(-\frac{1}{2}, \frac{\sqrt5-1}{\sqrt5}\right)$ $n\left(\frac{1}{2}, \frac{4-\sqrt5}{4}\right)$

mn a pour pente $\frac{\frac{4-\sqrt5}{4} - \frac{\sqrt5-1}{\sqrt5}}{1} = \frac{4\sqrt5 - 5 - 4\sqrt5 + 4}{4\sqrt5} = -\frac{1}{4\sqrt5} = -\frac{\sqrt5}{20}$

Donc mn est parallèle à la tangente en f.
et est donc perpendiculaire à kf.

mn coupe ef au point d'ordonnée: $\frac{\frac{\sqrt5-1}{\sqrt5} + \frac{4-\sqrt5}{4}}{2} = \frac{4\sqrt5 - 4 + 4\sqrt5 - 5}{8\sqrt5} = \frac{8\sqrt5-9}{8\sqrt5}$

La droite mn a pour équation $y = -\frac{\sqrt5}{20}x + \frac{8\sqrt5-9}{8\sqrt5}$

elle coupe l'horizontale de base au point p'': $x = \frac{8\sqrt5-9}{8\sqrt5} \times \frac{20}{\sqrt5} = \frac{8\sqrt5-9}{2}$

4,44

Donc mn et la tangente en f sont des droites parallèles coupant l'horizontale de base la 1ère au point p'': $ep'' = 4{,}44$
la 2e au point p': $ep' = 8{,}94$.

Si l'on mène par i la parallèle à gf elle rencontre fp' en f_1
et si de f_1 on mène la parallèle $f_1 i_1$ à fi on obtient un nouveau triangle $i f_1 i_1$ semblable à gfi dans le rapport $\frac{pi}{pg} = \frac{8{,}0496}{10{,}062}$ # $\frac{4}{5} = 0{,}8$

Calculations for Le Corbusier's *Le modulor* (see page 71)

SEINEN SCHÜLERN EIN FÜHRER AUF
❏   DIESEM KUNSTGEBIETE VON   ❏

OTTO WAGNER,

ARCHITEKT, (O. M.), K. K. OBERBAURAT,
PROFESSOR AN DER K. K. AKADEMIE DER
BILDENDEN KÜNSTE, EHREN- UND KOR-
RESPONDIERENDES MITGLIED DES KÖN.
INSTITUTES BRITISCHER ARCHITEKTEN
IN LONDON, DER SOCIÉTÉ CENTRALE DES
ARCHITECTES IN PARIS, DER KAISERL.
GESELLSCHAFT DER ARCHITEKTEN IN
PETERSBURG, DER SOCIÉTÉ CENTRALE
D'ARCHITECTURE IN BRÜSSEL UND DER
GESELLSCHAFT ZUR BEFÖRDERUNG DER
❏   BAUKUNST IN AMSTERDAM ETC.   ❏

III. AUFLAGE.

WIEN 1902
VERLAG VON ANTON SCHROLL & Co.

Title page from the third edition of Otto Wagner's *Moderne Architektur* (see page 138)

Architectural Theory

Books

ALEXANDER, C. *Notes on the Synthesis of Form*, Cambridge (Mass.) 1964.

ALLSOPP, B. *Art and the Nature of Architecture*, London 1952.

BALJEU, J. *Attempt at a Theory of Synthesist Plastic Expression*, London 1963, New York 1964.

BANHAM, R. *Theory and Design in the First Machine Age*, London 1960 (1970 p.b.). The important post-war summary of Modern Movement events.

BØE, A. *From Gothic Revival to Functional Form*, Oslo and Oxford, 1957.

BONTA, J. P. *Architecture and its interpretation*, London, New York, 1979.

BORISSAVLIEVITCH, M. *Les Théories de l'architecture*, Paris 1926.

BORISSAVLIEVITCH, M. *The Golden Number*, London 1958.

BOURGEOIS, V. *L'architecte et son espace*, Brussels 1955.

BROADBENT, G. *Design in Architecture*, London 1973.

BROADBENT, G. and WARD, A. *Design methods in Architecture*, London 1969.

CHOISY, A. *Histoire de l'architecture*, 2 vols, Paris 1899.

COLLINS, P. *Changing Ideals in Modern Architecture*, London 1965.

DANBY, M. *Grammar of Architectural Design. With Special Reference to the Tropics*, London 1963.

DELEVOY, R.L. *et al, Rational Architecture*, Brussels 1978. Essays by Vidler, Krier, Scolari, etc.

DIJKEMA, P. *Innen und Aussen: Die Frage nach der Integration der Künste und der Weg der Architektur*, Hilversum 1960.

DOXIADIS, C. *Architecture in Transition*, London 1963. Now with little more than peripheral relevance.

FERRAN, A. *Philosophie de la composition architecturale*, Paris 1955.

GHYKA, M. *A Practical Handbook of Geometrical Composition and Design*, London 1956.

GROOT, J.H. DE, *Voormharmonie*, Amsterdam 1912.

GUADET, J. *Éléments et théories de l'architecture*, 4 vols, Paris, n.d. (1902–4).

GUTTON, A. *Conversations sur l'architecture*, 6 vols, Paris, n.d.

HUDNUT, J. *Architecture and the Spirit of Man*, Cambridge (Mass.), 1949.

JONES, J.C. & THORNLEY, D.G. (eds). *Conference on Design Methods*, Oxford 1963. A collection of papers presented at the conference on Systematic and Intuitive Methods in Engineering, Industrial Design, Architecture and Communications, held in London 1962.

LETHABY, W.R. *Architecture, Mysticism and Myth*, London 1892. Later reissued, see section on Lethaby.

LETHABY, W.R. *Architecture*, London 1922. And later revisions.

LEWIS, W. *The Caliph's Design. Architects! Where is Your Vortex?*, London 1919.

LICKLIDER, H. *Architectural Scale*, London 1965.

LURÇAT, A. *Formes, composition et lois d'harmonie*, 5 vols, Paris, n.d. (1953–7).

MOHOLY-NAGY, L. *The New Vision from Material to Architecture*, New York, n.d. (2nd edn 1938). An English translation by D.M.Hoffmann of the original Bauhaus Book No.14, 1930. 3rd edn: *The New Vision*, New York 1946 (6th printing 1964), includes autobiographical essay by Moholy-Nagy entitled 'Abstract of an Artist'.

MOHOLY-NAGY, L. *Vision in Motion*, Chicago 1947. A posthumously published extension of the previous book.

MÜLLER-WULCKOW, W. *Aufbau-Architektur!*, Berlin 1919 (p.b.). In the series 'Tribüne der Kunst und Zeit', No.4.

NORBERG-SCHULZ, C. *Intentions in Architecture*, London 1963.

PFLEIDERER, W. (ed.). *Die Form ohne Ornament*, Stuttgart 1925. In the series 'Bücher der Form', No.1.

PHILLIPPS, L.M. *The Works of Man*, London 1911. Classic work on aesthetics.

PHILLIPPS, L.M. *Form and Colour*, London 1915.

RASMUSSEN, S.E. *Experiencing Architecture*, London 1959 (1964).

REILLY, C.H. *The Theory and Practice of Architecture*, London 1932.

SCOTT, G. *The Architecture of Humanism*, London 1914 (2nd edn 1924) (Also p.b.).

SLEBOS, J.C. *Fundamentals of Aesthetics and Style*, Amsterdam 1939.

TAFURI, M. *Teorie e storia dell'architettura*, Rome, Bari, 1968 (1976, p.b.). English version: *Theories and History of Architecture*, London, New York, 1980.

VENTURI, R. *Complexity and Contradiction in Architecture*, New York, 1966 (Large p.b. 1979).

VOYSEY, C.F.A. *Individuality*, London 1915.

WITTKOWER, R. *Architectural Principles in the Age of Humanism*, London 1959.

ZEVI, B. *Poetica dell'architettura Neoplastica*, Milan 1953 (p.b.).

ZEVI, B. *Architecture as Space*, New York 1957 (Rev. edn. p.b. 1974).

ZEVI, B. *Architettura in Nuce*, Florence 1972.

ZEVI, B. *The Modern Language of Architecture*, Washington 1978.

ZURKO, E.R. DE, *Origins of Functionalist Theory*, New York 1957.

Magazine articles

ALEXANDER, C. 'Perception and Modular Co-ordination', *RIBA Journal*, October 1959, pp.425–9.

BANHAM, R. 'The Machine Aesthetic', *Architectural Review*, April 1955, pp.255–8.

BANHAM, R. 'Ornament and Crime. The Decisive Contribution of Adolf Loos', *Architectural Review*, February 1957, pp.85–8.

BANHAM, R. 'Mondrian and the Philosophy of Modern Design', *Architectural Review*, October 1957, pp.227–9.

BANHAM, R. 'Futurist Manifesto', *Architectural Review*, August–September 1959, pp.77–80.

BANHAM, R. 'Vitruvius Go Home!', *Architectural Association Journal*, March 1960, pp.146–56.

BANHAM, R. 'The History of the Immediate Future', *RIBA Journal*, May 1961, pp.252–60, 269.

BANHAM, R. 'History of the Immediate Future', *The Listener*, 23 February 1961, pp.347–9. The broadcast version of the talk given to the RIBA.

BANHAM, R. (ed.). A series of articles on the future of architecture in the *Architectural Review:*

1. 'Stocktaking', February 1960, pp.93–100.
2. 'The Science Side', March 1960, pp.183–90.
3. 'The Future of Universal Man', April 1960, pp.253–60.
4. 'History under Revision', May 1960, pp.325–32.
5. 'Propositions', June 1960, pp.381–8.

BETTINI, S. 'Semantic Criticism and the Historical Continuity of European Architecture', *Zodiac 2*, 1958, pp.7–25.

Within the image: GROTESKE GEGEND MIT BEARBEITETEN BERGSPITZEN

'Grotesque region' from Bruno Taut's *Alpine Architektur* (see page 128)

BONFANTI, E. 'Emblematica della tecnica', *Edilizia Moderna*, No.86, 1965, pp.14–29.

COLQUHOUN, A. 'The Modern Movement in Architecture', *The British Journal of Aesthetics*, January 1962, pp.59–65.

DOXIADIS, C. 'Architecture in Evolution', *RIBA Journal*, September 1960, pp.429–38. Part 2, October 1960, pp.469–79.

GIEDION, S. 'History and the Architect', *Zodiac 1*, 1957, pp.57–61.

GOLDFINGER, E. 'The Sensation of Space', *Architectural Review*, November 1941, pp.129–31.

LINDHAL, G. 'Von der Zukunftskathedrale bis zur Wohnmaschine', *Idea and Form*, Stockholm 1957, pp.226–82.

MUMFORD, L. 'Monumentalism, Symbolism and Style', *Architectural Review*, April 1949, pp.173–80.

PEVSNER, N. 'Modern Architecture and the Historian or the Return to Historicism', *RIBA Journal*, April 1961, pp.230–40.

PEVSNER, N. 'Return of Historicism in Architecture', *The Listener*, 16 February 1961, pp.299–301. Broadcast version of RIBA talk.

READ, H. 'The Aesthetics of Architecture', *Architectural Association Journal*, May 1960, pp.202–9.

ROWE, C. 'Mannerism and Modern Architecture', *Architectural Review*, May 1950, pp.289–99.

RUDOLPH, P. 'The Six Determinants of Architectural Form', *Architectural Design*, May 1957, pp.149–50. Originally in *Architectural Record*, Oct. 1956.

SMITH, D. 'Towards a Theory', *Architectural Review*, February 1965, pp.101–4.

SMITHSON, A. & P. (eds). 'Team 10 Primer', *Architectural Design*, Special No. December 1962. Issued as separate publication, London 1965.

SMITHSON, A. & P. (eds). 'The Heroic Period of Modern Architecture', *Architectural Design*, Special No., December 1965.

STERN, R. 'PSFS: Beaux Arts Theory and Rational Expressionism', *Journal of the Society of Architectural Historians (USA)*, May 1962, pp.84–95.

SUMMERSON, J. 'The Case for a Theory of Modern Architecture', *RIBA Journal*, June 1957, pp.307–13.

ZUCKER, P. 'The Paradox of Architectural Theories at the Beginning of the "Modern Movement"', *Journal of the Society of Architectural Historians (USA)*, October 1951, pp.8–14.

COLLECTION DE " L'ESPRIT NOUVEAU "

LE CORBUSIER

CROISADE

ou

le Crépuscule des Académies

LES ÉDITIONS G. CRÈS ET Cie
11, RUE DE SÈVRES, 11
PARIS

Cover of Le Corbusier's *Croisade* (see page 70)

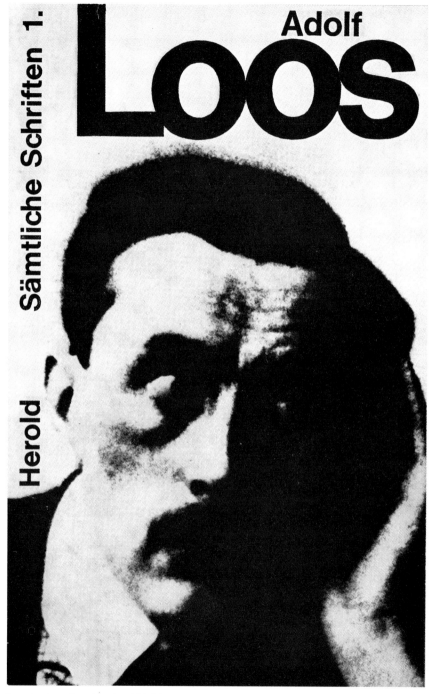

Cover for the collected works of Adolf Loos, vol.1 (see page 77)

Aesthetics, Architecture and Society

ABERCROMBIE, J.M.L. *The Anatomy of Judgement*, London 1960.

ANDERSON, D.M. *Elements of Design*, New York 1961.

ARNHEIM, R. *Art and Visual Perception*, Berkeley 1954, London 1956 (Also p.b.).

BIEDERMAN, C. *Art as the Evolution of Visual Knowledge*, Minnesota 1948.

BOSANQUET, B. *A History of Aesthetic*, London 1892.

CARRITT, E.F. *The Theory of Beauty*, London 1914 (1962, p.b.).

COLLINGWOOD, R.G. *The Principles of Art*, Oxford 1938.

CRANE, W. *Ideals in Art*, London 1905.

DEWEY, J. *Art as Experience*, London 1934.

DORNER, A. *Way Beyond Art*, in the series: Problems of Contemporary Art, New York 1946.

FRY, R. *Vision and Design*, London 1937. Reprinted 1962 (p.b.).

GILBERT, K., & KUHN, H. *A History of Esthetics*, London 1956.

GOMBRICH, E.H. *Art and Illusion*, London 1960 (1962), New York 1961.

GREEN, T.M. *The Arts and the Art of Criticism*, Princeton 1940.

GREENHOUGH, H. *Form and Function*, New York 1947.

HULME, T.E. *Speculations*, London 1936.

KEPES, G. *The New Landscape*, Chicago 1956.

KEPES, G. (ed.). *Education of Vision*, New York, London, 1965.

KEPES, G. (ed.). *The Nature and Art of Motion*, New York, London, 1965.

KEPES, G. (ed.). *Structure in Art and in Science*, New York, London, 1965.

LANGER, S. *Philosophy in a New Key*, Cambridge (Mass.) 1942 (2nd edn 1951).

LANGER, S. *Feeling and Form*, London, New York, 1953.

LANGER, S. *Problems of Art*, New York 1957 (p.b.).

MORRIS, C.W. *Foundations of the Theory of Signs*, Chicago 1938.

MUMFORD, L. *Technics and Civilisation*, London 1934 (5th edn, 1955), New York 1963.

RADER, M. *A Modern Book of Aesthetics*, New York 1952.

READ, H. *Art and Industry*, London 1934; Bloomington, Indiana, 1961 (p.b.).

READ, H. *Art and Society*, London 1937.

READ, H. *Education through Art*, London 1943, New York 1958 (p.b. 1961).

READ, H. *The Psychopathology of Reaction in the Arts*, London, n.d. (Pamphlet published by the Institute of Contemporary Arts.)

READ, H. *The Forms of Things Unknown*, London 1960.

ROOKMAAKER, H.R. *Synthetist Art Theories*, Amsterdam 1959.

SCRUTTON, R. *The Aesthetics of Architecture*, London 1979 (Also p.b.). See also same author, *Art and Imagination*, London 1974.

SEDLMAYR, H. *Art in Crisis*, London 1957.

THOMPSON, W.D'ARCY, *On Growth and Form*, 2 vols, Cambridge 1917 (1 vol. 1962).

VENTURI, L. *History of Art Criticism*, New York 1936.

WHITTICK, A. *Symbols, Signs and their Meaning*, London 1960.

WÖLFFLIN, H. *Principles of Art History*, London 1932. (English trans. by M.D.Hottinger.)

Art nouveau-Jugendstil source books

BOTT, G. (ed.). *Jugendstil, Art Nouveau, Modern Style, Nieuwe Kunst, Kunsthandwerk um 1900*, Darmstadt 1965. An illustrated catalogue of the Hessisches Landesmuseum, No.1.

BRUNHAMMER, Y. *et al. Art Nouveau Belgium France*, Houston 1976. Exhibition catalogue (p.b.).

CASSOU, J., LANQUI, E., & PEVSNER, N. *The Sources of Modern Art*, New York, London 1962.

CREMONA, I. *Il tempo dell'Art Nouveau*, Florence 1964.

GRADY, J. 'A Bibliography of the Art Nouveau', *Journal of the Society of Architectural Historians* (USA), XIV, No.2, 1955, pp.18–27.

LENNING, H.F. *The Art Nouveau*, The Hague 1951.

MADSEN, S.T. *Sources of Art Nouveau*, Oslo 1956, New York 1957 (p.b.). New paperback edn. New York, 1976.

PEVSNER, N. 'Beautiful and, if need be, useful', *Architectural Review*, November 1957, pp.297–9. (A review of Madsen's *Sources of Art Nouveau*.)

READE, B. *Art Nouveau and Alphonse Mucha*, London 1963 (p.b.).

RUSSELL, F. (ed.). *Art Nouveau Architecture*, London 1979.

SCHMALENBACH, F. *Jugendstil*, Würzburg 1935.

SCHMUTZLER, R. 'The English Origins of Art Nouveau', *Architectural Review*, February 1955, pp.108–16.

SCHMUTZLER, R. 'Blake and the Art Nouveau', *Architectural Review*, August 1955, pp.90–2.

SCHMUTZLER, R. *Art Nouveau-Jugendstil*, Stuttgart 1963, London 1964. The classic work.

SELING, H. *Jugendstil, der Weg ins 20. Jahrhundert*, Heidelberg 1959.

SELZ, P., & CONSTANTINE, M. (eds). *Art Nouveau: Art and Design at the Turn of the Century*, New York 1959. (Revised, p.b. 1975).

BORSI, F. *Brussels 1900*, Brussels 1974.

BORSI, F. & GODOLI, E. *Paris 1900*, London, New York, 1978.

The Bauhaus

The following is a selection of the main items connected with the Weimar and Dessau years of the Bauhaus. See also biographical section on Walter Gropius.

Bauhausbücher
Originally published by Albert Langen Verlag, Munich, 1925–30. Re-issued by Florian Kupferberg Verlag, Mainz, 1965–
1. GROPIUS, W. *Internationale Architektur*, 1925 (2nd edn 1927).
2. KLEE, P. *Pädagogisches Skizzenbuch*, 1925 (2nd edn 1928). English translation *Pedagogical Sketchbook*, London n.d., New York 1944 (p.b.).
3. MEYER, A. (ed.). *Ein Versuchshaus des Bauhauses in Weimar*, 1925.
4. SCHLEMMER, O. *Die Bühne im Bauhaus*, 1925. English translation *The Theater of the Bauhaus*, Middletown, Conn., 1963.
5. MONDRIAN, P. *Neue Gestaltung*, 1925.
6. VAN DOESBURG, T. *Grundbegriffe der neuen gestaltenden Kunst*, 1925. English version *Principles of Neo-Plastic Art*, London, Greenwich (Conn.), 1969.
7. GROPIUS, W. (ed.). *Neue Arbeiten der Bauhauswerkstätten*, 1925.
8. MOHOLY-NAGY, L. *Malerei, Photographie, Film*, 1925. (2nd edn *Malerei, Fotographie, Film*, 1927). English version *Painting, Photography, Film*, London, Cambridge (Mass.), 1969. (Reprinted Cambridge (Mass.) 1973 p.b.).
9. KANDINSKY, W. *Punkt und Linie zu Fläche, Beitrag zur Analyse der malerischen Elemente*, 1926 (2nd edn 1928). English trans. *Point and Line to Plane*, New York 1947.
10. OUD, J.J.P. *Holländische Architektur*, 1926 (2nd edn 1929).
11. MALEVICH, K. *Die gegenstandslose Welt*, 1927. English translation: *The Non-Objective World*, Chicago 1959.
12. GROPIUS, W. *Bauhausbauten, Dessau*, 1930.
13. GLEIZES, A. *Kubismus*, 1928. Trilingual edn *And Cubism*, Basel 1962.
14. MOHOLY-NAGY, L. *Von Material zu Architektur*, 1929. English translation: *The New Vision from Material to Architecture*, New York 1930 (6th printing 1964).
N.B. Schlemmer's *Bühnenelemente* announced in original prospectus was never issued; later published as *Der Mensch*, Mainz 1969 (English version *Man*, London, Cambridge (Mass.), 1971).

Key books on the Bauhaus

BAYER, H. *Herbert Bayer*, New York, London, 1967.
BAYER, H., & GROPIUS, W. and I. *Bauhaus 1919–1928*, New York 1938; London 1939 (2nd printing 1952). German version, Stuttgart 1955. Re-issued Boston 1956 (p.b. 1975).
FRANCISCONO, M. *Walter Gropius and the Creation of the Bauhaus in Weimar*, Urbana 1971.
GROPIUS, W. *The New Architecture and the Bauhaus*, London 1935 (also p.b.). P.Morton Shand's translation of Gropius's German text which was not published in Germany until 1965.
HARMON, R.H. *The Bauhaus: Art and architecture in harmony*, Monficello 1980. A selected Vance bibliography.

Cover for *Bauhausbücher* 1 (see page 159)

HIRSCHFELD-MACK, L. *The Bauhaus, an Introductory Survey*, Victoria (Aus.) and London 1963 (54 pp. p.b.).

ITTEN, J. *Design and Form. The Basic Course at the Bauhaus*, London, New York, 1964. A description of the introductory course at the Bauhaus by its originator.

NEUMANN, E. *Bauhaus and Bauhaus People*, New York 1970.

SCHEIDIG, W. *Weimar Crafts of the Bauhaus*, London 1967.

WINGLER, H.M. *Das Bauhaus 1919–1937: Weimar, Dessau, Berlin*, Bramsche 1962. An exhaustive history of the Bauhaus written by Dr Wingler, Director of the Bauhaus Archiv, Berlin. An essential reference book. US edition (1969). Now in paperback, Cambridge (Mass.) 1979.

Wassily KANDINSKY (1866–1944)

Born Moscow, 1866. Died Neuilly-sur-Seine, Paris, 1944.
It may appear strange to some people that painters are included in a bibliography on modern architecture. I have included Kandinsky and Paul Klee because of their connexions with the Bauhaus and also because of the generic importance of their books on modern art.
After studying law and economics at Moscow, Kandinsky took up painting at the age of 30. In 1896 he went to Munich to study at the Academy. He later became a member of the Berliner Sezession. In 1911 the 'Blaue Reiter' group was founded at an exhibition in Munich and close links were established with Moscow for a few years. In 1914 Kandinsky returned to Russia. In 1921 Walter Gropius offered him the post of Professor at the Bauhaus. He left the USSR for Weimar in 1922. After 1933 he settled in Paris.
Kandinsky's book *On the Spiritual in Art* (to use its American title) first appeared in Munich in 1912, although it was written as early as 1910. It appeared in American, English and French editions after his death.

KANDINSKY, WASSILY. *Über das Geistige in der Kunst*, Munich 1912. English trans: *The Art of Spiritual Harmony*, London 1914; *On the Spiritual in Art*, New York 1946.

KANDINSKY, WASSILY. *Punkt und Linie zu Fläche*, Bauhaus Book, No.9, Munich 1926. English translation *Point, Line and Plane*, New York 1947.

GROHMANN, W. *Kandinsky*, Cologne, London 1958.

Paul KLEE (1879–1940)

Born Munchen-Buchsee, nr Bern, Switzerland, 1879. Died Muralto, nr Locarno, 1940.
From 1898 to 1901 he studied painting at Munich. After a few years' travelling he returned to live in Munich in 1906. Exhibited with the 'Blaue Reiter' group in 1911. Friendship developed with Kandinsky. Met Robert Delaunay in Paris, 1912. He joined the Bauhaus staff in 1920. In the mid-twenties he made up the fourth member of the 'Blue Four' group – the others being Kandinsky, Feininger and Jawlensky. In 1930 appointed to Düsseldorf Academy but was dismissed in 1933. He then returned to Bern.

The famous *Pedagogical Sketchbook* (originally published as Bauhaus Book No.2, Munich, 1925) has been excellently transferred into English by Sibyl Moholy-Nagy (London and New York). The 1924 Jena lecture is published under the title 'On Modern Art'. The books on Klee are almost as magical as his paintings and drawings and the publishers and graphic designers who produced *The Thinking Eye* are to be complimented on producing one of the finest books of the twentieth century.

KLEE, PAUL. *Pädagogisches Skizzenbuch*, Bauhaus Book No.2, Munich 1925. English translation: *Pedagogical Sketchbook*, New York 1944; London, n.d. Introd. and trans. by Sibyl Moholy-Nagy. Original layout is retained.
KLEE, PAUL. *Über die Moderne Kunst*, Bern 1945. English translation: *Paul Klee on Modern Art*, London 1948. Translated by Paul Findlay. Introd. by Herbert Read.
KLEE, PAUL. *Tagebücher 1898–1918*, Cologne 1956. English translation: *Paul Klee's Diaries 1898–1918*, London 1965.

GROHMANN, W. *Paul Klee*, Stuttgart, New York, London, 1954.
GIEDION-WELCKER, C. *Paul Klee*, London 1952; Stuttgart 1954.
SPILLER, J. (ed.). *Das bildnerische Denken*, Basel 1956. English translation: *Paul Klee Notebooks Vol.1: The Thinking Eye*, London, New York, 1961. See bibliography pp.523–4.
SPILLER, J. (ed.). *Unendliche Naturgeschichte*, Basel 1970. English translation: *Paul Klee Notebooks Vol.2: The Nature of Nature*, London, New York, 1973.

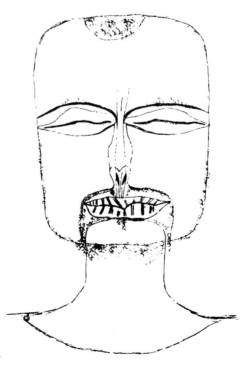

Paul Klee: *Self-portrait*

National bibliography

This section is devoted to books and articles that indicate the modern architectural climate in various countries. The list by its very nature needs to be kept under control and only 'key' source material has been noted. An exploration of building types has not been attempted nor has it been the compiler's intention to include books in this section on the work of individual architects except where this is indispensable, i.e. where an architect has been involved in making a wide national survey of architectural developments.

All the items in this section are arranged in alphabetical order under the name of the author. Again, first dates of publication and original place of publication have been noted whenever possible.

Austria

BROOK, D. 'Karl Marx Hof', *RIBA Journal*, August 1931, p.671 ff.
HOLME, C. (ed.). *The Art-Revival in Austria*, London, Paris, New York, 1906. A *Studio* publication. See article, 'The Architectural Revival in Austria' by Hugo Haberfield.
MISC. *Wiener Neubauten in Stil der Sezession*, 6 vols, Vienna 1908–10.
MÜLLER-WULCKOW, W. *Wiener Werkstätten 1903–1928*, Vienna 1929.
SCHWANZER, K. *Wiener Bauten. 1900 bis heute*, Vienna 1964 (p.b.). A useful guide to buildings in Vienna arranged in date order.
SOTRIFFER, K. *Modern Austrian Art*, London 1965.

Czechoslovakia

BENESOVA, M. 'Pioneers of modern architecture in Czechoslovakia', *Architects' Journal*, Vol.145, No.25, 1967, p.1456.
DOSTAL, O.J., PECHAR, V. *Modern architecture in Czechoslovakia*, Prague 1967 (1970).
GIOVANNI, P. DE, SETNIOKA, J. 'Architettura nuova in Cecoslovacchia', *Casabella*, No.2, 1935, p.18.
KOVLA, J.E. *Nova ceska architettura a jeji vyvej ve XX stoleti*, Prague 1940.
MARGOLIUS, I. *Cubism in Architecture and the Applied Arts*, Newton Abbot 1979. See also author's article in *AA Quarterly*, Vol.8, No.4, 1976, pp.51–9.
PECHAR, J. 'Bauen in der Tschechoslowakei', *Deutsche Bauzeitung*, No.5, 1968, p.320.
PERSITZ, A. 'Tchécoslovaquie – Documents d'architecture contemporaine.', *L'Architecture d'Aujourd'hui*, No.10, 1938, p.30.
SHARP, D. 'Czechoslovak Modern', *RIBA Journal*, May 1970, pp.200–3.
SLAPETA, V. 'Tsekkilaisesta funktionalismista', *Arkkitehtiopisbelija*, Otaniemi, No.3–4, 1977, p.26.
SOKOL, J. 'L'architecture tchécoslovaque', *L'Architecture d'Aujourd'hui*, No.5, 1933, p.4.
TEIGE, K. *Moderni architettura v Ceskoslovensku*, MSA 2, Odeon, Prague 1930.
TEIGE, K. *Modern architecture in Czechoslovakia*, Prague 1947.
VOKOUN, J. 'Czech Cubism', *Architectural Review*, Vol.139, No.829, 1966, p.229. Reprinted in Richards, J.M. and Pevsner, N. (eds), *The Anti-Rationalists*, London 1973, pp.106–10.

Denmark

FABER, T. *New Danish Architecture*, Stuttgart, London, 1968.
FINSEN, H. *Ung Dansk Architektur 1930–1945*, Copenhagen 1947.
FISKER, K. & YERBURY, F.R. *Modern Danish Architecture*, London 1927. An important illustrated survey of Danish architecture.
HIORT, E. *Contemporary Danish Architecture*, Copenhagen 1949 (2nd edn 1958).
HIORT, E. *Housing in Denmark since 1930*, Copenhagen 1952.

MISC. *The Architecture of Denmark*, London 1949. The book version of the special
no. of *Architectural Review*, November, 1948.
SKRIVER, R.E. & STARKE, G. (eds). *Guide to Modern Danish Architecture*,
Copenhagen 1964 (p.b.).

Finland

BANHAM, R. 'The One and the Few: The Rise of Modern Architecture in
Finland', *Architectural Review*, April 1957, pp.243–59.
BECKER, H-J. & SCHLOTE, W. *Contemporary Finnish Houses*, Stuttgart 1958.
BECKER, H-J. & SCHLOTE, W. *New Housing in Finland*, London, Stuttgart, 1964.
Expansion of the author's earlier book above.
MISC. *Helsinki Architectural Guide*, Helsinki 1963. Issued by the Museum of
Finnish Architecture.
PETÄJÄ, K. (ed.). *Helsinki: Architectural Guide*, Helsinki 1965
RICHARDS, J.M. *Modern Architecture in Finland*, London, n.d. (20 pp). A pamphlet
produced by the Finnish Travel Information Centre. Its size belies its value.
RICHARDS, J.M. *Guide to Finnish Architecture*, London 1966.
RICHARDS, J.M. *800 Years of Finnish Architecture*, Newton Abbott 1978.
SCHILDT, G. *Finnish Architecture*, Helsinki 1961. An illustrated pamphlet
indicating the chronological development of Finnish architecture.
SCHULTÉN, M.af 'Recent Architecture in Finland', *Architects' Year Book*, No.7,
1956, pp.79–99.
WICKBERG, N.E. *Finnish Architecture*, Helsinki 1959.

France

AMOUROUX, D. *et al. Guide d'architecture contemporaine en France*, Paris 1972.
GIEDION, S. *Bauen in Frankreich*, Leipzig 1928.
GINSBURGER, R. *Frankreich*, Vienna 1930. In the series 'Neues Bauen in der
Welt', No.3.
GINSBURGER, R. *Junge französische Architektur*, Geneva 1930.
MAUCLAIR, C. *L'Architecture va-t-elle mourir?*, Paris 1933.
MORANCÉ, A. (publisher). *L'Architecture Vivante en France*, Paris, n.d. (*c.*1930–5).
A considerable number of volumes appeared in 'L'Architecture Vivante'
series on French architecture, e.g. see biographical section: Le Corbusier,
Tony Garnier.
PICCINATO, G. *L'architettura contemporanea in Francia*, Bologna 1965. In the series,
'L'architettura contemporanea', No.3.
ROBERTSON, H. & YERBURY, F.R. *Examples of Modern French Architecture*, London 1928.
SCHEIN, I. *Paris construit*, Paris 1961. A pictorial guide to contemporary
architecture in Paris.
SCHIMMERLING, A. (ed.). 'Architecture and Planning in France, 1952–1962',
Special No., *Architectural Design*, April 1963.
U.I.A. (publisher). *Cent œuvres d'architecture contemporaine de la région Parisienne*,
Paris 1965. A photographic record compiled for the U.I.A. Paris conference 1965.
ZAHN, L. *Moderne Pariser Bauten*, Berlin, c.1930.

Germany

ADLER, L. *Neuzeitliche Mietshäuser und Siedlungen*, Berlin 1931.

BEHNE, A. *Der Moderne Zweckbau*, Munich 1926. New edition, Berlin 1964. In the series 'Ullstein Bauwelt Fundamente' (p.b.). A classic work.

CAMPBELL, J. *The German Werkbund*, Princeton 1978.

CONRADS, U. (Introd.). *Modern Architecture in Germany*, London 1963. Translation by J. Palmes.

CONRADS, U. (Introd.). 'Berlin. Dokumente europäischen Bauens', Special No., *Bauwelt*, 41/42, 16 October 1961.

FEUERSTEIN, G. *New Directions in German Architecture*, New York, London, 1969.

FRIES, H. DE, *Junge Baukunst in Deutschland*, Berlin 1927.

GROHMANN, W. *Zwischen den beiden Kriegen*, Frankfurt/M 1953. In the series 'Bildende Kunst, Architektur', Vol.3.

HAJOS, E.M. & ZAHN, L. *Berliner Architektur der Nachkriegszeit*, Berlin 1928. A guide to the built work of Berlin architects.

HENNING-SCHEFOLD, M. and SCHAEFER, I. *Frühe Moderne in Berlin*, Winterthur 1967.

HOFFMANN, H. *et al*. *New German Architecture*, London 1956.

KORN, A. *Glas im Bau und als Gebrauchsgegenstand*, Berlin 1929. A pictorial survey of the use of glass in modern buildings.

LANE, B.M. *Architecture and Politics in Germany 1918–45*, Cambridge (Mass.), 1968.

MARGOLD, E.J. *Bauten der Volkserziehung und Volksgesundheit*, Berlin 1930.

MISC. 'Germany', Special No., *Architectural Design*, June 1963.

MORANCÉ, A. (publisher). *L'Architecture Vivante en Allemagne*, 4 vols, Paris, n.d. (*c.*1930–5).

MÜLLER-WULCKOW, W. *Bauten der Arbeit und des Verkehrs*, Königstein-im-Taunus and Leipzig 1929 (p.b.).

MÜLLER-WULCKOW, W. *Bauten der Gemeinschaft*, Königstein-im-Taunus 1929 (p.b.).

MÜLLER-WULCKOW, W. *Wohnbauten und Siedlungen*, Königstein-im-Taunus, 1929 (p.b.). Three volumes in the series 'Deutsche Baukunst der Gegenwart'. All three are excellent pictorial records of German architecture from the first decade of this century to 1929.

PEHNT, W. *German Architecture 1960–70*, London 1970.

RAVE, R. & KNÖFEL, H.J. *Bauen seit 1900. Ein Führer durch Berlin*, Berlin 1963 (p.b.). An excellent comprehensive guide to buildings in Berlin. Revised 1968.

SCHEFFLER, K. *Die Architektur der Grossstadt*, Berlin 1913.

SCHULZE, K.W. VON, *Glas in der Architektur der Gegenwart*, Stuttgart 1929.

SENGER, A. VON, *Krisis der Architektur*, Zürich 1929.

ZUCKER, P. *Theater und Lichtspielhäuser*, Berlin 1926. Concerned almost entirely with examples of theatre and cinema buildings in Germany.

Cover for *Bauhausbücher* 10 (see page 159)

Holland and Belgium

BAKEMA, J.B. 'Dutch Architecture Today', *Architects' Year Book*, No.5, London 1953, pp.67–82.

BEHNE, A. *Holländische Baukunst in der Gegenwart*, Berlin 1922.

BEKAERT, G. and STRAUVEN, F. *La Construction en Belgique 1945–1970*, Brussels 1971. Book based on exhibition held in Brussels in 1970 for 25th anniversary of CNC.

BERLAGE, H.P. & OTHERS. *Modern Bouwkunst in Nederland*, 20 monographs, Rotterdam 1932–5.

BLIJSTRA, R. *Netherlands Architecture since 1900*, Amsterdam 1960.

FENELLI, G. *Moderne Architectuur in Nederland 1900–1940*, The Hague 1978. The definitive history (previously published in Italian, 1968) with English abridged text.

HOUSDEN, B. (ed.). 'M.Brinkman, J.A.Brinkman, L.C. van der Vlugt, J.H. van den Broek, J.B.Bakema', *Architectural Association Journal*, Special No., December 1960.

JAFFÉ, H.L.C. *De Stijl: 1917–1931. The Dutch Contribution to Modern Art*, London 1956.

MIERAS, J.P. & YERBURY, F.R. *Modern Dutch Building*, London 1931.

MIERAS, J.P. *Na-oorlogse bouwkunst in Nederland*, Amsterdam 1954.

MORANCE, A. (publisher). *L'Architecture Vivante en Hollande*, 2 vols, Paris, n.d. (*c*.1930–5).

PUTTEMANS, P. and HERVÉ, L. *Architecture moderne en Belgique*, Brussels 1974.

RIETVELD, G. 'Post-War Architecture in Holland', 'The Evolution of Dutch Architecture', two articles in Special No., *Werk*, November 1961.

ROBERTSON, H. 'Modern Dutch Architecture', *Architectural Review*, August 1922; September 1923. The first features de Klerk and the second Kramer and Dudok.

ROBERTSON, H. & YERBURY, F.R. 'The Modern Movement in Holland', *Architect and Building News*, 6, 13, and 20 April 1928.

SHARP, D. 'Progress and Tradition in Modern Dutch Architecture', *RIBA Journal*, March 1965, pp.136–41.

VAN LOGHEM, J.B. *Bouwen, Holland*, Amsterdam 1936.

VRIEND, J.J. *Reflexen. Nederlands bouwen na 1945*, Amsterdam 1959.

WATTJES, J.G. *Modern Dutch Architecture*, London 1928.

YERBURY, F.R. *Modern Dutch Buildings*, London 1931.

Italy

ALOI, R. *Nuova architettura a Milano*, Milan 1959.

AMBASZ, E. (ed.). *Italy: The New Domestic Landscape*, New York 1972.

BANHAM, R. 'Neoliberty: The Italian Retreat from Modern Architecture', *Architectural Review*, April 1959, pp.231–5.

BANHAM, R., ROGERS, E. & OTHERS. 'Neoliberty: The Debate', *Architectural Review*, December 1959, pp.341–4.

BOTTERO, M. (ed.). 'Italia'. Special issue of *Zodiac*, No.20, 1970.

FILLIA, L. (ed.). *La nuova architettura*, Turin 1931 (1935).

GREGOTTI, V. *New Directions in Italian Architecture*, New York, London, 1969.

KIDDER SMITH, G. *Italy Builds: Its Modern Architecture and Native Inheritance*, London 1955.

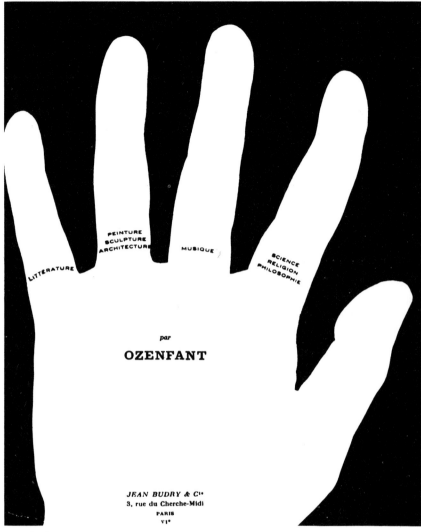

Cover for Ozenfant's *Art* (see page 99)

MAZZOCCHI. G. *et al. 28/78 Architettura* (Cinquanta anni di architettura italiana dal 1928 al 1978), Milan 1979. A unique survey of Italian modernism by the editor of *Domus* for the city of Milan exhibition held in 1979 (p.b.). Includes sections on Castiglioni, Mangiarotti, Mollino, Moretti, Nervi, Ponti and Scarpa.

PAGANI, C. *Italy's Architecture Today*, London 1955.

PICA, A. *Nuova architettura Italiana*, Milan 1936. An important, well illustrated survey of the Italian 'Rationalists'.

PICA, A. *Architettura Italiana Recente*, Milan 1959. English translation, *Recent Italian Architecture*, London 1960.

REGGIONI, F. *Milano 1800–1943*, Milan 1947.

Japan

ALEX, W. *Japanese Architecture*, London 1963.

DREXLER, A. *The Architecture of Japan*, New York 1955, London 1963 (1966).

ENGEL, H. *The Japanese House. A Tradition for Contemporary Architecture*, Rutland, Vermont and Tokyo 1964.

HARADA, J. *The Lesson of Japanese Architecture*, London 1936 (2nd edn 1954). A classic work on Japanese architecture.

ISHIMOTO, Y., TANGE, K. and GROPIUS, W. *Katsura: Tradition and Creation in Japanese Architecture*, New Haven 1960.

KOIKE, S. *Contemporary Architecture of Japan*, New York 1954.

KOIKE, S. (ed.). *Japan's New Architecture*, Tokyo 1956.

KULTERMANN, U. *Contemporary Architecture of Japan*, New York 1960.

RICHARDS, J.M. *An Architectural Journey in Japan*, London 1963.

SADLER, A.L. *A Short History of Japanese Architecture*, Tokyo 1962. A useful background book.

SEIKE, K. & TERRY, C.S. *Contemporary Japanese Houses*, London 1965.

Latin America

ARANGO, J. & MARTINEZ, C. *Arquitectura en Colombia*, Bogota 1951.

CETTO, M. *Moderne Architektur in Mexico*, Stuttgart 1960.

GOODWIN, P.L. *Brazil Builds, Architecture New and Old 1652–1942*, New York 1943. Photographs by G.Kidder Smith.

GRAHAM, G. 'Modern Architecture in Brazil', *Architects' Year Book*, No.7, 1956, pp.72–8.

HITCHCOCK, H.-R. *Latin American Architecture since 1945*, New York 1955. An admirable general survey.

MINDLIN, H. *Modern Architecture in Brazil*, New York 1956.

MISC. 'Brazil', *Architectural Review*, Special No., March 1944.

MISC. 'Mexico', *Architectural Design*, Special No., Sept. 1963.

MYERS, I.E. *Mexico's Modern Architecture*, New York 1952.

WAISMANN, M. (ed.). *Documento para una historia de la arquitectura argentina*, Buenos Aires 1978 (p.b.). An excellent survey including notes on the major architects.

Spain

BOHIGAS, O. *Arquitectura Modernista*, Barcelona 1968.

BOHIGAS, O. *Arquitectura espanola de la segunda republica*, Barcelona 1970.

BOTTERO, M. (ed.). 'Espana'. Special issue of *Zodiac*, No.15, 1965.

DOMENECH, L. *Arquitectura Espanola Contemporanea*, Barcelona 1968.

FLORES, C.F. *Arquitectura Espanola Contemporanea*, Bilbao 1961.

HERNANDEZ-CROS, J.L. *et al. Arquitectura de Barcelona*, Barcelona 1973. An excellent guide published by the Official College of Architects of Catalonia. Second edition much expanded. Foreword by Oriel Bohigas.

MISC. *Arquitectura Contemporanea en Espana*, Madrid c.1933. A series including volume on Blanco-Soler and Bergamin.

RAFOLS, J.F. *Modernismo y Modernistas*, Barcelona 1949.

Sweden

AHLBERG, H. *Swedish Architecture of the Twentieth Century*, London 1925. Preface by F.R.Yerbury.

KIDDER SMITH, G.E. *Sweden Builds*, London, New York, 1950 (2nd edn 1957).

MISC. 'Sweden', Special No. *Architectural Review*, September 1943.

MISC. *Ny Svensk Arkitektur*, Stockholm 1939. English and Swedish text.

RASMUSSEN, S.E. *Nordische Baukunst*, Berlin 1940. On Swedish and Danish modern architecture.

S.A.R. *Ten lectures on Swedish Architecture*, Stockholm 1949.

S.A.R. (publisher). *Guide to Modern Architecture in Stockholm*, Stockholm 1959. A guide to buildings in Stockholm produced by Svenska Arkitekters Riksförbund.

Switzerland

BACHMANN, J. & VON MOOS, S. *New Directions in Swiss Architecture*, New York, London, 1969.

BILL, M. *Moderne Schweizer Architektur 1925–1945*, Basel 1944.

BLUMER, J. 'Modern Swiss Architecture since 1945', *Architects' Year Book*, No.10, 1962, pp.124–45.

GIRSBERGER, H. & ADLER, F. *Architectural Guide to Switzerland*, Zurich 1969.

KIDDER SMITH, G. *Switzerland Builds*, London 1950.

MISC. *Moderne Schweizer Architektur*, 10 vols, Basel 1940–6.

MISC. 'Swiss Architecture', *Architectural Design*, Special No., September 1962. Introduction by Hans Curjel.

ROTH, A. 'Swiss Architecture, Yesterday and Today', *Architects' Year Book*, No.3, 1949, pp.106–14.

VOLKART, H. *Schweizer Architektur*, Ravensburg 1951.

GUBLER, J. *Nationalisme et Internationalisme dans l'architecture de la Suisse*, Lausanne 1975.

United Kingdom

BOTTERO, M. (ed.). 'Great Britain'. Special issue of *Zodiac*, No.18, 1968. Includes survey by H.-R. Hitchcock of period 1900–39.

BRUCKMANN, H. & LEWIS, D.L. *New Housing in Britain*, London 1960.

DANNATT, T. *Modern Architecture in Britain*, London 1959. With an introduction by John Summerson.

GOULD, J. *Modern Houses in Britain, 1919–1939*, Newcastle 1977 (Architectural History Monograph, No.1, p.b.).

HITCHCOCK, H-R. & OTHERS. *Modern Architecture in England*, New York 1937.

HOWE, J. 'New Schools in Britain', *Architects' Year Book*, No.4, 1952, pp.64–79.

HUGHES, N., GRANT, L. & WESLEY, T. *Cambridge New Architecture*, Cambridge 1964 (p.b.).

LAMBERT, S. (ed.). *New Architecture of London. A Selection of Buildings since 1930*, London 1963.

LANDAU, R. *New Directions in British Architecture*, London, New York, 1969.

MARS GROUP. *New Architecture*, Catalogue of the MARS Group exhibition, New Burlington Galleries, London 1938 (p.b.).

MCCALLUM, I. *A Pocket Guide to Modern Buildings in London*, London 1951 (p.b.).

MILLS, E.D. *The New Architecture in Great Britain, 1946–53*, London 1953.

MUTHESIUS, H. *Die englische Baukunst der Gegenwart*, Leipzig 1900.

MUTHESIUS, H. *Das englische Haus*, 3 vols., Berlin 1904–5 (1908–12). (*The English House*, London, New York, 1979).

PEVSNER, N. 'Nine Swallows – No Summer', *Architectural Review*, May 1942, pp.109–12. English architecture from 1900 to 1914.

RICHARDS, J.M. Introduction to catalogue, *Architecture Today*, London 1961. Published by The Arts Council.

SUMMERSON, J. Introduction to catalogue, *Ten Years of British Architecture*, London 1956. Published by The Arts Council.

WILLIS, P. *New Architecture in Scotland*, London 1977 (p.b.).

YORKE, F.R.S. 'The Modern English House', Special No., *Architectural Review*, December 1936.

YORKE, F.R.S. *The Modern English House*, London 1937.

U.S.A.

ALFIERI, B. (ed.). 'America'. Special issue of *Zodiac*, No.8, 1957. Articles on Kahn, Wright, Saarinen, etc.

BLOC, A. (ed.). 'USA 65' Special No., *L'Architecture d' Aujourd'hui*, No.122, 1965.

BOSSOM, A.C. *Building to the Skies. The Romance of the Skyscraper*, London 1934. A rather dated book but still a fascinating early study of the 'high' building.

BURCHARD, J. & BUSH-BROWN, A. *The Architecture of America. A Social and Cultural History*, Boston, Toronto, 1961; London 1967.

CIUCCI, G., DALCO, F., MANIERI-ELIA, M., TAFURI, M. *The American City: From the Civil War to the Deal*, Cambridge (Mass.) 1979; London 1980.

CONDIT, C. *The Rise of the Skyscraper*, Chicago 1952.

CONDIT, C. *The Chicago School of Architecture*, Chicago 1964.

DIXON, J. *Architectural Design Preview, USA*, New York 1962. A collection of project drawings.

ECKARDT, W.VON (ed.). *Mid-Century Architecture in America*, New York 1961.

HEYER, P. (ed.). *Architects on Architecture: New directions in America*, New York 1966 (London 1967). Important statements by contemporary architects.

HITCHCOCK, H.-R. & DREXLER, A. (eds). *Built in USA: Post-War Architecture*, New York 1952.

JORDY, W.H. 'The Formal Image: USA', *Architectural Review*, March 1960, pp.157–65.

MCCALLUM, I. *Architecture USA*, London 1959.

MCCOY, E. *Five Californian Architects*, New York 1960.

MOCK, E. (ed.). *Built in USA, 1932–44*, New York 1944.

MISC. *Chicago Tribune Tower Competition*, Chicago 1923. A record of the entries for the most famous international competition of the twenties.

MUMFORD, L. *Sticks and Stones*, New York 1924.

MUMFORD, L. *The Brown Decades*, New York 1931.

MUMFORD, L. *Roots of Contemporary American Architecture*, New York 1952. Thirty-seven essays tracing the development of modern architecture in America – from Greenhough to Nowicki. Introduction by Mumford. Many biographies. Indispensable. (Also available as p.b.).

ROTH, L.M. *A Concise History of American Architecture*, London 1979. Contains useful bibliography.

SCHUYLER, M. *American Architecture and Other Writings*, 2 vols, Cambridge (Mass.), 1961. Schuyler's writings edited by William Jordy and Ralph Coe. (Re-issued in one volume, 1964).

STERN, R. *New Directions in American Architecture*, New York, London, 1969.

174

U.S.S.R.

ARKIN, D. *Modern Western Architecture*, Moscow 1932.

CARTER, E.J. 'Soviet Architecture Today', *Architectural Review*, November 1942, pp.107–14.

FEO, V.DE, *U.R.S.S.: architettura 1917–1936*, Rome 1963.

LISSITZKY, EL. *Russland. Die Rekonstruktion der Architektur in der Sowjetunion*, Vienna 1930. Vol.1 in the Schroll series 'Neues Bauen in der Welt'. New edition with important additional Appendices, *Russland: Architektur für eine Weltrevolution*, Berlin, Frankfurt/M, Vienna 1965 (p.b.). See Biographical Section.

LUBETKIN, B. 'Soviet Architecture. Notes on Developments from 1917 to 1932', *Architectural Association Journal*, May 1956, pp.260–4.

LUBETKIN, B. 'Soviet Architecture. Notes on Developments from 1932–1955', *Architectural Association Journal*, September–October 1956, pp.85–9.

MISC. 'Russia', Special No., *Architectural Review*, May 1932. Includes article by Berthold Lubetkin.

MORANCÉ, A. (publisher). *L'Architecture Vivante en U.R.S.S.*, 3 parts, Paris, n.d. (*c.*1930).

QUILICI, V. *Architettura sovietica contemporanea*, Bologna 1965. No.4 in the series 'L'architettura contemporanea'.

QUILICI, V. *Città Russa e città Sovieticà*, Milan 1976 (p.b.).

SENKEVITCH, A., Jr. *Soviet Architecture 1917–1962*, Charlottesville 1974. An excellent bibliographical guide to source material.

SHARP, D. & COOKE, C. Special issue on Russian/Soviet architecture, *AA Quarterly*, Vol.II, No.2, 1979. With contributions from Starr, Kirichenko, Schvidkovskii, etc.

TSCHERNYKHOV, J. *Architectural Fictions*, Leningrad 1933. Includes 101 coloured 'Constructivist' prints.

A select list of architectural periodicals

The periodicals included in this list are those concerned with the main developments in the Modern Movement in architecture. However in some cases the magazines noted also include articles on the other arts; nearly all of them have a particular ideological point of view that relates to general Modern Movement developments. Due to the number of title changes in magazines over a period of time, I have noted the current (or last) title first and have indicated the previous history of the magazine below the main title. Many of these magazines have now been reissued either in separate yearly volumes (e.g. *L'Esprit Nouveau*) or as fascsimile reprints of single issues (e.g. *ABC*). An asterisk indicates where there are known reprints. In addition to the reprints of architectural journals and periodicals, copies of which can be found in most national library collections, a number are also available on micro-film.

Name of periodical	Place of publication	Dates of publication
ABC: Beiträge zum Bauen (*Reprinted: Delft, Eindhoven, Dortmund)	Zürich	1924–5
Abstraction-Création	Paris	1933
Academy Architecture	London	1889–1931
Archigram	London	1961–77
The Architect (1971–79), formerly *Architect and Building News*	London	1869–1979
Architects' Journal	London	1919–
Architects' Year Book	London	1945–75
Architectura	Amsterdam	1881–1917
Architectural Association Quarterly (1968–) formerly *Architectural Association Journal* (1905–65), *Arena* (1965–68). Earlier, *Architectural Association Notes* (1887–1905)	London	1905–
Architectural Design (1947–) previously *Architectural Design and Construction* (1935–46)	London	1935–
Architectural Forum (1965–73) New format Vol.122; previously *Architectural forum* (1892–64)	New York	1892–
Architectural Record	New York	1891–
Architectural Review	London	1897–
Architecture, Mouvement et Continuité (*AMC*). Published by SADG	Paris	1967–
L'Architecture d'Aujourd'hui. Absorbed *Architecture*	Paris	1929–
Architecture in Greece	Athens	1967–
L'Architecture Vivante	Paris	1923–33
Der Architekt	Vienna	1895–1922
Archithèse (see also *Werk*)	Zurich	1972–76, 1980–
L'Architettura, Cronache & Storia	Rome	1955–
Arkhitektura published by Moscow Architectural Society (2 issues only)	Moscow	1923
Arkitectura	Prague	1939–
Axis	London	1935–6
Bauen und Wohnen. See *Werk: Bauen + Wohnen* 1979–	Zurich	1946–79
Bauen und Wohnen	Ravensburg	1946–79

Name of periodical	Place of publication	Dates of publication
Der Baumeister	Munich	1902–
Bauwelt (1952–) previously, *Bauwelt, Zeitschrift für das Gesamte Bauwesen* (1910–45) and *Neue Bauwelt* (1946–52)	Berlin	1910–
Building previously *The Builder*	London	1842–
Byggekunst	Oslo	1919–
CA (SA) superseded by *Sovetskaia Arkhitektura* in 1931	Moscow	1926–30
Cahiers d'Art	Paris	1926–
Le Carré Bleu	Paris	1958–
Casabella (1964–) previously *La Casa Bella* (1928–32); *Casabella* (1933–7); *Casabella-Costruzioni* (1938–9); *Costruzioni-Casabella* (1940–3, 1946); *Casabella-Continuità* (1954–64)	Milan	1928–
La Cité (Organ of SBUAM) Supplement *Tekhné* (1927–)	Brussels	1919–35
De 8 en Opbouw	Amsterdam	1932–43
De Stijl	Leiden	1917–32
Deutsche Bauzeitung	Munich	1867–
Domus	Milan	1928–
Edilizia Moderna	Milan	1931–
L'Effort Moderne	Paris	1924–7
Ekistics	Athens	1955–
* *L'Esprit Nouveau*	Paris	1920–25
Focus (four issues only)	London	1938–9
Die Form (Magazine of the Deutscher Werkbund)	Berlin	1922, 1925–35
Forum (New version 1980)	Amsterdam	1946–
Frühlicht previously as a supplement to *Stadtbaukunst alter und neuer Zeit*, Berlin (1920–21)	Magdeburg	1921–2
'G'. Zeitschrift für elementare Gestaltung	Berlin	1923–6
Das Kunstblatt	Berlin, Weimar, Potsdam	1913–32
Lotus International, formerly *Lotus*	Venice	1968–
Metron	Rome	1945–54
Der Moderne Stil	Stuttgart	1899–1905

Name of periodical	Place of publication	Dates of publication
Das Neue Frankfurt. Later *Die Neue Stadt* to 1933	Frankfurt-a.-M.	1926–31
Oppositions: A Journal for Ideas and Criticism in Architecture (published by the Insitute for Architecture and Urban Studies)	New York	1973–
Plan (Student publication ASA)	London, etc.	1943–51
Plan (1970–) previously *Bouwkundig Weekblad*, Amsterdam (1881–1969)	Amsterdam	1881–
Plastique (Nos. 1–5)	Paris	1937
Praessens (2 issues only)	Warsaw	1926–30
Progressive Architecture (1944–) previously *Pencil Points* (1920–42) and *New Pencil Points* (1942–3)	New York	1920–
Red (Three yearbooks 1927–28, 1928–29, 1929–31)	Prague	1927–31
Stavba	Prague	1922–38
Stavitel	Prague	1919–32
Studio International (1963–76) previously *The Studio* (1893–1963). Now occasional	London	1893–1976
Der Sturm	Berlin	1910–32
Styl	Prague	1908–38
Techniques et Architecture	Paris	1942–
Ter es Forma	Budapest	1928–
Vers Sacrum	Vienna	1898–1903
Volneshery	Prague	1898–1948
Wasmuths Monatshefte (1933–42) previously *Wasmuths Monatshefte für Baukunst* (1914–29); *Wasmuths Monatshefte für Baukunst und Stadtbau* (1930–2)	Berlin	1914–42
* *Wendingen* (An English edition appeared in 1921–4) Reprinted by Da Capo, New York	Amsterdam	1918–31
Werk: Bauen + Wohnen (1979–) previously *Werk-Archithèse* (1977–79) previously *Werk* (1913–77)	Zurich	1913–
Zodiac (Yearbook)	Milan	1957–73

Index of architects and authors

Jordy, W. H. 62, 174

Kahn, Louis 63, 64
Kandinsky, Wassily 159, **161**
Katan, E. and R. 64
Kaufmann, E. 142, 147
Kaufmann, Jr., E. 126
Kawazoe, N. 127
Kemper, C. 124
Kepes, G. 157
Khan-Mahomedov, S. O. 73
Kidder-Smith, G. 82, 169, 172
Kiesler, Frederick 64
Killick, J. 106
Klee, Paul 159, **161, 162**
Kleiner, L. 60
Klerk, Michel de 65
Klingborg, A. 124
Klotz, H. 135
Knofel, H. J. 167
Koch, A. 80
Koike, S. 171
Koninck, Louis H. De 65, 66
Korn, Arthur 66, 67, 167
Kornwolf, J. D. 20
Kostelanetz, R. 90
Kotera, Jan 67, 68
Koulermos, P. 36
Kovla, J. E. 165
Kramer, P. 65
Krejcar, Jaramir 68
Kudelka, Z. 44
Kuhn, H. 157
Kulka, H. 77
Kultermann, U. 79, 127, 148, 171
Künstler, G. 77
Kysela, F. 50

Labo, G. 17, 131
Lambert, S. 173
Lancaster, C. 52
Landau, R. 173
Lane, B. M. 167
Langer, S. 157
Lanqui, E. 158
Lauterbach, H. 58
Le Corbusier 48, **68, 70, 71,** 99
Leitner, B. 148
Lenning, H. F. 158

Leonhardt, F. 25
Leonidov, Ivan 72
Lescaze, William 61
Lethaby, William Richard 73,
141, 151
Lewis, D. L. 173
Lewis, W. 151
Licklider, H. 151
Lindahl, G. 154
Lindner, W. 148
Linze, G. 26
Lissitzky, El 75, 175
Llewelyn-Davies, R. 37
Loghem, J. B. van 75, 169
Longatti, A. 112
Loos, Adolf 76, 77
Los, S. 112
Lubetkin, Berthold 77, 79, 175
Lucas, Colin 32, 33
Luckhardt, Hans 79
Luckhardt, Wassili 79
Lurçat, A. 151
Lux, J. A. 95, 139

Mackintosh, Charles Rennie 79
Macleod, R. 73, 80
Madl, K. B. 68
Madsen, S. T. 61, 158
Magalhães, A. 34
Makinson, R. L. 52
Maldonado, T. 23
Malevich, K. 159
Manieri-Elia, M. 174
Manson, G. 126, 142
Mantero, E. G. 131
Marchi, V. 148
Marek, P. 68
Margold, E. J. 167
Margolius, I. 165
Mariani, L. 112
Marilaun, A. 77
Markalaus, B. 77
Markelius, Sven 19, **80, 82**
Marks, R. W. 45
Mars Group 173
Martinell, C. 48
Martinell y Brudet 48
Martinez, C. 171
Mauclair, C. 166

190

Photo credits